JUST HELP
YOURSELF

For the wonder of you

My grandchildren, Bradley, Liberty, Brittany

JUST HELP YOURSELF

*TOM JONES, THE SENATORS
AND THE ROAD TO STARDOM*

VERNON HOPKINS

Seren is the book imprint of
Poetry Wales Press Ltd
57 Nolton Street, Bridgend, Wales, CF31 3AE
www.serenbooks.com
Facebook: facebook.com/SerenBooks
Twitter: @SerenBooks

First Published in 2012

ISBNs
Paperback– 978-1-78172-476-7
Ebook – 978-1-78172-477-4
Kindle – 978-1-78172-478-1

A CIP record for this title is available from the British Library.

The publisher acknowledges the financial assistance
of the Welsh Books Council.

Front cover image courtsey of Pictures In Mind

Printed by Bell & Bain Ltd, Glasgow.

Contents

1. EARLY DAYS

Naked in every sense of the word, I was thrust into daylight kicking and screaming, which was how I was to make my way in life. The timing could have been better. The skies above war-ravaged Britain were heavy with German Bombers, hundreds of them, dropping their deadly payloads on cities and towns all over the country. Weighing in at ten and a half pounds, my birth must have been a rather painful experience for my mother, and with the war being fought on the Home Front, my life expectancy must have given her pause for thought too. My parents had spent most of that year under the kitchen table, listening to the terrifying drone of German planes criss-crossing the skies.

My first cries rang out in the tiny bedroom of 16 Gwilym Street, Rhydyfelin, a small village two miles down the road from Pontypridd. The terraced house was close to the banks of the River Taff, and its gurgling black water was probably the first sound from the outside world to reach my ears. The filthy coal-black river had once teemed with trout, but those days were long gone. The Rhondda Valleys were packed with coalmines and coal-tips. The Welsh rain filtered through the huge pyramids of slag and coloured the green, green grass a charcoal black.

My parents, Evan and Eva Hopkins, along with my five-year old brother lived in what was known locally as the apartments. Number 16, a two bedroomed house, was owned by Mr and Mrs Evans, a kindly old couple. The downstairs had a front room, middle room and back kitchen. My family lived in the tiny middle room reached along a dark passage, and an even tinier back bedroom. I shared a single bed with my brother Norman, and my parents were in the three-quarter-sized bed where I was born.

Aged three, I attended Hawthorn Infants School, and my recollection of my first day is of trying to escape the playground and run after my mother. I got my head stuck in the school railings, which was every bit as traumatic as seeing my mother waving goodbye and brushing a tear from her eye. A year or so later, when the war finally came to an end, my young life almost ended too. I almost departed this earth with a bladder full of pee soaking my Sunday-best trousers.

Every Sunday morning, Norman and I would attend Sunday School at Bethlehem Chapel, half a mile from home. My mother would give us both a penny each for the collection plate. My brother, who was aged around nine or ten, always had other ideas as to where those two pennies would end up. Inevitably it would be two lovely ice-cream cornets on our way back home. Our Sunday School teacher always warned us, that if we ever got up to any mischief – the wrath of God would punish us. Before buying our ice-cream Norman would sometimes decide to knock on somebody's door and run away. We called it Rat-tat-ginger, and I pestered him to let me have a go. Banging on the knocker, in my excitement I ran down the garden path and out into the main road.

I can clearly remember Norman screaming out behind me – "Stop! Stop!"

Thank God I listened. I stopped in the middle of the road. Glancing to my right, a large double- decker bus was bearing down on me. To my left was a lorry hurtling towards me. I shut my eyes and felt the slipstream from both vehicles, as they rushed past on either side. Eyes shut tight; I heard an almighty crash and peed myself. The lorry, laden with rationed butter, had skidded into a telegraph pole, ripping it from its foundations. It was a hot summer's day and the slabs of butter had spilled onto the road. Telephone cables were draped over the wrecked lorry, its bonnet embedded in the pole. I remember running for home, as fast as my legs would carry me, with Norman in hot pursuit. Needless to say my parents were not best pleased, and contacted the police. I got a fierce telling off about the accident, but my parents were also relieved that I'd come to no harm.

If I hadn't stopped that day, in all likelihood I wouldn't have survived, and the events that unfold in this memoir wouldn't have come to pass. There wouldn't have been a Tommy Scott and The Senators. No fascinating stories to tell, no anecdotes, and probably no knighthood. In fact, no Tom Jones at all, if truth be told. But I'll get to that…

What follows are my recollections of my years as a professional musician with Tom Jones. It is a candid view of the music industry and the ruthless people who inhabit it. My journey begins in the South Wales Valleys, buying my first guitar, forming a band and bringing in a singer who would eventually become one of the greatest superstars in the world. Success came slowly for Tom Jones and The Squires (originally Tommy Scott and The Senators) until we were spotted by a ruthless manager, Gordon Mills, and catapulted into the London music scene of the Sixties.

The group became caught up in the world of Fleet Street gossip, groupies, sex and drugs. Although we all started out as a tight-knit bunch of mates from Ponty, it quickly became clear that Tom had his own agenda. Tom was the star, and had a streak of callousness that led him to neglect the other members of the group, his young wife, and everyone who stood in the way of his success.

The band struggled on with Tom for eight life-changing years, in pursuit of recognition and stardom. We left the green Valleys for the stark concrete and rat-infested slums of Ladbroke Grove. We starved together but survived together, and through sheer persistence and hard work we broke through.

'It's Not Unusual' changed our miserable existence, but sadly it revealed a darker side to Tom Jones. There have been several biographies written about him, but no-one was closer to Tom during those formative years than me. Inseparable in many ways, for so long, in the end we couldn't have been further apart.

Some of the comments in these pages will no doubt alienate me to Tom Jones' legions of fans, but I make no apologies. Sometimes the truth casts an unflattering spotlight on the behaviour of people we think we know. But generally we are blinded by the glare of stardom and we see what we are meant to see, what is manufactured for public consumption. I got to stand behind the curtain with Tom, this is my story.

2. BIRTH OF THE SENATORS

My parents were married in 1935, at St. Mary's Church, Glyntaff, Pontypridd. My father was a qualified piano tuner and repairer, my mother in service as a housemaid. During the war my father was seconded to work on the local trading estate. Being deft of hand, he was put to work on the line assembling engine parts for fighter planes. Mercifully, he wasn't designated for military service, much to my mother's relief and his great disappointment.

Two years after the war ended, we left Gwilym Street and moved to a brand new council house in the same village, 2 Glyndwr Avenue. My mother had recently given birth to my sister, June, and in 1948 my other sister Heather was born. My father continued with his trade, repairing the actions (inside workings) of pianos in an outhouse attached to the property.

The three-bedroom house was vast by comparison to the cramped apartment we had vacated. These days number 2 is owned by my nephew and his wife, Lee and Mel Hopkins. Number 2 Glyndwr Avenue was important in bringing The Senators together as a band, particularly the tiny front room. Perhaps one day in the future, a commemorative plaque may find itself onto an outside wall. After all it's where it all began for Tom Jones and The Senators.

As a four or five-year old, music was something that came out of the wireless or gramophone. I didn't have the faintest idea about what made those magical sounds. My parents took me to see a revue show in Pontypridd's Town Hall. The orchestra in the pit struck up and the curtain opened. I wasn't remotely interested in what was happening on stage. I was transfixed by the music emanating from the strange objects handled by the men in black suits. It was a revelation, I was hooked. With no television in those days, I had never seen a gathering of musicians before. I remember feeling overwhelmed and absolutely fascinated.

After that experience, I took complete charge of the family's wind-up gramophone. My father had a collection of 78rpm records which I would play for hours. I didn't care, nor was I even aware of, what kind of music was on the records; all that mattered was that it was the same kind of sound that I had heard from the orchestra in the Town Hall. A good few years later I would learn to differentiate between the bands. My father's collection was a mix of bands from the Twenties, Thirties and Forties, and a range of solo singers. Stan Kenton's 'Peanut Vendor', Jimmy Lunceford's 'White Heat', Glenn Miller's 'In the Mood', Gene Krupa's astonishing drum solos, the list of riches was endless. I must have almost worn out the gramophone needle listening to Judy Garland, Vera Lynn, Al Jolson, Edmundo Ross and a load of other records. My father, being an accomplished pianist, was overjoyed that we had enough room for a piano at the new house. Apart from a kazoo, it was the first instrument I ever had a crack at. I played the two-fingered bass line to 'Mule Train' while my father knocked out the melody.

Leaving Hawthorn Senior School, aged fifteen, I started work as an apprentice compositor at *The Pontypridd Observer*, a weekly newspaper. Years later, when I formed The Senators, I would coax the editor, John Lewis, into giving the band valuable publicity in his newspaper. He duly obliged and we got numerous favourable mentions right up until we left for London in 1964. But my first real interest in music came about when I was seventeen. My father paid eight pounds for a second-hand Spanish guitar. The guitar belonged to a former school friend, John Lawrence, but he had lost interest in playing it. After mastering the basics, and suffering sore fingertips, I just knew this was for me. I would never, to this day, lose my interest in playing one of the greatest musical instruments ever invented.

Like most other teenagers of that time I thought rock 'n' roll was king, and Elvis Presley was the King of rock 'n' roll. But 1959 was a very black year for me. Buddy Holly, The Big Bopper and Richie Valens were killed in a plane crash, and Eddie Cochran died in a car crash. Their tragic deaths were mourned the world over, but closer to home it was a tragic time for our family also. My mother Eva died from cancer on December 5th that same year, aged forty-seven. Her passing left a chasm in all our lives. But something happened in the following year that would eventually help me to come to terms with the heart- breaking loss. I had been tinkering with the idea of forming a band for some time, and my father had been aware of it. In February 1960, he was tuning a piano for a local family and noticed that their sixteen-year-old son, Jeff Maher, was very adept at playing the guitar. My father mentioned that I was keen on forming a band. Jeff contacted another sixteen-year-old guitarist, Keith Davies, and before very long they called on me.

I opened the door of number 2 Glyndwr Avenue to two boys carrying guitars, and with the same stars in their eyes as mine. It was the birth of The Senators. By an amazing coincidence, the three of us all owned blonde Hofner guitars. Jeff's model was a 'President', Keith's a 'Club' and mine was called a 'Senator'. We spent days trying to think of a name for the band and eventually settled on 'The Senators'.

It wasn't very long before The Senators developed into a five-piece band, adding a drummer, Brian Price, and a good looking singer, Tommy Pitman, who had just completed his National Service in the RAF. The fashion for bands at that time was to have a lead singer with the rest of the band singing backing harmonies, emulating the likes of Cliff Richard and The Shadows, Buddy Holly and The Crickets, Bill Fury and The Tornadoes, Gene Vincent and The Bluecaps etc... Our singer sounded like Elvis, so there was a good slice of The King in our repertoire.

My father allowed the band to rehearse in the front room, or parlour as it was quaintly referred to back then. You could just about swing a cat in it, but the five of us managed to squeeze in, along with our amplifiers, guitars and snare drum. We all had day jobs and would practice every Wednesday night. Sometimes halfway through a pounding rock number, the electricity would fail, creating a dead stillness, followed by the chink of a shilling being dropped into the electricity meter courtesy of my father. The music would resume but not before my father bellowed out, "Right you lot, that's another shilling you owe me when you become famous, boys!" We derived a great deal of satisfaction experimenting with popular music. It was a tough musical education as we improved our technique, starting to become more established playing in and around Ponty.

I was keeping busy between the band and my job as a compositor for the local newspaper. John Lewis and his charming sub-editor wife, Margaret were a happy-looking couple, always smiling and welcoming. But beneath their charming personalities, the stress of running a newspaper was becoming apparent in the dark shadows forming below their eyes. They were very generous in giving the band free publicity and keeping up with our progress. The staff photographer supplied some great shots of us in action. On one occasion we were given a banner headline announcing in the newspaper that The Senators were appearing on a TWW television show called *Discs a Go-Go*. The programme was fronted by the famous Canadian disc-jockey, Kent Walton.

The band appeared alongside Screaming Lord Sutch and Monty Sunshine's Jazz Band. Madcap Sutch was enjoying a number of freaky-sounding hit records themed on vampires and Count Dracula. He came on after our performance, appearing out of a coffin, swathed in dry ice. The lid opened on cue, with his hand appearing, then his black top-hat, followed by a chalk-white face with theatrical blood dripping from his mouth. Rising from the coffin, wrapped in a flowing black cape, he leapt out and proceeded to frighten the living daylights out of his young audience, and the millions watching at home.

The television appearance did the band a world of good, and we got a lot of respect up and down the valleys back home. Television is a great vehicle for getting a toehold on that ladder to fame. We all quickly realised that having one isolated appearance wasn't going to be enough, but it certainly encouraged us to stick at it and press on with the dream.

We continued to play the dance halls in 1961, and became increasingly popular. We even scored with business acumen: after all it's not just show, its business as well, we started hiring out our own halls and putting on dances. We profited from the entrance fees, cloakroom tickets, light refreshments and such. We thought we were the bee's knees – entrepreneurs!

John Lewis, bless him, continued publicising the band in *The Pontypridd Observer*. My job at the newspaper sometimes entailed having to operate the keyboard on the linotype, churning out columns of typeface matter for the presses. There was one article of news copy that caught my attention. It was information about a band from Liverpool, that was being tipped to hit the big time. When I reached the part that spelled out their name, I almost fell out my chair laughing. It was the most ridiculous name for a band I had ever heard – The Beatles. They must be joking I thought, but as history testifies, they were certainly no joke!

Those several years working at *The Observer* left me with many happy memories and naturally a few sad ones too. One memory that's stayed with me, and illustrates just how much working conditions have changed for the better, concerns an ex-miner employed as a lackey on a measly wage. Bill Enoch was forced to quit mining after almost a lifetime underground. Poor Bill had developed emphysema, causing severe breathlessness. All those years of breathing coal dust had cut short his career at the coal face. He hadn't yet reached retirement age so he was very grateful to *The Observer* for employing him.

Bill was a typical miner, short, stocky and his arms and face were scarred purple with coal dust tattoos. One of his 'easier' jobs at *The Observer* was manhandling the heavy reels of blank newsprint paper, getting them ready to attach to the huge letterpress machines. Other times, he would pack bundles of newspapers and carry them out to the vans ready for distribution. Often these duties left him wheezing and literally choking for breath. As a young apprentice, it was distressing to see this proud, likeable old man doing such heavy work. But the saddest sight of all – and in no way should he have been doing it – was witnessing him collecting old columns of typeface for recycling. The recycle foundry was situated in a claustrophobic windowless room. The temperature there must have been well over a hundred degrees, and it was impossible to be in there for any length of time. Bill's job was to fill the foundry with used type, made up of tin, antimony and lead. When it became molten he'd open a valve and pour it into moulds. Once the metal had cooled, Bill would hurl the mould to the floor and to release the ingots. The recycled metal resembled bars of gold. The fumes from the dross floating on the molten metal were choking and irritated the eyes. I found it incredible that a man with emphysema was made to work in such a suffocating environment. From the mines to this, it was tragic, poor man.

Pontypridd is the gateway to the Rhondda Valleys and there was always plenty of news around to fill *The Observer*'s pages, it kept us printers very busy. Ponty was a market town surrounded by a number of collieries and mountains. Its greatest claim to fame is that it was the birthplace of Evan James and James James, father and son composers of the Welsh national anthem, no less. It's also the birthplace of a notable singer, Sir Tom Jones, but more about him later.

As for The Senators and our dreams of stardom, we were going from strength to strength. We had plenty of gigs lined up throughout the Valleys and we invested the money we earned in buying better gear. We all had day jobs so upgrading our equipment was affordable. Compared with today's amplification, the volume of decibels our equipment produced was very low. The legendary American guitarist, Duane Eddy, whose hits included

'Shazam', 'Peter Gunn' and 'Dance with the Guitar Man', used one of the most powerful amplifiers available at that time. All 30 watts of it, and that was when he was performing on stage! Our amplifiers were pitiful in comparison. Amplification in venues today amounts to thousands of watts of power. The average household stereo set produces more volume than we were producing as a whole band back then. The drum kits were also pretty basic and generally consisted of a small diameter bass drum, modest high-hat cymbal and one mediocre crash cymbal and snare drum. Modern kits have so much equipment that the drummer is almost lost behind it all, and on top of that the kit is usually miked with all the instruments going through the mixer creating a perfectly balanced sound. The Senators reckoned we were pretty loud back in the day!

The most prestigious venue to play was Ponty's Regent ballroom. We were incredibly nervous and apprehensive the first time we played there. It was a cavernous hall with a wide, high stage, with bunches of flowers skirting its edge. A big dance band was resident most weekends, about fifteen musicians in all, with trumpets, trombones, piano, saxophone, the lot. Mr Berriman, the owner of The Regent, had seen our write-ups in *The Observer* and wanted to experiment with how a rock 'n' roll band would be received. Up until that point ballroom dancing was all that had ever been held there. He gave us a midweek booking, crossed his fingers, and hoped for the best. I remember we stood behind the plush curtains, tensely awaiting Mr Berriman to announce us,

'Welcome to the Regent Ballroom everyone. For the first time ever on stage, a pop group for your entertainment. Pontypridd's very own Senators!'

We heard cheering and clapping filtering through the heavy curtains, and they swished open. There we stood, in front of a sea of faces. We kicked off with an Elvis number, Tommy Pitman singing and gyrating just like The King. It was a thrilling, unforgettable experience and we seriously thought we were going places. We were playing the fabulous Regent Ballroom, for Christ's sake. That was something else, man!

Mr Berriman was also on a high. The rotund middle-aged grey-haired businessman thought all his Christmases had rolled up at once. With such a phenomenal turn-out on the night he knew he was on a winner, and began booking a host of other groups for the venue. During the years that followed, the Regent was visited by Brian Poole and The Tremeloes, Freddie and The Dreamers and many famous bands from the era. The Senators were there first and had started it all.

We were in high demand. During those heady *Discs a Go-Go* and Regent Ballroom days, we were the first rock 'n' roll band playing the Valleys; we were unique in that sense. Then other bands began sprouting up. Cardiff had their fair quota of impressive bands doing the rounds in their own territory, but never venturing north of the City.

The Valleys Teddy Boy culture was very popular at the time, and none were more aggressive than Ponty's gangs. They hated the Cardiff Teds and vice versa. Cardiff bands like The Raiders, starring a then unknown singer-guitarist Dave Edmunds, The Heartbeats, The Afro-Cuban Combo, all stayed well clear of the Valleys if they didn't want their equipment and possibly their heads kicked out of recognition.

There was one really violent confrontation between the Cardiff and Ponty Teds at the town's railway station. Ponty station has the longest platform in Wales, and one Saturday night in 1960 around a hundred Cardiff Teds pitched up, with knuckle-dusters, bicycle chains, coshes. Some were even armed with old fashioned cut-throat razors. Their intention was clear; they wanted to sort out the Ponty boys for good. All hell broke loose. The Ponty Teds got wind of the invasion and were out in force to meet them. With only a few Bobbies on the beat, the warring gangs were uncontrollable.

The fighting lasted for around two hours with both sides beating the hell out of each other and the railway station. Police reinforcements finally arrived forcing the Cardiff gang onto the next train, outclassed by Ponty's 'elite' Teds. I say 'elite' with my tongue planted firmly in my cheek. There was nothing elite about the Teds who prowled around the streets of Pontypridd in feral packs of six or seven. Their sideburns, velvet collared drape suits, boot lace ties and drainpipe trousers marked them out for trouble, and boy did they go looking for it!

I will always be proud of my home town. Many of my ancestors lived and were buried or cremated in Glyntaff Cemetery. My parents married in the church there. Ponty also boasts a stunningly beautiful War Memorial Park, with tennis courts, swimming pools, cricket ground, golf course, and bowling green. The town also hosts a vibrant annual music festival, Ponty in the Park, which attracts the cream of British bands and solo singers.

As a very young child the Park held only one attraction for me and other kids: the open air junior swimming pool. My parents would take me there often, relaxed in the knowledge that I couldn't wander off. As I grew in height, so did my yearning to test the water in the nearby senior pool. It was a whopping seven foot six inches at its deepest end, and resplendent with a three-tier diving board. Diving from that top plank was a pretty scary proposition. I must admit the closest I ever came was holding my nose and jumping.

Up until my tenth birthday I was a rather skinny child, not undernourished, but far from robust. My condition was put down to frequent attacks of tonsillitis, and of course deprivation through rationing during the first five years of my life. Out came the offending tonsils, along with the adenoids for good measure, and all was well. I remember my mother telling me after that I practically sprang up like a bean stalk. I entered my teens sturdy, bright eyed and no longer a slave to religious beliefs. I had put the Chapel fire and brimstone behind me and had my sights set on rock 'n' roll.

My hometown was my world, cradled by protective mountains, with coalmines in every direction. Unemployment was very low and people wanted somewhere to relax. Rock 'n' roll was just breaking through. Jiving was all the craze and dance halls were springing up all over town: The Ranch, The Jive Club to name two. Even established dance halls like The Coronation and St Patricks opened their doors to the rock 'n' roll fever sweeping the land.

It wasn't all sunshine and light, there was a fair underbelly of violence pervading the town back then too. I abhorred every aspect of it. The Ted battle at the railway station wasn't an isolated incident. Fights were quite common in Ponty's dance halls, pubs and streets. After working hard all week I looked forward to the weekend, with a couple of pints on Friday and Saturday nights before heading for one of the dance halls. The intention was always to score with a pretty girl. But it was all undermined by one simple fact. Whenever you were lined up on the edge of the dance floor, you had one eye on the girls and the other trying to see through the back of your head. Predictably a gang of Teds would saunter into the hall and eventually cause havoc, giving everyone a hard time.

They were always looking for a reason to start a fight. I picked up my fair share of black eyes and bruises. But my father had taught me how to defend myself from an early age, and I was six feet tall, twelve stone and as fit as a fiddle. I didn't come off so bad, people who picked on me once, seldom did again.

During the years before I formed The Senators I didn't know of anyone else in Ponty that played guitar. I was always on the lookout for someone who could perhaps teach me some new chords and so on. It was around 1958 when I heard through the grapevine that a young singer, who also played guitar, was regularly performing at The Wheatsheaf, a local pub located near the foot of the Graig hill. The community living on the Graig have their own natural border. To enter the Graig from the southern end of the town centre you have to travel under the railway station platform. The tight-knit community that lived beyond looked out for each other, especially when the mines were going strong. For me as a teenager to venture onto Graig territory wasn't advisable, unless it was completely unavoidable. The young bucks, who lived there, especially the Teds, didn't take kindly to young strangers wandering around their turf. But that didn't deter me; I wanted to know more about this singer, Tommy Woodward, and what I might pick up from his guitar playing.

I thought that visiting The Wheatsheaf on my own would cause a lot less aggravation than if I went along with a couple of friends. It was a really warm summer's evening and the pub's door was wide open. I could hear music filtering through the open windows upstairs. I entered and made my way through the crowded bar and up a flight of stairs. As I entered the room the music stopped. I had arrived just in time for the interval. The room covered most of the first floor, rows of folding wooden chairs, about twenty in all, were lined up facing the far end. A sunburst acoustic 'Hawk' guitar was leaning against an empty chair. The place was pretty full, with a clutch of Teddy Boys in the mix. I ordered a pint, took a seat, and quietly waited.

Today, if The Wheatsheaf were still standing, it would probably host an evening of karaoke. Back then there were no backing tracks to sing along to, you either accompanied yourself on the battered honky-tonk piano or just sang your heart out to a foot-tap or hand-clap. But Tommy Woodward on the other hand was a very rare sight, he had a guitar.

I clearly remember a rather tubby, ruddy faced kid performing a couple of Frankie Laine numbers in the second half. He was attired in full Teddy boy gear, his moon face sweating and lashings of Brylcreem greasing his hair. He sounded so much like Frankie Laine that I was very impressed. A couple of other singers got up and sang well, but I was impatiently waiting for Tommy Woodward to sling that guitar over his shoulder. I really wanted to see what he could do with it.

Eventually his name was announced. I didn't have a clue what he looked like until he loped past my chair and picked up his guitar. Tommy was about 5′10″ or 11″, with tight jeans and an open-necked shirt; he was not at all what I had imagined. He had a shock of black curly hair with a Teddy boy quiff and a large broken nose and crooked teeth. He had a good physique and an intimidating presence.

I can't remember the song he started with. I may have been too engrossed with his guitar playing. At that time it hadn't crossed my mind to form a band. I was still trying to get the hang of my guitar. I recognised that Tommy had a powerful voice and was getting a good response from the crowd. But I didn't hang around too long. I could see that he only knew two or three chords and he wasn't any more advanced than me, to be quite honest. Once he had finished his short spot, ending with a rock 'n' roll number, he headed for the bar downstairs. I followed him out heading for home. I was a little bemused to see Tommy blocking my way at the bottom of the stairs. There were three or four girls cosying up to him. I couldn't see what the attraction was, what with the broken nose and all. I made my excuses squeezing past, and left the pub. I remember thinking that it must have been his tremendously rich macho voice that was the attraction for pulling the girls, it certainly wasn't his looks.

Later, when I had decided on forming a band my interest in singers became more acute. I took myself along to a couple of workingmen's clubs where Tommy Woodward was appearing. I had the idea of him joining The Senators. It was a different ball game to performing at The Wheatsheaf. There he had the Graig neighbourhood encouraging him. But the clubs were filled with hardened miners and some of them were fine tenors and baritones. Tommy would lope on stage, the epitome of a Teddy boy, wearing a powder-blue drape jacket with velvet collar, drainpipe trousers, lace tie and crepe-soled beetle crushers. He would stand centre stage and belt out a selection of Frankie Laine songs: 'I Believe', 'Ghost Riders in the Sky', 'Lucky 'Ole Sun' and then some rock 'n' roll numbers. The bulk of his set was Jerry Lee Lewis hits, and he didn't move an inch, concentrating mainly on his guitar chords. The entire image he portrayed, especially with the broken nose, was pretty dire. He needed working on badly. You're nobody until you're somebody, and Tommy Woodward was certainly that. Back then some were very critical of him, though not to his face. But once out of earshot they said he shouted and that his singing was all over the place. 'Why can't he sing those songs straight, like every other singer around here,' was the usual complaint. In reality the 'singing all over the place' was Tommy's interpretation of a song. When I tried to explain that he was giving some cool phrasing, people just scratched their heads in bewilderment, 'Phrasing? What the bloody hell's that? A right bloody noise if you ask me!' If his audiences had only known then just how famous he would later become.

The few times I watched him perform in those clubs I had the feeling that he didn't particularly want to be there. But he was making a few quid from each gig and he had a wife and young child to support. Tommy had married when he was just sixteen to his childhood sweetheart, Linda Trenchard. I didn't think he had much drive in him, back then, to become a star. He was just drifting along, drinking, singing and eyeing up the local talent, with the occasional rumble along the way with his Teddy Boy buddies.

I mentioned to him once or twice that I was forming a band, but I didn't get any response. I think he realised that joining a band meant sharing the fees, which would have affected his earning power. But as The Senators became more established, especially after appearing on television, Tommy would always enquire about how the band was getting along. I got the impression that he would have liked to be part of the action. By then we had recruited the other Tommy, Tommy Pitman, as our singer. But something happened that would change all our lives.

Around the spring of 1962 The Senators had a regular Friday night booking at the local YMCA, situated at the top end of town near the Old Bridge. The three storey red-brick building first opened its doors in 1910. I used to love playing there. The windowless concert room was deep within the building, and held about two hundred people, who liked nothing better than rocking their socks off every Friday night. There was a roomy stage with red velvet curtains and the acoustics were fantastic. Our fee, shared between the five of us, wasn't so great. The YMCA relied on donations and had little money to spare. We weren't that bothered as it was such a pleasure to play there. The girls used to throng around the front of the stage and make a real fuss over us, who wouldn't enjoy that?

Our singer, Tommy Pitman, was a huge Elvis fan like the rest of us. He used to emulate The King with his leg shaking and pelvis swinging. The rest of the band would join in with some harmony on certain numbers. We used to give Tommy a break by playing The Shadows' entire song book of instrumentals, along with The Ventures and some Duane Eddy hits.

Then some uninvited gremlins interrupted the band's easy-going rhythm and we struck a few bum notes. The bum note was Tommy Pitman's continuing absences. It started with his not attending rehearsals, and then occasionally not turning up at gigs. Eventually we found out that Tommy's penchant for playing cards for money was becoming more profitable than sharing the eight pounds fee we got at the YMCA. In a nutshell he had become disenchanted with singing in the band. This kind of thing happens in every band sooner or later. We were disappointed because he was a good singer and a hell of a nice guy.

That fateful Friday the YMCA was packed to bursting point. Tommy hadn't shown up again: we had lost out to a game of cards. Facing up to another night without our singer we got through the first set. We were looking forward to our half hour break but dreading the second set, our only option was to play a number of repeats and hope nobody would notice.

Tommy Woodward's regular haunt on a Friday night was The White Hart Hotel on the other side of town, near the Graig. It was a safe bet he would be propping up the bar with his buddies. I told the band my intentions and with a window of about twenty minutes before we were due back on stage, I raced the half mile along Taff Street. The White Hart was situated on 'The Tumble', the most vibrant part on entering town from Cardiff. All roads lead through it and onto the Graig, the Rhondda Valleys and back through town to the YMCA. It's an open area surrounded by five pubs and the railway station. The pubs were The Clarence, The Greyhound, The Half Moon, The Criterion and the one I was dashing for, The White Hart. It's hardly surprising the area was called 'The Tumble' with all the boozing that went on there!

I charged into The White Hart and Tommy was there, as anticipated, and propping up the bar along with the other Teds. He was dressed in his trademark powder-blue drape suit with all the necessary Ted requisites. He looked deep in thought supping his pint, whilst his friends were in animated conversation. Maybe he was dwelling on the fact that he was absolutely in a rut as far as his singing was concerned. The Liverpool sound had recently caught on. It was all the rage, and bands had never been more fashionable. We were turning down bookings we were so busy. Poor Tommy was a solo act, strumming his guitar, singing his heart out in social clubs to indifferent audiences who didn't know or care about phrasing and thought Tommy's singing was all over the shop. The Senators by contrast were on the up, appearing on television and building a loyal following. Tommy's future in the music business looked bleak.

I tapped him on the shoulder and he came out of his trance. 'Hey, Tommy,' I said breathlessly. 'Pitman hasn't turned up at the YMCA. How about joining us for the second half? We're due back on stage in about ten minutes. There's a couple of quid in it for you if you're interested.'

He was visibly taken aback; perhaps a little stunned that The Senators wanted him right there and then to sing with them. The bar was silent with anticipation while Tommy gathered his thoughts. Coughing nervously into his hand he replied in his rich gravelly voice, 'Yeah, Vern, Okay. I'll do it for a couple of quid.'

He quickly gulped down his pint and was heading for the exit when a thought struck him: 'Hold on, the YM doesn't serve booze.'

'I know, its run by the Young Christian Association, they're not allowed to serve booze,' I said.

'Oh, I don't know then,' he tut-tutted, shaking his head. 'It's Friday night, I'm out for a good drink Vern. You know, out with the boys like.'

I wasn't going to leave it at that, especially after belting all the way across town, 'Look,' I said, 'what if I buy you some light ales and smuggle them in. Will that be okay?'

He didn't hesitate. 'You're on,' he chuckled. 'Get them in and let's piss off!'

We were out of the pub and tearing back to the YM in no time. It was such a mad dash back that I was surprised Tommy had the breath left to sing a note. The band was waiting for us nervously behind the curtain. I dumped the light ales backstage, and we were just in the nick of time for the second set. Tommy was twitching a bit, having never sung with us before.

'What are we going to kick off with?' he asked. 'Christ we've never even practised together.'

I didn't have the heart to tell him that it was only recently The Senators had acquired two new members: guitarist Mike Roberts and drummer Alva Turner. Our previous members had decided to form their own band, The Strollers. It had to be said that Mike and Alva were a vast improvement on the two that left. But Tommy didn't know that at the time, and to be quite honest we were all of us twitching a bit. Especially as regards unfamiliarity and how these changes would go down with our audience at the YMCA.

Tommy seemed less tense when I suggested we stick to classic rock 'n' roll and twelve bar blues, like 'Linda Lou', 'Lawdy, Miss Clawdy' and Fats Domino. I thought with no fancy stuff, and if we stuck to songs with three or four chords we'd do okay.

With only a few seconds before the curtains would open, I asked Tommy what he'd like to kick off with. Without hesitation, he quickly replied, 'Great Balls of Fire.'

'What key?' we all chorused, adrenaline pumping through our young bodies.

'It's in C,' sniffed Tommy, legs wide apart, his hand holding the microphone in a steely grip. Next moment, the curtains opened and we were off!

The YMCA members seemed stunned by the spectacle. All two hundred of them stared open-mouthed at Tommy the Ponty Ted, his face contorted as he belted out the aggressive music and lyrics. Those youngsters had never seen anything like it. Tommy Woodward standing stock still with an intimidating stance, chest out and legs positioned as though he were about to leap off the stage into the crowd.

There was no applause after the first number, nor the second or third. He was just too much for those kids to take in. What with his huge voice, huge presence and scary persona they didn't know how to react. We ploughed through song after song. Then something magical happened to Tommy. Having no guitar to deal with he began to command the stage, moving from one end to the other and giving some rhythm to his body.

The audience latched onto it and soon they were all dancing. Tommy took a break halfway through the set and polished off the light ales. We carried on with some instrumentals. When he came back a little glassy-eyed, there was no holding him back. He was like a man possessed. The band was steaming along cranking out the rhythm and Tommy was streaming sweat and jumping all over the stage. We finished the night to huge applause and there was a great sense of relief all around: we had cracked it!

I gave Tommy his couple of quid and thanked him for standing in. He was off like the clappers, hurrying back to The White Hart, before last orders were called.

As we packed away our equipment I had to say what was on my mind. I told the band that I wanted Tommy to be part of the line-up. There was no doubt in my mind that he would jump at the chance, especially after the way we had jelled on stage that evening. A couple of the boys weren't in agreement, they argued that Tommy's image was crass, he was always fighting and some accused him of being a petty thief. They wanted to give Tommy Pitman another chance. The band was unsure about broken-nosed Tommy Woodward. But I was pretty persuasive and stuck to my guns. Who would have guessed that four bottles of light ale would play such a pivotal role in the ascent of Tommy John Woodward to Sir Tom Jones, superstar!

There was now something of a crisis within the band. I lay awake that night wondering how I could convince the other members to let Tommy Woodward join. Although he was a bit of a rough diamond, I recognised instantly that his singing far outshone the other Tommy. We simply couldn't rely on Tommy Pitman anymore, he was a great friend, but he would only turn up for gigs when he wasn't embroiled in a massive card game down at his local pub.

Over the following days I kept at it, but my pleas fell on deaf ears. I simply couldn't get everyone to agree to letting him join. Finally I decided that the best way forward was to hold a meeting at my house. On the fateful night we all trooped into the little front parlour, where we used to practise our set. I instantly recognised my mistake: just imagine six tense young musicians, testosterone oozing from every pore, crammed into a tiny room, jockeying for position. In retrospect it would have been better to hold the meeting down the local pub. You could have cut the atmosphere with a knife. I had visions of tempers, tantrums and turmoil erupting before the end of the evening.

Tommy Pitman could handle himself. He was especially fit after recently finishing his national service. Tommy Woodward had a reputation for nutting people. He didn't get his broken nose by accident. I wondered how I would stop the pair of them going for each other's throats if things got out of hand. One of them was going to be disappointed with the outcome of the meeting. I persuaded my sisters, June and Heather, to provide some tea and sandwiches in an effort to keep things civilised.

Nothing was mentioned to Tommy Woodward regarding his rough edges. The meeting was mainly focussed on whether we should reinstate Pitman. I had already made my views known about that, and spoke up for why I thought Tommy Woodward should join The Senators. But by the end of the evening we were still at stalemate, with two votes for Pitman and two for Woodward. Someone then suggested we have two singers in the band. I instantly rejected that as a non-starter. Tommy Woodward hadn't come to the meeting to be told that, and who could blame him. It was imperative that a decision was made that evening or The Senators were in danger of splitting up. No one would budge, so I took a deep breath and said, 'Look boys. I'm the one who set up this band, so I think it's only fair that I make the final decision, either that or we're going to be here till the cows come home!'

I was chancing my arm a bit, but thank God nobody challenged me on it. I turned to Tommy Pitman, I'm sure he knew what was coming, especially as my eyes filled up a bit.

'Tom,' I said, 'I know you still want to be part of the band. Otherwise you wouldn't have bothered coming here tonight. But I don't think you feel the intensity anymore. The spark isn't there for you. Otherwise we wouldn't be playing second fiddle to a game of cards.'

He shrugged his shoulders and lowered his head. He didn't deny it. I held out my hand and he shook it, 'Yeah Vern, you're right,' he said. He turned to Tommy Woodward and shook his hand.

'Looks like you're in Tommy.'

The room was deathly silent. It was an awful moment and I

felt sick to my stomach. I'll never know how I managed to go through with it. But there it was, we were now on a new track. That's how Tom Jones came to join The Senators.

3. THE LADDER TO STARDOM

The ladder to stardom is a slippery climb at the best of times. Tom joined The Senators and we all felt that we'd taken our first steps on that journey. None of us were under any illusions about how difficult a climb we were embarking upon. Along the way there would be tears of joy and heartache, laughter and sorrow, and love and anger.

Having Tom on board was a massive step forward. As 1962 progressed the band went from strength to strength. I used to spend every Saturday afternoon at Cliff Terrace, where Tom, wife Linda and young son Mark, lodged with Linda's mother, Vi Trenchard. The family lived in the basement and in the ground floor room above Tom and I would listen to the latest music hitting the record shops.

Tom had a great selection of records, mainly of his hero Jerry Lee Lewis, and other rock 'n' roll legends like Chuck Berry. But sometimes he would radically change tack and play more sophisticated artistes and music: Brook Benton, Ray Charles, Chuck Jackson, real quality singers. He introduced me to a whole world of music that I had no idea existed. It was a pleasure to listen to them on Tom's two and a half watt Dansette portable record player.

Tom would often ask me to pop a hundred yards up the road with him to visit his mother, who lived a couple of streets away. Freda would always welcome me with a cup of tea and a biscuit, and an enquiry about how the band was getting on. 'Tom never tells me anything,' she would scold. 'I have to drag the information out of him.'

'We're getting there Mrs Woodward,' was my usual refrain. 'We'll be in the charts one day, just you wait and see.' I remember being fascinated by all the huge brass plates decorating the walls, along with the shire horse brasses on wide leather belts. There were brass ornaments everywhere. On the sideboard, the mantelpiece, nest of tables, wherever you looked there was a brass figure or music box. Everything was highly polished – it was a bit of an Aladdin's Cave. Where on earth Freda found the time to keep it all dust free and sparkling I'll never know. She must have been keeping Brasso in business.

At that time Tom was working at Treforest Trading Estate, on the paper mill where they made huge rolls for dispatch all over the United Kingdom. The band would usually arrive at his house at 7p.m. to pick him up for a gig. On the pavement outside 3 Cliff Terrace was a metal grill that protected the kitchen window below. Tom would be finishing his dinner after work and one of the boys would stamp on the grill, shouting for him to hurry up. Inevitably he would appear about fifteen minutes later, wiping shaving cream off his neck with a towel, and chewing on a piece of bread.

The neighbours must have cursed us like hell, rattling on that grill, it set off all the dogs in the area, barking and howling. Tom used to get into the back of the van and immediately fall asleep. While the rest of us were generally too wired by the impending gig, Tom just lay there, out for the count. We always had a hell of a job waking him up when we arrived at the venue.

After Tom joined The Senators we had drawn up a fresh list of material. With a little coaxing we made further changes. We persuaded Tom to drop his Teddy boy image, and he decided on a black leather outfit, Gene Vincent style. It gave him a sexier appearance and was less intimidating for our audiences. I also changed his surname to Scott; Woodward just wasn't very rock 'n' roll. One sunny afternoon we were having a few beers in the Upper Boat Inn. Tom wasn't very keen on the names we were trying to come up with. I nipped out of the pub and into one of those now redundant red telephone boxes close by.

I went through page after page of names. It being Wales, a good three quarters of the phone book comprised of Joneses, so I discarded that early on! I finally came up with a tight name, Scott, which I thought would ring with The Senators. Tom immediately took to it and we had some new business cards printed: *THE SENATORS, with twisting Tommy Scott.*

We still had our residency at the YMCA, and were booked into dances up and down the Valleys. One of our regular venues was Newbridge Memorial Hall, 'The Memo', in the Rhymney valley. If any one of us had fallen off that stage it would have been curtains: it was that high. But it was also high on our list of great venues to play; they used to love us there. It was a large venue with plenty of space to move around. Our lead guitarist Mike Roberts was a happy go lucky character who worked for BBC Wales Television in Cardiff. He was involved in camera work and always looked on the bright side of any situation. If the band were feeling down for whatever reason, Mike would be the positive one, 'C'mon, it's only a blip, get over it,' he would say. I liked him immeasurably; he was great for the band's morale. Not only that, Mike could play a mean guitar solo, with the guitar behind his head, not even looking. Not that he had any option; we would always goad him into doing this during a gig, the audience used to love it.

Mike had a sexy middle-class girlfriend at the time, Carol.

Tom tried it on a couple of times but nothing ever came of it. In fact we all had girlfriends except our drummer. Alva was small in stature, with large protruding ears; he was cruelly christened Dumbo, after the cartoon elephant. I think he secretly took to it, after all the elephant is the largest land mammal, and Alva only weighed in at about eight stone soaking wet. His power lay in his arms; he would beat the hell out of his drum kit. He was a perfectionist as a musician and in his personal life as well. Always neat and tidy, always taking care of his drum-kit, polishing it after every gig and carefully stashing it away. His father, Horace, was also a perfectionist and would eventually become our 'manager'. Horace found us work in social clubs and up market hotels like The Angel, in Cardiff. Horace worked hard for us, refusing to take any commission, other than a small remuneration for petrol expenses when he oversaw gigs some distance away from his home in Treharris. He was married to Pearl, a tiny lady with a sweet soft voice who you had to strain to hear. Sadly the whole family are no longer with us.

Keith Davies had been with The Senators from the beginning, he was a rhythm and lead guitarist and a huge fan of The Shadows. Keith could cover their instrumentals to perfection. He had only just left grammar school when the band was formed. Tall and lean, he was softly spoken, and inclined to be a bit morose at times. But you had a job to stop him chuckling when something tickled his fancy. After all these years, and all the water under the bridge, we still keep in touch. He calls in to see me in Pontardulais, and vice-versa, when I'm over his way in Rhydyfelin. Keith married his girlfriend, Tegwyn, a pretty brunette. I've known their children, David and Debbie, since they were born.

As for Tommy, he was going through the throes of puberty

when he was struck down with tuberculosis. He had to stay in bed for close on two years. Unfortunately he lost out on much of his schooling and although he was tutored at home, his spelling was atrocious. Later, when we found ourselves living in London, Tom would ask one of us to help compose letters to Linda, who was back in Wales. He could read pretty well, but spelling was a nightmare for him. He might not have been the sharpest when it came to academia, but streetwise he certainly was. Having married at the tender age of sixteen, and with a wife and child to support, he was old in the head for his years. There were no flies on Tom. He had a good grasp on how to get the most out of things, especially the girls.

Although married, he couldn't keep his eyes or his hands off them. He was rampant, and an expert at getting laid. The band learned a lot from him, especially how to go about chatting up. Tom was an extrovert alright, nothing like his father Tom Snr, who was a quiet, unassuming character. He always sat in the background whenever I called around to Tom's parents' house in Laura Street.

Sheila, Tom's elder sister, his mother, Tom and I, would be gassing away ten to the dozen and Mr Woodward Snr would be taking everything in, but did not utter a single word. The only time I ever heard him speak was if we passed each other in the street. He was always smartly dressed in a beige suit and brown trilby hat; 'Nice now, innit,' he would say, and off he'd pass, usually on the way to the Wood Road Social Club. He was a miner, and a shrewd one too, I think much of that streetwise shrewdness was passed onto his only son.

Tom had told me about when he told his father that Linda was pregnant. The old man had hit the roof. After he had calmed down he shoved a wad of pound notes into his hand and told him, 'get your arse down to Cardiff Docks and join the bloody merchant navy'. The idea of scrubbing decks at dawn was not an attractive proposition for Tom, and he chose marriage as the better option.

Today, Tom Jones lives in the rarefied atmosphere of super stardom. After decades partaking of the finer things in life and travelling the world, he's delved into the encyclopaedia of life in a way that would have seemed impossible back then. Tom was always very single-minded, that is to say that in his thinking, everything was, 'It is or it isn't.' A very black and white approach with no shades of grey. Tom's shrewdness rarely took any prisoners; right from the start self-preservation was paramount. When the authors of his biography, Stafford Hildred and David Gritten, asked Tom what his most precious possession was he replied, 'My health, because although I love my mother, I love my sister, I love my wife, I love my son and daughter-in-law and grandchildren, they are all very important to me but if I don't have me I don't have them. The most important thing is my well-being.'

You might argue that there's an innate egotism in that remark, but it's that thinking that illustrates Tom's driven self-preservation. Tom was always out for Tom and inevitably left in his slipstream a trail of callous and ruthless decisions that adversely affected those around him. Looking back on our time together with the band, he was seemingly unconscious of the physical, emotional and financial sacrifices we all made.

Back then Tom was always quite laid back, even though he had a bit of a reputation as a lout, in trouble and for fighting. But with the band he was dedicated, never missing rehearsals and gigs. Before joining The Senators he hung around the Teds from the Graig. Roy Nicholls was probably the closest to him, along with Dai Perry, who Tom eventually employed as his minder. Tom sacked Dai after he punched someone in South America and the authorities didn't take too kindly to the assault. After having a glamorous job travelling the world, Dai returned to Pontypridd a broken man, ushered onto the first flight home, and quickly forgotten by his famous school friend. He lived out the rest of his short life alone in a pokey flat in Treforest. His body was found on the mountainside where he and Tom used to play as school kids. Georgie Toms, Johnny Cleaves, and Alan Barratt were all Tom's buddies from that time. They were all part of a formidable gang off the Graig that looked out for each other whenever trouble came their way.

Those close ties with his pals began unravelling quite early on, due to his commitment to the band. We had an abundance of work thanks to Horace Turner. He had had the idea of forming a concert party around Tommy Scott and The Senators. (We had dropped the twisting Tommy bit.) The party consisted of Tom, The Senators, comedian Bryn Phillips and a sweet young female singer. Around that time our guitarist, Keith Davies left. He and Tegwen had decided to tie the knot and wanted to settle down and have kids. He didn't cut ties with the band altogether, always popping up to where we were playing and helping with the equipment.

We auditioned a few guitarists and settled on a diminutive, good-looking young fella, Dave Cooper, or Dai as he was known. His parents ran the Thorn Hotel in Abercynon, which eventually became our rehearsal space. Much later, by a quirk of fate another Welsh band used it for the same purpose: The Stereophonics. The residents around 2 Glyndwr Avenue, where we usually rehearsed, were chuffed to pieces; they almost threw us a street party. They had peace for the first time in years.

Once we had the concert party up and running we were a force to be reckoned with, our bookings went through the roof. The first act on was The Senators minus Tom. We used to warm up the audience with the Coasters' 'Yakety Yak', and a few instrumentals. Then Tom would join us on stage and belt out thirty minutes of power ballads, pop songs and finish with some rock 'n' roll. This was always well received by the audience, with Tom really giving it some welly and leaping about the stage. Then it was the turn of the comedian Bryn Phillips, or 'Bryn the Fish' as he was called around Abercynon. Bryn had a fish round there, delivering fresh cod, haddock and other sea creatures from door to door. His transport was a distinctive green Morris van, with sliding front doors and double back doors from which he would trade his smelly fish.

In the future, long after we had departed for London, Bryn would achieve fame with *The Comedians*, the popular 70s TV show, starring the likes of Bernard Manning, Frank Carson, Mike Reid and other well-known comics of the era. When he was performing with us he used to arrive on stage dressed as a Hawaiian dancer, with nothing on but a bra, raffia skirt, and long black wig. To say that Bryn was a little on the large side would be an understatement. He loved his beer and his stomach reflected his taste for it. He used to sing along to a tape recorder playing popular Hawaiian tunes, with his great big belly flopping all over the place. It was some sight to behold. Bryn always had a slight pong of fish about him, even though he'd scrub himself pink in the bath before every gig. He came to the rescue of the band on more than one occasion when our van broke down. Once he picked us up in his van straight after work. By the time we got to the club we stank to high heaven of haddock. That evening neither Tom, nor the rest of the band had a cat's chance of scoring with any girls. Bryn the Fish smelt even worse than us and nobody would go near him. Even the club's cat beat it out of the back door!

A little prank we used to set up for the interval, was to get little Dai, our guitarist, to crawl inside the bass drum case back in the dressing room. Then we'd roll him out to the side of the stage, pretty well unnoticed, Dai must have felt like a hamster in a rotating wheel. When the audience was settled down after getting their drinks in, Dai would burst out dressed in a gorilla suit, thumping his chest, roaring and growling. There wasn't a woman in the clubs who stayed in their seats. Dai would chase them around the room, screaming hysterically, and right out into the car park. Drinks would be spilt, chairs knocked over, it was chaos. The whole concert party would be doubled up with laughter, even though we'd seen the same routine a thousand times. It was hilarious and we always looked forward to it as the highlight of the night. Poor old Dai would return to the dressing room and climb out of the gorilla suit, bathed in sweat and exhausted. 'Was that okay boys?' he used to gasp. 'Quick fetch me a pint, I'm burning up.'

One memorable night we played a club in Ystrad Mynach, about five miles from Ponty. After the show Tom and I got chatting to a couple of girls we recognised as hairdressers. They had a shop situated on The Tumble, back in Ponty. Ignoring the pleas from the rest of the band to hurry up, they got fed up and left without us. Tom just smiled and said we'd find our own way home.

THE LADDER TO STARDOM

We were so busy necking with the girls that we didn't notice that the club had been locked up. The car park was deserted, we were stranded. It was a chilly night and overcast, and we had no option other than to walk the five miles back to Ponty. We had only gone about a mile along the winding country road when it began to pour with rain. The only cover I could make out in the pitch darkness was some kind of shed on stilts. I could just about see it, illuminated by a distant lamp post, in an allotment beside the road. The four of us made a dash for it, taking shelter under the shed. Lying low in the dark, waiting for the rain to subside one thing led to another and we got down to some serious hank-panky. Afterwards, what with the effects of the beer Tom and I had consumed and the shorts the girls had been knocking back, we all fell asleep, with the rain battering the shed above.

We were abruptly awoken at the crack of dawn by a bloody great cockerel crowing in the allotment. The rain had finally stopped and the sun was up. Rubbing the sleep from our eyes, we heard a soft coo-cooing from above and the pattering of tiny feet. I could just about make out movement through the inch wide gaps in the wooden planked floor above and the sound of fluttering wings. We had taken shelter under a bloody pigeon cot. The girls had a right fright and started screaming. We were all covered in pigeon shit. They must have been bombing us through the gaps in the floor throughout the entire night. The stuff was in our hair and splattered all over our clothes and faces. We stank of ammonia. Bryn and his fish couldn't hold a candle to the terrible stench.

We crawled out from under the shed. The girls were weeping, beating the shit out their clothes and trying to shake it from their hair. Tom and I caught sight of each other, covered head to toe in pigeon shit, and couldn't help but see the funny side: we fell about laughing. The girls were not amused though, hitting us with handbags and kicking us in the shins with their pointed high heels. They called us everything under the sun, but we couldn't help ourselves. The cockerel was still crowing its head off, and passing motorists were slowing down and craning their necks to catch the show.

Eventually the girls calmed down and we began the long trek back to Ponty. We tried to hitch a ride, but drivers would slow down, take one look at us covered in bird shit and speed off. The most embarrassing part of the long trek home was passing the many chapels and churches along the way. It was a Sunday morning and the Sabbath was in full swing. The rather prudish congregations arriving at their places of worship stopped to stare open mouthed. The girls both looked like they'd been dragged through a hedge backwards and they were limping along high heels clutched in one hand and handbags in the other.

The sun blazed overhead and the four of us stank to high heaven. There was no Sunday morning bus service in those days and Tom was becoming a bit agitated. There were white pigeon stains all over his creased jeans. He was in a bit of a state, not only visually but mentally as well. He would have some explaining to do when he got home. What could he say? 'Sorry love, I got delayed. I've been sleeping with a few birds, alright? You know the feathered…' Linda would have gone ballistic. Setting the cat amongst the pigeons would have been putting it mildly.

For the life of me, I can't remember what excuse Tommy made when he got home. But it must have been a cracking one, that's for sure, because he rocked up to the next gig smiling.

On another occasion the band was playing at a club near Merthyr Tydfil, without the rest of the concert party. Fochriw Workingmen's Club was always packed on a Saturday, all the clubs were back then. It was heaving this time with a wedding party, and with the summer temperature soaring it was suffocating inside. We came offstage after the first set soaked in sweat; it felt like we'd been swimming. Tom, after prancing and gyrating all over the stage, was in a right state, the sweat was running off him and forming a pool around his feet.

During the interval the entertainment secretary appeared, carrying a large freshly killed chicken on a silver platter. It was a prize ready for cooking by the lucky person with the winning raffle ticket. The secretary placed it beside a box of chocolates and a bottle of whiskey at the foot of the stage. The intention was to raffle them at the end of the evening.

We went on for the second half, belting out a load of rock 'n' roll numbers, and before long we were drenched again. The audience were well worked up too and were dancing on the floor, on the tables and even on the bar, it was crazy. With the heat and the beer, always a combustible mix, suddenly it all went off like a rocket.

To be quite honest it wasn't unusual back then to witness a punch up from the safety of the stage. A great many of our valleys audiences comprised mostly of miners, who worked hard and played hard. The band used to have fun rating the venues. Sometimes it was entertaining to see the fists flying and heads butting, they used to knock seven shades of shit out of each other. It was like a cabaret spot. The band was never that bothered, as long as we weren't involved.

Unfortunately on this occasion it was no ordinary punch up. It just went on and on, tables and chairs and pint glasses flying all over the place. It was a battleground, totally out of control. Every man in the place was involved in the melee, including the entertainment secretary and the rest of the committee.

We stopped playing when they started fighting at the foot of the stage, and used our microphone stands to keep them from spilling onto the stage. It was like Rorke's Drift. The curtains were suddenly closed and we started packing up our equipment like our lives depended on it, which they probably did. It was bedlam: we couldn't hear each other as we carried the equipment back to the van. They were still fighting as we drove off, lucky to get out in one piece.

We headed back to Ponty in silence. We were all pissed off about losing out on our wages for the evening. I was up front and Tom and a couple of the boys were in back. Suddenly a loud gravelly voice boomed out of the darkness, 'I'm 'aving chicken tomorrow, boys!'

That was back in 1963. Imagine my surprise when I opened my morning newspaper in early 2010. I almost choked on my bacon and eggs. The headline read: 'Village lifts ban on Tom Jones!' The article went on to declare that the village of Fochriw in South Wales had decided to end the banning of superstar Tom Jones from entering the village. "Almost forty-five years previously, Jones was the chief suspect in stealing a fresh chicken that was meant to be raffled on behalf of the Fochriw Workingmen's Club. The chicken went missing during a brawl in the club and was never seen again. But the finger of suspicion pointed at Tom Jones. Now that the singer is about to enter his seventh decade, the villagers have decided to lift the ban, and not take the incident any further. The villagers went on to report that there was no danger of a citizen's arrest being made and Tom was welcome back at the club, and perhaps he might like to perform a couple of songs!"

The report brought tears of laughter and vivid memories of that barnstorming night. Tom's hands were forever wandering somewhere they shouldn't have been, and not only in connection with girls he used to chat up. Nicking things had been part of his rebellious nature, right from his youth. I remember being at home in Glyndwr Avenue one sunny weekend in 1963. Suddenly a car horn blared impatiently outside. I remember thinking, 'who the bloody hell's that idiot?' The horn kept blaring causing the net curtains to twitch in every window up and down the street. Finally I went to the front door to see what the fuss was about.

I got the shock of my life. There was Tom, beckoning me from the driver's seat. He was driving a spanking new red Ford Corsair, his face a picture of happiness. I ran down the garden path and opened the passenger door, 'What the hell are you doing Tom,' I said, 'you haven't passed your bloody test, you can't drive to save your life.'

'Oh shut up Vern and hop in, we're off to Barry island,' he said.

The car belonged to Tony Thorne, Tom's brother-in-law, who had only bought it the week before. I remember saying, 'What the hell is he thinking, letting you of all people take it out for a spin?'

'He doesn't know I'm taking it for as spin does he, he's in bed sleeping one off. Come on Vern, get in, we're wasting time. I'll have to have it back outside the house in a couple of hours.'

I thought 'well on your head be it', he was a damn sight madder than I thought, and I hopped in.

Tony Thorne was married to Linda's younger sister, Rosalind. He had struck lucky with the football pools and won £3000, a considerable amount of money at the time. The first thing he'd splashed out on was the red Corsair. It was his pride and joy. The day he bought it he rocked up to one of our band rehearsals to show it off; he was so excited he took us all out for a spin in it. I've never been so scared in my life; he was tearing along the winding country roads, taking the scenic route to Cardiff. Tony pushed the car flat out, racing down the valley high on the side of the mountain with cliff-edge-drops of hundreds of feet whizzing below us. What Tony hadn't realised was that the newly produced Corsair was prone to losing control, due to a very light rear end. Tom and the rest of us were clinging on for dear life, as the back end slewed across the road. It was white knuckle stuff.

By the time we reached Cardiff, my stomach was in my mouth. I was close to throwing up. Then the finale. On approaching Cardiff Castle, the road bends sharply, Tony was still driving like a maniac, foot to the floor. Taking the corner, the back end spun out of control and we crashed smack into the castle wall. We were badly shaken up, but thankfully there were no injuries. Tony had to take the car to the panel beaters to get the dents beat out.

Now I was sitting in the very same car with Tom at the wheel, driving down to Barry Island. Tom was uninsured, unlicensed, inexperienced and travelling in a vehicle without the owner's consent. I was also now aware that the car had a dangerous fault and was in dire need of modification.

Was I scared? You bet. Did I let on to Tom? No way, I was too proud.

Fortunately Tom took the direct route to Cardiff and then on to Barry. To his credit he didn't behave like his maniac brother-in-law and it was all plain sailing. Tom took it slow and was focused intently on keeping on the right side of the road; he was no doubt worried about damaging it, or worse, writing the car off.

With our hearts in our mouths we arrived at Barry seafront all in one piece. Behind the Greek pillars was a penny arcade and numerous fish and chip cafes. Barry catered for the hordes of Valleys folk who used to make a beeline for the beach at the first sign of hot weather. From an age almost too young to remember, my parents would take us kids there on the Sunday School outing and we'd be enthralled by the funfair.

Leaving the Corsair parked on the front we treated ourselves to ice-creams and made our way down to the sandy beach. It was a lovely sunny day and we fell to talking about the band and making the big time. Living so far away from London and the bright lights, we both realised our chances of being discovered were pretty remote. We could only dream and continue plugging away.

The sea was mirror calm that day and we both found ourselves collecting pebbles and skipping them across the water and out to sea. I clearly remember saying to Tom, 'I'm desperate to get away from Ponty and the Valleys, we're working off the radar, we need to get recognition farther afield, it's the only way,' I sighed, 'besides making it with the band, I've been nowhere, done nothing. I feel suffocated.'

Tom agreed. We were packing them into the clubs and dance

halls, but we didn't have a clue about how to take the next step. Today, we would have made a cracking demo and sent it off to record companies. But back then there were no small recording studios, no home recording facilities to produce anything of quality. We believed we had everything talent-wise, but no one to guide us in the right direction. Horace Turner was a loveable character, straight as a dye, but like us he didn't know how to step up the ladder. He was great at finding us work up and down the valleys, but we longed to spread our wings.

Together on the beach, with the expanse of the ocean in front of us, we both realised we'd have to stretch out across that void if we were to make anything of ourselves. Each deep in thought, we climbed back into the Corsair. Tom crunched the gears into first and we were off back to Ponty. Tom was worried about getting the car back before his brother-in-law missed it, and he gave it some stick on the journey home. There were a few hair-raising moments along the way, but we got back safely and Tom dropped me off at number 2 and raced off for Treforest, a mile away.

I learned the following day that about two hundred yards from his destination, Tom was flagged down by a police officer. He was immediately arrested. Tony Thorne had reported the vehicle stolen from outside his home that morning, and Tom was in deep trouble, with no driving licence, no insurance and without L plates. I had warned him of the risk.

Tom went to court and was fined. He was spitting feathers about it, and thought Tony, being his brother-in-law, would have been able to get him off. But the wheels of justice are merciless. After the court case I heard from one of the band that Tom wasn't very happy with me. He'd been moaning to the boys that he expected me to pay half the fine, as I was in the car with him prior to his being pulled over. I thought this was rather cheeky and told him so, he only had himself to blame and had reaped what he'd sown. He gave me a right black look, but as I pointed out, he was earning good money with the band and could afford the fine. And it wasn't like I hadn't tried to talk him out of taking the car in the first place.

Tom's escapade with the car rubbed off on me and I became interested in owning a car of my own. Later that year my brother Norman sold me his 1947 brown Morris 11. At thirty quid you couldn't go wrong. He fondly called it 'Old Bess'. But I didn't notice any tears of nostalgia when he handed me the keys. He seemed glad to be shot of it. I subsequently learned that 'Old Bess' was an apt nickname and she should have been put out to pasture years before.

But it was my first car and I thought I was the bee's knees, especially sitting behind the steering wheel, stationary outside 2 Glyndwr Avenue. I had to be stationary as I hadn't passed my test and didn't even have a provisional licence. I couldn't afford a tax disc or insurance. But it was mine and one day after I had saved enough cash I would obtain all those things.

It stood there for months on end, gathering cobwebs on the wing mirrors.

Being young and foolish I was tempted to do what Tom did and drive it without all the necessary paperwork. I started tentatively at first, driving it about a hundred yards up the road and back again. It was addictive and I did it more and more often, getting a greater buzz each time. Pretty soon I was driving 'Old Bess' all over the place, without a care in the world.

I began picking the band up, while our new volunteer roadie,

Chris Ellis, drove the van with all our equipment to the gigs. What a blast, now the band was travelling in luxury.

On one particular evening the band were booked to appear at Wattstown Workingmen's Club in the Rhondda. It was a filthy winter's night and the rain was lashing down. We were crammed in like sardines. Poor 'Old Bess' was struggling up the steep Rhondda hills, engine labouring, really struggling with the weight of the band. The wipers were barely operating and my nose was pressed against the misted windscreen. My passengers were all deadly silent, bracing themselves to tumble over the edge of the mountain road and into the abyss below.

We all breathed a huge sigh of relief when the blurred sign for Wattstown appeared out of the driving rain. The car was travelling at around 20mph and backfiring badly every few hundred yards. A single headlight on full beam cut through the darkness ahead of us. Through the dazzle of the full beam we could just about make out the ominous profile of a police officer. He was standing next to his motorbike and flagging us to stop.

My heart leapt into my mouth. 'Oh shit,' I groaned, 'they're going to throw the book at me. I think you're going to have to find another bass player for the gig. I'll be in the nick in no time.'

I pulled up in front of the police officer and buried my head in the steering wheel. The first thing he would probably notice was the lack of a tax disc, and that would inevitably lead on to everything else. I was well and truly done for. The officer tapped on the window. I wound it down and a blast of wind and rain rushed in.

'Excuse me sir,' said the officer in a muffled voice, 'would you mind stepping out of the vehicle. I need your details. Are you aware that both your sidelights are not operating?'

I was about to get out of the car when the officer lifted his goggles up over his crash helmet.

'You bastard,' I screamed in surprise.

The boys were startled and little Dai, our guitarist piped up, 'Vernon button it, you're going to get life talking to the law like that.'

Then I started laughing hysterically, the band must have thought I'd gone into shock.

Tom leaned across the seat and shouted in my ear, 'Calm down Vern, it's not the end of the bloody world man!'

I relaxed and said, 'It's okay boys, this is my brother Norman. He's had me good and proper.' I introduced Norman to the band, and there was relief all around.

Norman was on duty that evening and was aware that we would be on his patch in Wattstown for our gig. He had been waiting patiently in the rain for 'Old Bess' to come chugging along, having previously taken me aside and warned me on more than one occasion that I was taking a risk with no licence and insurance. This was his way of teaching me a lesson. He had decided to show me the consequences of my actions.

After everyone had stopped splitting their sides with laughter, Norman got on his motorbike, gave us a little wave and sped off into the stormy night. We went on to the club and played a great gig.

Afterwards we decided to head for Cardiff. You would have thought I'd learned my lesson earlier. But since I'd been driving it was becoming a bit of a regular thing to do on a Saturday post-gig. We liked to head for Cardiff for a curry and finish the evening at the Haven Club. That evening the South African singing star, Danny Williams, was appearing. At that time he was riding high in the charts with 'Moon River'.

On the way to Cardiff, travelling down the A40, the road slopes down from the mountains and into the flat suburbs on the outskirts of the City. This was always my opportunity to let 'Old Bess' off the leash and get some real speed up. The long slope was perfect for pushing the car to its maximum. That evening we broke our past record and reached just over 50mph. The whole car was shuddering violently and the band was egging me on to see if we could go any faster.

Halfway down the incline we sped past two stationary vehicles on our left. The first was obstructing a decent view of the other, which turned out to be a police patrol car. Two officers leapt into the patrol car and gave chase. I remember thinking just my luck: twice in the same evening, although this time I wouldn't be let off by my brother. To make matters worse, Dai our guitarist had been putting pint after pint away back at the club and was absolutely legless. He was leaning half out the window, with his finger pointing at the police car and firing imaginary bullets; he could have been on a stagecoach being chased by Apaches, for all I knew!

At the bottom of the incline were a set of traffic lights, luckily they were on green and I took a sharp left almost on two wheels. A hundred yards ahead was another set of lights, and they turned red as we careened through them. 'Old Bess' was now overheating badly. I knew I had to stop soon or the car would blow a gasket. I turned down a quite side street and coasted to a halt in front of a couple of cars. I turned off the engine and the lights, and we all ducked down. The flashing light from the patrol car washed over us, and it sped past, its siren peeling out enough to wake up the entire neighbourhood.

It was a very narrow escape, and we all gave Dai a right rollicking for his John Wayne impression.

We finally made it to the curry house and had the works. Then it was onto the Haven Club. It was a fairly small venue and when we rolled up, Danny Williams was just about to go on stage. We all stood near the bar, Tom propping himself up. Like Dai he'd sunk a good few pints and was glassy eyed.

Danny Williams was diminutive man with a lovely silky voice. He began rolling off his hit songs and received a fantastic response from the audience. Then he began to sing 'Moon River' and the room fell completely silent, this was by far his biggest hit to date.

Then it happened. I was standing beside Tom. He put his pint to his lips, took a sip, cleared his throat and began singing along with 'Moon River'. Danny was singing through the house system but Tom was singing even louder, leaning back against the bar, belting it out. Here we go, I thought, there may be trouble ahead.

Halfway through the number Danny finally conceded defeat and left it to Tom to finish off the song. I think in part the decision had been made for him. The audience had all turned in their seats and were staring intently at Tom propped up against the bar. As Tom finished the song the audience applauded. It was very naughty of him to have intruded on Danny's performance, but the star took it very well and said, 'Man, I know you Welsh folk can sing. But that was something else. They must be putting something in the water down here!'

It was a memorable evening. At the time I thought it quite surreal, it was like something you only see happening in movies. But it did demonstrate just how badly Tom craved attention. He was hungry for recognition; we all were. But boy did Tom get buckets of attention that night as the audience tried to drag him up on stage for an encore.

We finally left the club, and made our way back home. After the earlier incidents I drove very slowly and kept an eye out for patrol cars. I remember feeling utterly deflated as we reached the outskirts of Cardiff. A lone police constable flagged us down with his torch. It had been a long evening; I was exhausted and felt resigned to my fate.

'Here's prison looking at ya,' quipped Dai, probably getting his own back after the rollicking we had all given him earlier about his 'shooting Apaches' episode.

I would down the window expecting the worse and wishing I'd listened to my brother and gone straight home after playing our gig.

'Good morning sir,' said the constable, peering into the car and shining his torch in our eyes, 'out rather late aren't we?'

'Yes Officer,' we chorused sheepishly.

'Been anywhere interesting lads?'

'Not really,' I gulped, 'we've been for a curry, after going to the pictures,' I lied. 'Oh yes and what film was that then?'

Before I could think of an answer Dai slurred, 'Shnowight an the Sheven Dwarfs ofhiffer!'

'Very funny, 'snapped the constable, 'I suppose you're wondering why I flagged you down.'

Here we go, I cringed. After the evening's freakish events and near misses with the police I assumed they would throw the book at me.

'Get out of the vehicle son; you have some explaining to do.'

That's putting it mildly I thought. The constable grabbed my arm in a vice like grip and pulled me to the front of 'Old Bess', 'I have to caution you,' he said pointing at the headlights, 'your side lights aren't functioning. Get them fixed, now clear off.'

I never drove 'Old Bess' again; I'd definitely learnt my lesson. As for my brother Norman, he sure put the fear of God into me that night. But how could I not forgive him, it was Norman that got the band one of our first big breaks. He wrote a letter to the TV station that broadcast *Discs-a-GoGo* recommending they check out an exciting new band from Pontypridd.

4. THE GREEN FLY

Women defined Tom, even at that stage of our careers. Linda was his wife, but she didn't crave fame like he did, neither did she have his energy. He was a party animal and he was always on the lookout for new conquests, in that respect he was insatiable, even then.

All the Senators had girlfriends. I was going steady with Jean Evans, who also lived in Rhydyfelin. She and Tom's wife Linda wore identical hairstyles, very short and platinum blonde, in the style of the Hollywood actress Kim Novak. They were just about the only girls in town daring enough to sport such a vivid style; they certainly made heads turn. Jean was also very friendly with Tegwen, our guitarist's girlfriend. We all had some great laughs together. But rock 'n' roll got in the way of courtship, especially when the band headed for London in search of fame.

At that time the band had secured a residency at Bedwas Workingmen's Club, near Caerphilly. The venue was more commonly referred to as the Green Fly; it was curious name and nobody seemed to know its origin. We played there every Tuesday and Thursday in the packed concert room. Our fee for each night was £11 shared five ways. It was at the Green Fly that three individuals became involved in our lives, who were to prove a decisive factor in Tom and The Senators taking the next step.

Along with our guitarist, Keith Davies I was a hairs-breadth away from not making that particular gig. I had recently bought a 125cc Ariel Leader motorbike, a phut-phutter in canary yellow. I was a provisional driver, with L plates. One gloriously sunny morning, having the day off from work, I called in on Keith, who lived just down the road. We both decided a day trip to Bristol Zoo was on the cards. I whipped off the L plates, as it was illegal to take a passenger as a provisional driver.

There weren't any problems getting there, but getting back in time to play our gig at the Green Fly was another matter entirely. Somewhere between Bristol and Newport the bike got really noisy, and with every mile it just became louder and louder: we phut-phutted on at a slower pace to keep the rattle down. Then the exhaust pipe began bouncing up and down, the bolt holding it to the chassis worked itself loose and fell off. The pipe dropped, scraping along the road and throwing out a trail of sparks.

I pulled over and Keith had a stab at reattaching the damn thing with a piece of string. Every time we got going again the string snapped. Time was against us, the gig was looming and we were miles away from Bedwas. After our third attempt at fixing it failed, Keith yanked off the exhaust and slung it over his shoulder. We kept our eyes peeled for a garage that might be able to fix it. The bike began backfiring badly, the noise was like rapid machine gun fire, deafening.

By the time we came across a garage that was open, we realised we simply didn't have the time to get it fixed and make the Green Fly in time for the gig. There would have been hell to pay from the band if we missed it, not to mention the entertainment secretary, who might have cancelled our residency. We made the decision to push on. It was a miracle we weren't pulled over by the law, but we made it to the club with minutes to spare. Tom and the band were on pins, the place was heaving and they'd been wondering where the hell we'd got to. When they caught sight of the pair of us they fell about laughing. Not out of relief, it was our appearance. Keith and I had worn goggles riding the bike. We were filthy soot black from head to toe, and removing the goggles revealed the only bit of clean skin on us. We were desperate for a pee and a freshen-up, but there was no time, and we were bundled on stage. God knows what the audience thought. By the time we finished the first set my bladder was fit to burst.

As for the Ariel Leader. I came off it one icy morning close near the Old Bridge in Ponty, sliding across the road and into the path of an oncoming lorry. (What is it with me and lorries?) It was a close call and I got rid of it.

Chris Ellis came to the gig at the Green Fly that night. Chris was a TV engineer by trade. He had heard about Tom and The Senators, and how popular we were becoming. He had decided to form his own opinion. Dark haired and slightly built, Chris was a chain smoker and as wired as the TVs he repaired. He stood at the back of the concert room mesmerised by the band. Little did we know then how important he would become to Tom and the band, and that he and I would become friends for life.

Chris started coming along regularly to the Fly and befriended us. If one of our amplifiers played up, he was on hand to fix it. With his engineer's knowledge he would soon get rid of the buzz and have it working perfectly. Our amplifiers weren't the only thing that used to play up. Occasionally so did our van. When the inevitable happened and it was out of service for a few days Chris came to the rescue. He offered to drive us to gigs in his works van. A really close bond was formed, and from that day he became our roadie, working on TVs during the day and with us at night.

Unassuming to anyone who didn't really know him, he was a bit of a character: wiry, alert and as courageous as a Jack Russell. Chris could smell a rat a mile away. Many years later, long after Tom and I had acrimoniously parted company, Chris remained Tom's personal road manager. He took care of all manner of business on behalf of the star; he was incredibly loyal, and as close to Tom as his own shadow.

During that spell at the Fly, Tom was involved in a very serious accident. Although he was completely absorbed with The Senators and dreams of stardom, he still found some time to hang out with his Graig friends when the opportunity arose. One evening his mate Johnny Cleaves drove a bunch of them over to the Fly to see the band. They offered Tom a lift back home. Tom, Roy Nicholls (Nicko) and Dai Shephard all got into Johnny Cleaves' black Austin A70 and left the club after our set.

I was shocked to hear the following day that they'd been involved in a crash with another vehicle. Whilst rounding a bend on Nantgarw Hill there had been a nasty collision. All four passengers were ambulanced to the local Miners Hospital, near Nantgarw Colliery.

Roy Nicholls had broken his jaw, Dai Shephard had been sliced from ear to ear and needed 36 stitches, and Johnny Cleaves' ear was hanging off by a thread of gristle. Tom miraculously had escaped with just a nasty bump on his forehead. He had been in the back, and furthest away from the impact. Roy Nicholls was later transferred to Chepstow hospital where they specialised in facial injuries. Johnny Cleaves' head injuries were very serious, he walked around like a zombie for months afterwards and his speech was impaired, but eventually he made a full recovery. Tom had concussion, and his head pounded if he sang a note, so we cancelled a number of bookings. Singing demands a lot of straining to reach the top notes, and increases the blood pressure in the head. Knowing Tom was always going for gold, hitting the top of his register, it was just too risky. Some months later, after Nicko had fully recovered, he visited us at the Green Fly. His favourite song was 'FBI' by The Shadows. As soon as he walked in the club we broke into a loud rock rendition of it, much to his amusement.

We started earning good money and there was some discussion about quitting our day jobs and going full time with the band. After a lot of thought I decided to continue with the day job and gig at night. The rest of the band arrived at the same decision, with the exception of Tom. He packed in the day job and signed on the dole instead. He told me that from then on, his only job was going to be singing, and so it has remained to this day.

We all felt a real sense of momentum with the band; things were moving in the right direction. We were looking for that final piece of the jig-saw to fall into place. One night at the Green Fly, there were two student-type characters who stood out like sore thumbs from the rest of our usual crowd. Ray Godfrey and John Glastonbury approached us with an offer of management. The dark-haired Ray Godfrey was of medium build and height – the better looking of the two. John Glastonbury was smaller framed with lighter hair, thin lips. He was a bit sly of eye and hard of voice. They were both a few years older than the band and dressed fairly conservatively. Ray came from Ystrad Mynach and I believe John was from somewhere near Caerphilly, you could never be sure of anything he said: he could have come from anywhere.

We told them we'd need some time to think about it but the general consensus was, what did we have to lose? We didn't agree to anything there and then, but they returned the following week and convinced us they could get us a record deal with a major label. It wasn't very long before we signed a contract with them. They met us at the Thorn Hotel in Abercynon, where we rehearsed, and we put pen to paper.

We were young and naïve, and like lambs to the slaughter. Looking back it was like every cliché in every movie, right down to the dialogue of 'sign here kid and we'll make you a star'. About the only props missing were the fat cigars as they handed us their pens to sign the contract. As I recall, the two stand-out clauses were that they would share 10% of all we earned and they would take another 10% for any venues they arranged for us to play. To be completely honest none of us took much notice of the small print, there was so much of it, and it was full of words like 'perpetuity'. We would certainly come to regret that many years later, in London's Old Bailey Law Courts.

They were certainly a couple of oddballs. The radio comedy *The Goon Show* was very popular at the time, and they were huge fans. They'd ape the show and indulge in silly humour which didn't always come off. They didn't really click with the band; they were two squares in a circle of musicians. It transpired that they had no contacts in show business or any real knowledge of the music scene. They just saw an opportunity to exploit our talent.

The band nicknamed them Myron and Byron. I got on quite well with Byron (Ray Godfrey) he was quietly spoken and always respectful to the band. Myron (John Glastonbury) on the other hand was arrogant, brash and condescending. Overly fond of giving orders, he rubbed up the band the wrong way and created a lot of friction. Alva Turner, our drummer, disliked him so intensely he wanted out. He agreed to stay until we found another drummer, but he could hardly stand to be in the same room with Myron. Invariably there were fireworks when the pair clashed.

Good drummers were a scare commodity at that time. There were only two other bands in the Valleys, The Strollers and The Bystanders, and neither particularly wanted to give up their drummer. Then we heard on the grapevine about a talented kid, Chris Slade Rees. Chris had just left Pontypridd Grammar School and was working as an assistant in Clark's shoe shop in Taff Street.

Tom and I called into Clark's one afternoon and sure enough there was young Chris down on one knee, fitting a shoe on a customer. He was fair-haired, about five foot ten inches tall, slim and good looking. If he could play as good as he looked, we had found our new drummer. We arranged to call in at his home in Treforest later that evening. His mother answered the door and led us into the front parlour. Chris was already waiting for us, all set up at his drum kit. Tom asked him about his experience and if he had played with any bands. Chris screwed up his nose and scratched his head awkwardly, 'I've never been in a band Tom'. Tom looked at me and was preparing to leave.

Our hopes vanished. 'Oh dear,' I sighed, 'well we're here now, you might as well have a bash on the drums. Why not try a drum solo?'

'I've never tried a drum solo,' he mumbled.

'Well can you play anything we might know? Something from the charts maybe?' I said.

'I know the intro to 'Walk, Don't Run' by The Ventures,' he volunteered.

'Well go on then,' said an exasperated Tom, 'give it a bloody crack.'

Clearly nervous, poor Chris warmed up with a roll around the kit before steaming into the intro. The windows vibrated as did almost everything else in the room. The volume was awesome, especially considering how lightweight Chris was in stature. He beat the hell out of those drums. I winked at Tom and he nodded back. The intro Chris played wasn't particularly difficult for an average drummer. It was the way he had tackled it that put smiles on both our faces. Tight, aggressive, enthusiastic and stylish: we had found our new drummer.

Chris Slade not only performed all over the world with Tom Jones and The Senators, or The Squires as we later were called. He went on to join a number of super bands: Manfred Mann's Earthband, Uriah Heep, Led Zeppelin, AC/DC, Asia and other big names. When we played The Flamingo in Las Vegas in 1968, Elvis Presley came to watch us and was so knocked out by Chris's great drumming that he tried to recruit him for his comeback tour. It was a chance in a million, Chris was really keen, but our manager at that time, Gordon Mills, said no. It still haunts Chris, especially after how badly he was treated later by both Gordon and Tom.

With Chris on board The Senators were back on track. Myron and Byron had big plans for the band. They got us a great gig playing Porthcawl's famous Pavilion, supporting Billy J. Kramer and The Dakotas. Billy and the Liverpool-based band were riding high at the time and regularly making the hit parade with big sellers like 'Trains, Boats and Planes' and 'Little Children'.

Playing the Pavilion was a big deal for us; it was our best venue to date. We arrived early for our set-up and sound check. The Dakotas' roadies were busy checking out their amps, tuning the guitars, and even giving them a polish. It was a different world, pampered wasn't the word; we could hardly believe it being so used to lugging our own kit around.

Billy was on a roll at the time, and even though it was a large venue, they had to start turning people away; it was packed to the rafters. We were on first as the warm up and we went down a storm. The place was electric and the crowd went wild when Tom and the rest of us started leaping about the stage. It was pandemonium; we were used to getting a good reception from our audiences but nothing like this.

Billy and the Dakotas were watching us from the wings, and they didn't look entirely happy with how we were received by the audience. Tom couldn't help but notice, and winked at me. We were hell bent on showing them how a Welsh band could perform, and we really went up a couple of gears that night.

The band got so carried away that we over-ran our half hour spot. Even when we eventually finished, the audience wouldn't let us get offstage. They were demanding more. Finally it was Billy's turn and the place went wild as soon as The Dakotas took to the stage. In all honesty, compared with Tom's voice Kramer's was pretty timid, and I thought their act was a bit static. But still the girls in the audience were screaming and fainting as soon as he opened his mouth. However, after a few numbers their excitement seemed to fizzle out and you could practically feel the crowd begin to deflate.

There were no dynamics in their set to speak of, and once they'd exhausted their laid back hit singles, they ran out of steam. The Dakotas started to struggle to keep the audience's attention. The set finished on a low key and Billy and his band disappeared back to the wings. Quite suddenly the audience began chanting for us to come back on.

We had only been booked to play the one set. Kramer was booked to finish off the show. But the audience just kept on chanting for us and refused to leave the venue. The Pavilion's manager took us aside and asked if we would go back on stage. It didn't take us very long to reach a decision and we belted out another half hour of high powered music. We converted a lot of Dakotas fans to Senators fans that night!

Later, during the early 70s, Billy J. Kramer recorded a song I had written, 'Walking'. It was a brooding Tony Joe White style back beat number which told the story of an escaped convict with only one thing on his mind, to reach his girlfriend before the bloodhounds picked up his scent. It even had sound effects of chains dragging with his every step. Billy cut a great disc and I'll always be thankful to him for it.

After the success of the Pavilion gig, Myron and Byron put together a portfolio of the band in which they wanted to include a demo of four tracks. They thought this would be a great way of trying the major record companies. We recorded the songs on a portable eight track studio in the changing room toilet at Ponty YMCA. The band still had a residency there so it was easy to arrange and the acoustics were ideal, having an echo effect. Myron and Byron took the reel-to-reel tape up to London, promising us this was it, the big time. Unfortunately nothing came of it and they returned tails between legs.

That was the last we heard about the recording until 2008 when I read a newspaper headline: 'OUR TOM SINGING IN THE LOO UP FOR GRABS'. The article went on to report that a rare recording made by Tom Jones in the toilets of Pontypridd YMCA was expected to fetch thousands of pounds at auction. The four songs were recorded by 'Jones the Voice' two years before he became famous and were recorded by a soundman at the former TWW TV Company. The soundman wished to remain anonymous and placed the tape in a Rock and Pop memorabilia auction at Christies in London. It was the earliest known recording of Jones and the band to have survived. A spokesman from Christies said, 'These recordings have genuine historical significance as they mark the birth of the Tom Jones phenomenon.'

I obviously remember recording the tracks. But it was so long ago I can't remember which songs we put down. It was probably a couple of ballads and rock 'n' roll numbers. It would be interesting to hear them again, but unless the purchaser comes forward there's little chance of it happening.

At the time, Chris Ellis was driving us all around in a cream Morris J van. Chris had gone to town and carpeted the floor and the walls. He'd even put in a couple of sofas for us to stretch out on. Whenever we had the opportunity, we did a lot more than stretch out on them, and there were a lot of opportunities. We christened it the passion wagon and grew very fond of that van and its facilities. Soundproofed by the carpet inlay there were seldom any squeals or groans filtering from it to attract unwarranted attention. Needless to say the springs and suspension took a bit a battering.

We all went into mourning when the van skidded into a wall

on an icy road one night. It was a write-off. Myron and Byron forked out some cash on a replacement. But it was a clapped-out yellow Thames van. It was much smaller than the Morris and with none of the legroom for amorous encounters. The Senators were a lot less passionate about it, particularly Tom.

After getting a poor response from the major labels in London, Myron and Byron changed tack and decided to use an independent record producer, Joe Meek. Joe had a reputation as a raging homosexual with a violent temper. He was pretty far out there and the general consensus at the time was that he was mentally unstable. But he was a gifted record producer, and way ahead of his time. He was famous for composing the legendary instrumental 'Telstar', which was a massive hit for The Tornados, who topped the charts in both the UK and the US with it.

The 'Telstar' recording had a unique sound. Meek had experimented with combining a number of Copycat Echo Chambers and compressed the sound, giving it a searing atmospheric bite. He also had a number of other artistes on his books. The fair-haired John Leyton topped the charts with 'Johnny Remember Me', and Meek's live-in-lover, Heinz, had recently had a hit with 'Just like Eddie', a tribute to the great Eddie Cochran.

We were all pretty excited about working with him. When the recording was finally booked we piled into the van for the trip up to London. It was a ten-hour journey: there was no M4 motorway in 1963. With Chris Ellis at the wheel we made it as far as Shepherds Bush. Chris pulled over and refused to go any further, 'I'm bloody shattered and it'll be a maze from here. I'll be lost within two hundred yards. Let's unload the gear and get the Underground from here to Holloway Road.' We unloaded the van and carted everything across London, changing underground trains a few times to reach our destination in North London.

Joe Meek's flat and studio were above a leather shop, selling handbags and hold-alls. The building was a typical Victorian three-story terrace, number 304 Holloway Road. There was a separate entrance at the side of the shop with a steep set of stairs leading up to Joe's flat. It was a bit awkward for me to climb as I was on crutches at the time having broken my ankle a few weeks earlier on a coach trip to Barry Island to see Dave Edmunds and The Raiders perform. The venue was heaving and a fight broke out. I was flung down some stairs to the bottom, breaking my ankle. I'd been playing gigs in the valleys, leg in plaster, ever since. Now my arms were aching like hell after crutching it across London. But I didn't have to carry any of the gear, much to the boys' chagrin, so I was ready to play and looking forward to it.

Joe Meek introduced himself; he was black-suited, with the complexion of a corpse. We set up in his front room under his steely, shadowed gaze. There was a massive white mantle-piece and a cavernous fireplace. Joe had Chris Slade set up his drum kit there and explained that he got a better sound that way. The opposite wall had a huge glass pane fitted into it and gave a view of the bedroom.

We all of us stopped dead in our tracks midway through setting up. There, lying naked and spread out on the double bed, was Heinz. He was calmly observing us and gave us a little wink when he noticed our amazement. None of us knew where to look; it was uncomfortable to say the least. Meek and Heinz exchanged smiles. I had the impression that they'd deliberately set up the scene on the off chance that one of us could be persuaded to join in the fun in the bedroom after the session. Instead it left us feeling a little edgy.

Joe sensed our discomfort, nipped into the bedroom and closed the curtains. That was the last we saw of Heinz. This was all a bit risky back in 1963. Homosexuality was still illegal and frowned upon by the general public. God only knows what people must have made of Heinz, parading along Holloway Road with his peroxide blonde hair. He had no inhibitions whatsoever.

I plugged my Fender Bass into the amplifier and Mike Roberts and Dave Cooper followed suit. Chris was positioned in the fireplace as requested by Meek. Tom was ready with the microphone; we were all just waiting for the sound check. Joe was next door in the control room with the door ajar. We could see him fiddling around with switches and knobs and spools of tape, surrounded by echo chambers, control desks, amplifiers, speakers and all manner of strange looking gadgets. He looked like the Dr Who of music producers ensconced in his own tardis. He was in a whirl, wild-eyed and sweating profusely, a real genius at work.

There was no intercom between the control room and the front room. Joe shouted instructions through the door. We were just about ready to lay down the first track when he bounced in and snatched my guitar lead out of the amp and plugged it into a direct line to the control room. Un-amped I was unable to hear myself play. Off he went back to the control room leaving me totally baffled. When I protested that I couldn't hear myself play, he shouted back, 'Don't worry I can!' I don't know how I managed. He explained that the bass sounded better going through a direct line. It was all part of the special Joe Meek sound.

The session produced a number of songs. One in particular Meek had written about himself, 'Lonely Joe.' Another was written by the songwriter who had penned the Dusty Springfield hit, 'I Only Want to be With You'. We also laid down a couple of Jerry Lee Lewis numbers including 'Great Balls of Fire'. We ended the session with a song called 'Chills and Fever'. It was agreed that we would return in a few weeks to finish off the sessions, and the plan was to have several tracks.

Joe decided we needed some publicity photos taken. We tramped off to some nearby parkland. It was rather awkward for me, with my leg in plaster. I had to stand behind tree stumps, foliage and other stuff in the various photos to hide my broken ankle. Then back to the studio where we began packing away our equipment. Joe had been all over Tom like a rash from the onset. With the band out of the room, shifting the equipment downstairs, he made his move, 'You sound great Tom, but I haven't seen you perform, how about a little demonstration?'

'I can't do that now, come and see us at a gig. We'll play a pub nearby if you set it up,' replied Tom.

We'd all realised something was amiss when the bass drum came bouncing down the stairs and rolled across the pavement and into the road: closely followed by a clearly livid Tom Jones.

Tom told me later, on the long journey back to Wales, that, 'The bugger was giving me the come on. I couldn't believe it. He couldn't stop admiring my jeans, he kept telling me they fitted me like a glove.'

'You've get a nice set in there haven't you?' and the bloody bastard stroked my crotch, he just made a lunge for my balls Vern!' said Tom.

We were all in stitches but Tom was fuming: he didn't like it one bit.

A few weeks later we rocked up again for the second session. Tom had come to terms with Meek's nature at that stage and just wanted the session completed as quickly as possible, all business. We were midway through a song when Joe shouted through the door. He wanted Tom to sing a certain passage differently. Tom just rolled his eyes. Off we went again and Tom sang it just as before. Joe burst into the room clearly agitated and insisting Tom sing it differently. Tom being Tom stubbornly repeated his version on the next take.

Joe Meek stormed into the studio waving a gun, his eyes blazing. He levelled the gun at Tom and pulled the trigger. There was an almighty bang and Tom's face turned a deathly white. Meek let out a manic laugh and stood toe to toe with Tom, their noses practically touching, 'Now will you sing it the way I want?' he hissed through gritted teeth.

Only then did he inform us that the gun was a harmless starting pistol. On the next take Joe got his way.

Joe Meek was a law unto himself. Perhaps he was getting his own back after being spurned by Tom. We had hoped this was the final session but he insisted we return for one more recording. On that occasion we made the long journey to London to find the door to the studio answered by his landlady. 'Sorry boys, Joe must have forgot you were coming. He's down in Gloucester attending a family wedding. I'll tell him you called.'

Mrs Violet Shenton must have innocently thought we were living somewhere in London.

'Just called in, Mrs Shenton?' I wearily replied. 'We've been on the road for the last ten hours up from Wales. How about putting the kettle on?' She duly obliged and put a smile back on our faces.

Later, Joe Meek contacted Myron and Byron. He told them he'd made a deal with Decca and they would be releasing one of the songs in the next few months. Time dragged by – it was an eternity. Eventually he stopped taking calls when our managers pestered him for a release date.

Fair play to Myron and Byron they didn't let matters rest there. They charged up to the studio in London to confront Meek: arriving at 10 a.m. with black bags under their eyes after travelling through the night. They banged on his door and were met with a resounding silence. Refusing to give up they kept hammering away at the door. Eventually Joe appeared looking dishevelled and gave them a murderous scowl, demanding to know what the commotion was for.

Then he started screaming and ranting, and literally began pulling his hair out. There was to be no release date with Decca. He screamed that he was sick to death of Tom and The Senators and he was twenty pounds out of pocket after paying for the publicity photos. Myron and Byron informed him that they had been in contact with Dick Rowe, the boss at Decca, and he'd informed them he'd never heard of The Senators or any proposed release date. Meek went berserk. He ran upstairs wailing threats and reappeared waving our contract, which he ripped to shreds, spraying it like confetti and slamming the door in our managers' faces.

When Myron and Byron recounted the events to the band in Ponty, we were livid. It has been a colossal waste of time and energy. Tom was so angry he insisted on going to London to confront Meek. He was going to nut Joe and give him a good going over. Tom persuaded Chris Ellis to drive him to Meek's studio in his Mini. They managed to burst their way into Meek's studio and confront him. Tom went for him and Joe ran around his desk wailing. To escape Tom's clutches he climbed up onto the big mantelpiece out of harm's way. Tom later told me, 'He thought I was gonna kill him Vern. He was hysterical, crying don't touch me, leave me alone. It was pitiful so we left him to it.'

Tom and Chris searched through Meek's studio for the tapes, but came back empty handed. That was something we would all later regret.

I must give some credit to Myron and Byron. Up until this point they'd both given the band the best of their limited capabilities. It was a massive task trying to get a record contract for an unknown band, especially with so much competition in London. Getting Joe Meek to even take an interest in us had been remarkable, even though it proved to be a dead end. He was riding high in the business at the time. We must have seemed like a right bunch of country bumpkins to him: out of sync with contemporary music trends, and not at all sophisticated by London standards.

The whole episode was a body blow, a real set back. Myron and Byron were really disenchanted with the whole music business. Still, The Senators were not going to be defeated. We were five fingers on the same hand. No way were we going to call it a day and disappear back into the relative obscurity of the mountains of Wales. We bounced back and recorded more demos which Myron and Byron took to London. If the door won't open you got to keep on knocking.

5. THE TOP HAT CLUB

Myron and Byron discovered that the top disc jockey of the time, Jimmy Savile, often stayed in a hotel in Paddington. He needed to be close to Central London for his work at the BBC. They hatched a plan to get the demos to him in the hope that he would be able to pull a some strings and get us some exposure.

They'd been gone a few weeks trying to pin down Savile and we hadn't heard anything from them. They might have been gadding around Soho for all we knew. We were becoming impatient and it was decided that Tom should drive up to London with Chris Ellis and find out what was going on. They tracked our wayward managers down to the same hotel that Jimmy Savile frequented. Unfortunately they didn't have enough money for a room so Tom and Chris kipped in the Mini overnight. It must have been quite a squeeze. They woke at dawn hungry and as stiff as floorboards. They kept their energy up by pilfering two bottles of milk from a nearby doorstep.

Tom informed us when they came back to Wales that Myron and Byron might just as well have been Pinky and Perky for all the good they'd accomplished. They'd swanned around London and hadn't even spoken to Jimmy Savile. Later Tom got agitated and decided to give Myron and Byron a rocket to hurry things along – he hadn't enjoyed kipping in Chris's Mini. He rocked up to their hotel door one morning at 8 a.m. and kept banging on it to get a response. Quite suddenly, Jimmy Savile popped his head out of another room along the long corridor complaining about the racket. Tom was speechless but quickly regained his composure and had a chat with Jimmy, explaining about the band and asking his advice.

That evening Tom had a massive row with our errant managers. Tom and Chris stormed off and went for a few pints to calm down. Feeling more courageous as a result, they went back to the hotel and knocked on Savile's door. He welcomed them into his room, and Tom poured out his heart, explaining that he'd lost all faith in our managers. Savile sympathized and told Tom to call back the next morning with the demo tapes. He then 'fixed it' by handing the tapes to Peter Sullivan, the top record producer at Decca.

Shortly afterwards, Peter Sullivan made the journey down to Wales to see us in action. We obviously wanted to make a good impression and arranged for a coachload of our fans to come along to the gig and support us. Most audiences in Wales were used to seeing us on a regular basis; we had become part of the furniture. We paid for a coach out of our own pockets and it picked up a bunch of kids from outside the YMCA in Ponty and transported them over to the gig in Newport. Sure enough, when Peter Sullivan turned up the kids were raring to go. They put on a great show, hollering and screaming throughout our set. Sullivan seemed very impressed with the fan worship.

Afterwards, the London-based producer found himself locked out of the Cardiff hotel we had booked him into. He'd enjoyed the gig a little too much and misjudged his journey time from Newport to Cardiff, arriving too late to check in. He ended up spending the night sleeping in his posh car and wasn't best pleased. We felt like we were back on track and even though that was the last we heard of Peter Sullivan for a little while, he eventually became Tom Jones' recording producer.

It was the spring of 1964 when things shifted seismically. Gordon Mills entered our lives and nothing would ever be the same again. Gordon was born in Madras in 1935. His father had been born in the Valleys and joined the army as a young man where he was posted to India. Whilst there, he met and married an Anglo-Indian girl who was a lot younger than him. When the Second World War broke out the family moved back to Wales and settled in Tonypandy.

Gordon was an only child and left school at fifteen. He tried his hand at a number of jobs before being called up for National Service. He was very popular with his fellow soldiers and entertained them with his harmonica playing. Gordon had won a few competitions and played in a band with a school friend, Johnny Bennett.

When he was released from the army he got a job as a bus conductor in the Valleys. Just like Tom and The Senators, he dreamed of stardom and travelled to London in search of it. Hohner, the famous harmonica manufacturers, staged a British championship at the Albert Hall in which Gordon came second, and this gave him the incentive to leave home for good and to pursue his dream in London. Eventually he formed a group, The Viscounts. They were a close harmony vocal group and got plenty of work. Gordon learnt a lot about show business during this period: the wheeling and dealing, the cut-throat attitude of agents and managers, the general rat-race that is show business. He was a diligent student and much of it rubbed off on him as time went by.

Toward the end of the Fifties Gordon became very friendly with another artiste who was also aiming for the big time. His name was Gerry Dorsey, and despite his perseverance he was getting nowhere. Later, at Gordon's instigation, he would change his name to Engelbert Humperdinck. Gerry had a fine voice and Gordon was a whizz with the harmonica. They were both born to Anglo-Indian mothers, and shared a flat in Bayswater. It was a real dump with little furniture, and all the cooking was done on a single gas ring. Trains kept them awake at night, rumbling by outside the window, close enough to touch. As time went by they became so poor that the rent arrears got out of hand and they were forced to do a moonlight flit.

It was around this time that Gordon met his future wife, Jo Waring. Jo was a stunningly beautiful white Rhodesian. She had arrived in London after touring Europe as a dancer; her elegant blonde demeanour attracted a lot of attention and she was 'discovered' by a top modelling agency.

When Gordon married Jo, Gerry was the best man and Gordon reciprocated later when Gerry married Pat Healy, a secretary who lived in Leicester. They were inseparable and very close friends. Gordon and Jo settled down to married life in a nice flat in Campden Hill Towers, near Notting Hill Gate. Gerry and Pat moved to less salubrious surroundings and took a dismal flat above a branch of Times Furnishing in King Street, Hammersmith. They were living there in June 1964 when The Senators made the move to London in search of the big time.

I remember visiting them later that year. Pat was a smouldering eyed beauty of Italian descent. They were parents to two very young and striking children, and living in abject poverty. They had a few sticks of furniture and the stuffing was bursting out of a couple of easy chairs. The thunder of traffic from the main road, was deafening and the stench of exhaust fumes overpowering.

Poor Gerry was stick thin with sunken and shadowed eyes. He looked completely stressed out trying to make ends meet. Gordon was managing his old friend at this time and trying to get him a break in show business. I've always reckoned Gerry a great singer. He had a three-octave range and a voice as smooth and crisp as brushed steel. I remember thinking that surely the world would recognize those qualities eventually. And as Engelbert Humperdinck they eventually did. Gerry worked hard for his success and he deserved every bit of it.

Gordon Mills and his wife, who was pregnant at the time, decided to pay a visit to his parents in Tonypandy. Gordon had hit pay-dirt earlier that year. He'd written a song for Johnny Kidd and The Pirates – 'I'll Never Get Over You'. It went straight into the top ten and he received £3000 in royalties, which was a fortune back then. But he was aware that even that large amount wasn't going to guarantee him long term security. Gordon had been sniffing around London for a band to manage that would make those royalties seem like peanuts. He knew which way the wind was blowing and was only too aware of Brian Epstein and his success with The Beatles. Gordon was hungry for a piece of the action and he had the financial clout to invest in a promising act that he could mould into real star quality.

During his stay in Tonypandy two of his old school friends, John Bennett and Gordon 'Gog' Jones, spoke to him about The Senators. We were packing them in and had quite a reputation throughout Wales. Gordon wasn't convinced, but his friends persuaded him to check us out. They told him we were different to most of the bands on the circuit and we had a fantastic singer to boot. A couple of days later Johnny Bennett picked up Tom, rhythm guitarist Dave Cooper and me and drove us to the Lewis Merthyr Club in Porth, where he had arranged for us to meet Gordon and his wife. We arrived early and sat near the stage. There was a comedian performing and he had the club members in fits of giggles. None of us had much of a clue who Gordon Mills was at the time and he obviously didn't have much of a clue about us either. It wasn't the most auspicious start to proceedings when he strolled in with Jo and 'Gog' Jones and on seeing us turned to Gog and said, 'well, they're a scruffy bunch of bastards, especially that one with the broken nose!'

He wasn't at all impressed, but he didn't turn on his heel and leave. Instead he sat with us and watched the comedian go through his routine. Jo was the only woman in the club. It was a Sunday morning matinee performance and all the wives were at home preparing the archetypal Sunday roast. At one point the comedian said something a bit risqué and Gordon admonished him in a flash, wagging a warning finger at him, and glaring daggers. I remember thinking at the time it was a bit uncalled for as Jo didn't seem bothered in the slightest. It was a bit of an early indication of what was to follow. Gordon was a classic control freak.

Later outside the club, Johnny Bennett insisted that Gordon and Jo come along to the Top Hat Club in Cwmtillery that evening. We were due to play there with our concert party. Gordon was reluctant but Johnny eventually persuaded him. He gave a little wave, hopped into his gleaming convertible Ford Zephyr and zoomed off. I remember Tom looking wistfully after it and saying, 'I'll have myself one of those one day, Vern.' I don't recall if he was talking about the car or Gordon's model wife!

Gordon and Jo did come along to see us perform that evening. The full concert party was in attendance, including our old friend Bryn 'The Fish' Phillips. The Top Hat was heaving and it was a members-only night, with a strictly no visitors policy in force. Gordon and Jo were turned away on arrival but we were able to persuade the committee to let them in. I remember telling the entertainment secretary that, 'this important man has driven all the way from London to see us perform'. It did the trick. Unfortunately it was standing room only in the club and Gordon was not best pleased to find himself propping the bar up with Jo and Johnny.

Gordon was scowling at us as we took the stage so we thought we better soften him up a little. We opened up our spot with 'I'll Never Get over You.' Gordon's hit record with The Pirates. He seemed to appreciate that and his scowl disappeared. We ran through our set with songs like 'Spanish Harlem' and 'I Can't Stop Loving You.' Jo seemed mesmerised by the show, especially with Tom leaping about the stage.

Tom stayed in the dressing room after our first spot. He was very quiet, which was unusual. I knew he was twitching about Gordon's reaction. Linda tried to calm him down, but she was a bit tipsy at that point and seemed to make things worse. I also tried to get him to relax, along with our guitarist Mike Roberts, but Tom was a bag of nerves. It was finally decided that I go and speak with Gordon and get his feedback on the band.

Gordon was standing with Jo, Johnny Bennett and Gog Jones being bustled by a scrum of club members yelling to get served. They all looked uncomfortable and a bit intimidated by all the pushing and shoving. Bryn Phillips was on stage telling jokes and singing a song or two. He had a fair old voice did Bryn, but it wasn't a patch on Tom's.

I managed to push my way through the scrum at the bar and order a pint. I turned to Gordon and asked, 'What did you make of us Gordon?' He nodded toward the stage, his scowl fixed firmly back in place. 'What do I reckon? I reckon that comedian has a better voice than your singer.'

This guy's a real joker I thought. I didn't remonstrate with him. I thought I'd better just leave it at that. It was another disappointment to overcome. I grabbed my pint and was heading back to the dressing room to let the band know when Johnny Bennett grabbed my arm, all smiles, and congratulated me on our set. He asked me what Gordon had made of it and was astonished when I told him. Johnny turned to Jo and relayed Gordon's words. 'Nonsense,' she said, 'that's just Gordon's warped sense of humour. Tom is a fantastic singer and you guys are a great band.' She laughed: 'Do you really think Gordon would still be crammed in amongst these rowdy beer bellies if he didn't think you had talent? He'd be on his way back to London.'

I headed back to the dressing room to relay the conflicting signals. Our ex-guitarist Keith Davies was returning from the bar with a tray of drinks for the band, 'Great news innit, Vern,' he chuckled.

'What do mean, Keith?' I said.

'That Gordon Mills bloke just told me at the bar he wants to take the band on. He wants you to relocate to London.'

I was taken aback, but happy never the less. 'Come on, we'd better go and tell Tom and the rest of the band.'

Tom was too nervous to communicate with Gordon directly about the proposal. As with many of the big decisions that were to follow he left matters in the hands of the rest of the band to decide. I was band leader at that time and everyone was happy to go along with my judgment. After much discussion we all agreed that it was too good an opportunity to miss. What did we have to lose? Quite a lot, it would prove.

The night ended on a real high note with Gordon promising us the world if we stuck by him. He headed back to London with Jo. I remember Jo telling me much later that he pulled the car over somewhere along the way and with the engine ticking over he turned to her and said, 'I'm really excited by that singer. I have to do something with this band. This is just what I've been waiting for, this could be really big.'

In hindsight I've always wondered why Gordon was so off hand with me about Tom's voice at that initial meeting. I think it's fair to say that he was playing down his interest in Tom, and planting seeds of discontent even then, as all part of a divide and rule strategy.

Gordon was back in London and making plans: he was eager for Tom and the band to be under his wing. But we found ourselves in a quandary. We were already contracted to Myron and Byron, and they were in no mood to relinquish their control to Mills. The band pored over the agreement with them and by our reckoning there were only a few months left before it expired. Tom was proving a bit of headache, he was caught in two minds, unsure if it was the best course to sign with Gordon. We hardly knew the man at that stage, and for all of Myron and Byron's failings it might be a case of better the devil you know.

Tom said he respected my judgment concerning the best moves for the band. But on this occasion he was clearly apprehensive. We all were: it was a leap into the unknown. London seemed very far away and to make a permanent move there was a monumental decision. Tom also had Linda and Mark to think about.

I said to him, 'We're at a crossroads here. We can either hang about dithering on which path to take or we can follow our instinct. We may not get another chance like this. Gordon Mills has got a decent track record in the business. Myron and Byron have had their opportunity and we're no farther forward than we were before. I say it's time to move on and give it a shot.'

Tom recognized the opportunity and finally came around to our way of thinking. The band was all on board, taking that leap into the unknown. The next thing to be done was to face the music with Myron and Byron. A meeting was arranged at the Thorn Hotel. They tried everything to change our minds, finally falling back to their default position, and pointing out we were still under contract. But our minds were made up and we asked them to call Gordon and sort out the particulars with him.

Gordon travelled down from London for a meeting with Myron and Byron held in a workingmen's club. This allowed Gordon to sort out the log jam with the contract and watch the band in action again. Gordon did his best to smooth over the business part: 'Look I'm not trying to steal Tom and the band from you. I'm aware that you've spent a lot of time and money getting them to this stage. I'll make a deal with you. I'll have a separate contract drawn up, and I'm willing to give you both five per cent of the band.'

Myron and Byron recognized which way the wind was blowing and with only a few months left of the original agreement they jumped at the offer. I'm certainly no contract lawyer but I remember thinking at the time, what about dates? Five per cent from when to when exactly? didn't say anything at the meeting but I mentioned it to Gordon later. He just smiled and told me to worry about the music and leave the business to him.

Gordon was always determined to prove a point and would argue his case as long until you threw up your hands in resignation. Quietly spoken, he rarely raised his voice, but there was an unmistakable steely determination. He was constantly biting his nails when the pressure was on. They were always bitten down to the very quick; he seemed to live on his nerves.

In his eagerness to get Tom and the band under contract Gordon had made a pretty fundamental error. But as far as he was concerned five per cent of nothing is nothing. I don't believe he ever had any real intention of giving Myron and Byron a piece of the action. Gordon was on a high and it was infectious. He had convinced us to go home and pack our bags, we were off to London. Gordon's words were ringing in our ears: 'We're heading for the top!'

Unfortunately our guitarist Mike Roberts decided to quit the band. As soon as the practicalities of the move hit home, and he realised he'd have to forsake his job as a TV cameraman and move to London, he wanted out. But Dave Cooper quit his job and I waved a fond farewell to *The Observer*. As a parting gift the paper ran a big spread about the band and our move to London. We played a farewell gig in The White Hart the night before we left Wales and the beer flowed until the taps ran dry.

We had been stuck with one major problem before we could complete the move: finding a new lead guitarist willing to make the move with us. We organized auditions at the Thorn Hotel and finally settled on a twenty-one year-old Cardiffian, Mickey Gee. He was a red-hot guitarist and lived for music, the boy could play. At the age of eighteen he had travelled to New York and hitched a ride along the famous Route 66 all the way to Nashville, on a mission to meet his guitar hero, the legendary Chet Atkins. Mickey found out where Chet lived and knocked at his door only to be told that Chet was away on tour. He was clearly disappointed and explained how far he had travelled to meet his hero. He was presented with one of Chet's guitar strings which he treasured as if it was spun from gold.

Mickey could play finger-picking style just like the cream of Nashville. After parting with Tom Jones on the worst possible terms he went to work with Dave Edmunds, Shakin' Stevens and the legendary Bruce Springsteen.

Tom had finally come around to the idea of departing for London and was a bag of nerves at the prospect. He took me aside and said that perhaps he should have singing lessons before we departed. I told him not to be so soft as his voice was in phenomenal form. But he was adamant and mentioned my next door neighbour Brenda Warlow. Brenda was an opera singer and voice coach, and I told Tom I would have a word with her. In all honesty if Tom had decided to go down the opera route he might well have made it, it was well within his reach. Brenda was a lovely lady in her forties, and had the elegant bearing of a trained opera singer; we used to call her the 'Valleys Maria Callas'.

After setting up the meeting on Tom's behalf, I took him along to meet Brenda. I introduced them and went back next door to let them get on with it. Pretty soon I could hear Tom's muffled voice tackling the musical scales. After a while everything went very quiet and about forty minutes later a disheveled Tom fell into my house, his face flushed.

'Get the kettle on Vern,' stammered Tom. 'I could really do with a cup of tea, I'm gasping, man.'

I asked him how he had got on with Brenda and he rolled his eyes. 'Get on, well I got on great until she got on top of me.' I did a double take and thought surely not, my mind going off in all manner of directions. 'She told me if I wanted to be an opera singer I would have to forget about singing pop music. It's a completely different technique apparently'. I nodded and asked him if he was sticking with rock 'n' roll for the time being. 'Well yes, but she showed me how to breathe properly, you know to get the best out of my voice like'. Tom told me that Brenda had him lying flat out on the carpet and suddenly straddled his chest, 'this is great exercise for breathing', she had told him and suddenly started bouncing up and down, 'I thought I was gonna pass out, Vern, she never let up, bouncing away like a mad thing, I almost passed out I swear.' Thankfully the kettle boiled displacing the image of Brenda bouncing up and down on top of Tom and I served him a deserved cup of tea. Tom looked in shock and tea always helps in those situations.

6. BASEMENT BLUES

Chris Slade's mother always fussed over him as though he were made of china; she would make him wear a scarf and jumper when the weather turned nippy. So she was especially upset when our seventeen-year-old drummer kissed her goodbye on his way to London. She tearfully watched his suitcase into the back of the yellow Thames van. If she had only known the trials and tribulations that lay ahead she would probably have laid in front of it to stop him leaving. I wouldn't have blamed her: we were in for a very rude awakening.

Our final call was to see my grandmother Hannah Mills, who was staying with my Aunt Lilly, just down the road in Rhyd-yfelin. Having lost my mother in 1959 and having to break the awful news to my grandmother, we were very close. She had been a great comfort to me and the family, helping us to come to terms with the tragedy. I'll always remember that beautiful sunny day in late June with my grandmother waving us off as we drove away with a sharp blast on the horn. Finally, we were off to London, and our excitement was palpable.

We arrived at Gordon's flat in Notting Hill. Jo welcomed us with tea and biscuits, and Gordon got out a map and gave us directions to a rather grotty hotel nearby. He explained we'd only have to spend a couple of nights there as he was sorting us out accommodation in Clydesdale Road in Ladbroke Grove. After spending two nights at the flea-bitten doss house we couldn't wait to move in. It was a real pit, and the boys were scratching like crazy.

Gordon picked us up from there in his mighty impressive Ford Zephyr convertible. We made the short trip from Notting Hill down to the Grove. Halfway down the incline the wide leafy road was fronted with large affluent houses which gradually gave way to less salubrious surroundings. At that time the Grove was a notorious ghetto, an eclectic mix of West Indian, Greek, Portuguese and many other settlers. It was a real melting pot. It also had a well-earned reputation for drugs, prostitution and all manner of crime. We had left the green, green grass of home well and truly behind. I took a quick look around the car and the band looked shell-shocked. Their jaws were practically in their laps. The streets were bustling with hookers and pimps and drug pushers, it was a real carnival.

Gordon pulled over at Clydesdale Road, a fifty-yard row of four storey terraced buildings. To describe them as run down would have been an understatement. They looked like they were held up by string and a good wind would have flattened the entire terrace. He jumped out of the car all smiles and led us down to a basement flat. It looked pretty grim from the outside. Gordon said, 'This is all I could find available at the moment lads. But don't worry you'll soon be out of here. I've got big plans for Tom and The Senators. This is just a little blip on the road to stardom.'

Gordon turned the key in the lock and had to give the door some shoulder to force it open with a loud creak. We filed into the gloomy passageway and our senses were assaulted by a variety of vile smells: dry rot, mice droppings and the distinct scent of something long dead, which turned out to be a rotten mouse. The ancient wallpaper was sweating with damp and alive with a vibrant fungus. The cheap ragged carpet was so stained that the original pattern had long disappeared. I looked up to the heavens for inspiration and noticed the ceiling was bowing so much from damp it was practically touching my nose.

Our new manager led the way further into the dismal abode and we followed like zombies, in utter disbelief. There was a poky room with two single beds and a window with minimal daylight. The view was a set of stairs leading up to ground level. There was another slightly larger room and containing three single beds. The window had a glimmer of light fronting onto another building within arm's reach. Tom piped up, 'Gordon this flat is like the Black Hole of Calcutta!' It was an apt description. The name stuck and we referred to it as that from then on.

Gordon made his excuses and beat a hasty retreat. Left to our own devices we debated who was sleeping where. It wasn't much of a discussion considering that both rooms were equally bad. I settled for the back room and the bed nearest the door. Tom wanted the bed in the corner opposite me and Dai grabbed the bed under the window. Chris and Mickey were left with the front room, after removing the dead mouse.

That was our welcome to London. Bothered, bewildered, but definitely not bewitched. We had a heated debate about leaping into the van and heading back to Wales. But cool heads prevailed and we decided to slum it for a little while and see what materialized. After all, Gordon had assured us that this was just a blip and that he had big plans for the band.

We ventured out of the flat to look for a café. Apart from Jo's tea and biscuits we hadn't eaten since breakfast. The weather was hot and sultry, and the air was richly permeated with a sweet and heady scent. We'd later recognise it as top grade marijuana: the area was awash with it and supplied the whole of greater

London. Whenever we passed an open doorway the repetitive beat of reggae music sounded.

We headed for Portobello Market and stumbled upon a tiny Greek café. Its basic British menu was scrawled across the window. We dived in and were welcomed by 'Pete the Greek', a cheerful handsome Cypriot in his early thirties. The food was reasonably priced and we dug into egg and chips. Pete filled us in on our whereabouts and gave us the lay of the land.

'Never ever venture down All Saints Road,' he warned us, 'it's a no-go area for the likes of you boys. The police don't even venture there. If you get into trouble there you're on your own, so stay away.' He couldn't understand why any manager would let a band live in the Grove and advised us to get the equipment out of the van as soon as possible, if it had not been stolen already. With our bellies full we headed back to the flat. We drew a lot of stares, being the only white faces on the street. We quickly emptied the van and stashed our equipment in the passageway of the flat. We spent the next few days cleaning and trying to end the mice infestation.

After a few weeks our money dried up and we were flat broke. Gordon told us because we were under contract he would pay the band one pound a day between us. We were speechless, and we had to find food, toiletries and our laundry out of that. He pointed out that he was also paying the rent on the flat and he asked us to be patient – our big break would come soon.

We tried to budget for one main meal a day, one pint of beer at night and ten woodbines shared between the five of us. With our daily allowance and rent Gordon was spending around twenty pounds a week. After six weeks morale was at rock bottom and we were no nearer to getting a record deal than when we first arrived.

BASEMENT BLUES

We wanted to start lining up some gigs in and around London to pay our way. We missed being on stage and were itching to get back in front of a live audience. But Gordon was adamant that this wasn't part of his plan for getting us a record deal. He said he didn't want to overexpose us, and we needed to be patient. In retrospect, the reason Gordon wouldn't let us play live gigs was probably because he was paranoid that we would be discovered by someone with a bit more clout in the music business, and then we wouldn't need him. He had already done something similar in persuading us to leave Myron and Byron.

Pete the Greek had become a great friend and introduced us to all the locals. We had quickly become accepted in the Ladbroke Grove community. I remember one warm night, a jolly West Indian who had befriended the band invited us along to an illegal basement club, around the corner from the flat. Being relatively new to London we were unaware we were breaking the law by attending. The place was very dark inside and the walls throbbed to the music of Bob Marley and the Wailers. The familiar scent of marijuana permeated the room. We made our way through the bustling crowd of dancers to a small bar at the back of the room at which we were each served with a bottle of fruit juice. The air was so stale and humid in the club that I took a long thirsty swig. It almost blew my head clean off. The drink was about two-thirds imported Jamaican rum. The illicit drink was disguised as simple fruit juice to avoid any excise duty. We soon got a taste for it and it was much cheaper than anything legitimate a pub could offer. Once again we were the only white boys there, but we were becoming used to that. It wasn't very long before we were on the dance floor and mixing it with the best of them.

An hour later all hell broke loose.

We were so much under the influence of the 70 per cent proof rum that we weren't initially aware that the place was teeming with police officers. They had charged down into the basement and were now charging back out with men and women in arm and head locks, shepherding everyone into the waiting black maria police vans parked outside.

We just stood there goggle-eyed with the place in uproar. It was bedlam. A woman standing beside me snatched something out of her handbag and pressed it into my hands. Then she disappeared into the darkness. I examined the small scrunched up envelope. I didn't have a clue what it was and innocently stuffed it into my pocket. The police left as quickly as they had come, they seemed to know exactly who they were looking for in the swoop and didn't even give us a second glance. We didn't hang around to ask questions and decided to make a bolt back to the 'Calcutta' as fast as we could. We avoided those places like the plague after that.

The next morning, nursing an almighty hangover, the envelope fell out my jeans pocket as I was climbing into them. Inside were six blue tablets. I had no idea what they were. I later found out from Pete the Greek that they were Purple Hearts, amphetamines. I didn't know what the hell he was on about but decided to hang onto them in case they ever came in handy.

Autumn was now drawing in and we were still in limbo. Gordon would visit once a day and hand over one pound to share between us. But there was no good news to report whatsoever. Pete's Greek café was a godsend during that lean spell. It got us out of the flat for a while, and even though the limited menu consisted of either egg and chips or sausage sandwiches, the banter kept us in some spirits. Our weight was beginning to plummet though. Relying on just the one meal a day our clothes were hanging off us, and starting to wear a little thin to boot. Our shoes were pretty scruffy too, we contemplated saving up the food allowance and buying some shoe polish, but rumbling bellies put paid to that plan.

We tackled Gordon again about playing some gigs to bring in a little money, but he wouldn't budge. It was his way, or no way. We were beginning to neglect ourselves, not cleanliness wise, we did wash and shower regularly, but our general appearance was a little shabby. We had nothing to feel good about. It was almost as though we had been abandoned.

We tried to keep our spirits up and were forever winding each other up and playing practical jokes. The tatty shower unit in the flat was situated close to the kitchen, and the ancient gas stove took up most of the room. We tried not to use it as it was so unreliable, the gas would cut on and off at will. We were hanging around the flat one afternoon and Tom decided to take a shower. Off he went to the kitchen, closing the door behind him. He seemed to be gone for an age. On the clock ticked and there was no sign of him. Suddenly there was a tremendous crash followed by a commotion and Tom crying out in pain. We all rushed into the kitchen to see what the fuss was about. There he was, half hanging out of the cubicle, naked as the day he was born. The shower was still going strong and flooding the kitchen floor.

'Help us up, boys,' he groaned, 'I was having one off the wrist when I slipped on the soap. I was just about bloody getting there too!'

'That'll teach you Tom,' I chuckled, 'you can't leave it alone for five seconds. It'll be the death of you if you're not careful, you mucky bugger.' Roaring with laughter, we left him to it.

Tom had often mentioned that he should slow down on his sexual adventures. I'm sure that if he'd been a guest on *Desert Island Discs* back then and been allowed one luxury item, it wouldn't have been a pair of boxing gloves: more likely a bumper edition of *Playboy* magazine. Back then we were all forever warning him that he would go blind and grow hairs on his palms. But that didn't deter him in the slightest.

It wasn't any wonder that he was losing weight faster than the rest of the band. After three months of living on the breadline we had lost over two stone each, but Tom was looking like a scarecrow. We weren't getting enough of the right vitamins and minerals and big boils were breaking out on our emaciated bodies. Tom's back suffered terribly with them: there were massive eruptions which certainly looked painful. I think he was more susceptible to them because he had quite oily skin. That went hand in hand with his dark looks. He decided to take matters of nutrition into his own hands.

It has been well documented in biographies that Tom was a bit of a teenage tearaway, with all manner of petty thieving and fighting. But after joining the band, apart from borrowing that club's chicken and his brother-in-law's Corsair, he never put a foot wrong. He was friendly with every band member, easy going and laid back, and never lifted a finger aggressively during the eight years we were together. Well, apart from a petty altercation with our guitarist Keith Davies, but that was quickly forgotten. The band had become ever more loyal during those wretched months in the 'Calcutta'.

Through shared adversity we had formed a very close bond, so it came as a bit of a surprise when Tom slipped into old

My parents, full of smiles on their wedding day in 1935, with my Aunt Lilly, mother's younger sister.

My grandmother, Hannah Mills.

Norman became a police superintendent.

With my brother Norman.

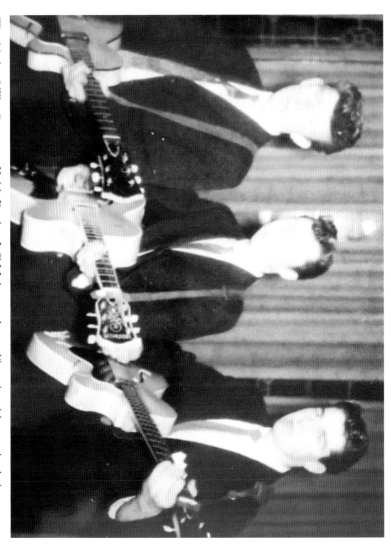

The birth of The Senators: Keith Davies, Jeff Maher and myself: a trio with stars in their eyes.

Performing at the Regent Ballroom. Now a five piece with drummer Brian Price and singer Tommy Pitman.

Tommy Scott and The Senators. Left to right: Alva Turner, Mike Roberts, Tommy Scott, Dave Cooper, myself. 1963.

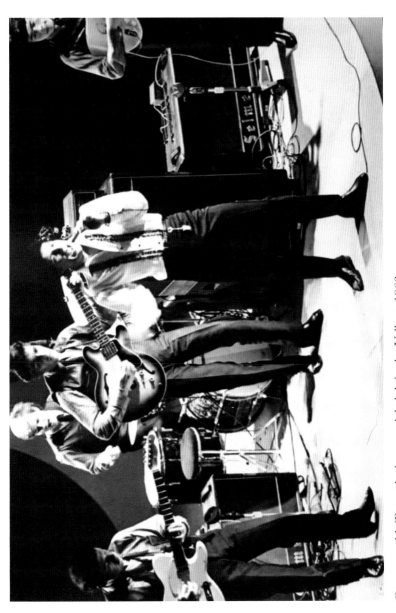

On stage with Tom, playing a social club in the Valleys, 1963.

All pals together, five fingers on one hand prior to the release of 'It's Not Unusual'.

The Senators with our new managers, after signing the contract with them at The Thorn Hotel, 1963. Far right: John Glastonbury (Myron) and Raymond Godfrey (Byron).

habits. Surviving on one light meal a day our young stomachs would be rumbling for food come nightfall. To relieve our hunger we would pool what was left from our daily pound to see if we could rustle up a snack. On this occasion we were pleased that we had just enough to buy two sausage rolls from Pete's café to share between the five of us. This early evening snack delivery was usually done on a rota and that night it was Tom's turn.

Time went by and there was no sign of him, it was like the shower incident all over again. We wondered where he'd got too. Our stomachs were rumbling like cement mixers, but pretty soon they were rumbling with anxiety. It was a pretty rough area after all; surely Tom wouldn't have been mugged for less than a shilling?

Finally the front door creaked and in he strolled, deviously wiping away any evidence of a crumb from around his mouth.

'Took the scenic route, Tom?' I asked.

'No boys, you're not going to believe this,' he said rather sheepishly, 'I'd just arrived outside the café and you know that bloody big drain. Well some bugger bumped into me and the lot fell down the drain.'

'Every penny,' we all groaned in unison.

'Every bloody penny, on my life,' he said.

'You lying bastard, you've got crumbs all down your shirt,' we wailed.

Naturally we all sent him to Coventry for the rest of the week, and it was never his turn to go on the snack run again. Looking back I can see the funny side, but we gave him hell at the time. Little did we realize it was a harbinger of what was to come.

Nights at the 'Calcutta' could become unbearably long and depressing, so we would sometimes take a stroll up to the Gate, calling in on Gordon and Jo, hoping for some good news. Our intention was to kill a little time and walk around the area for a while before heading back down to the Grove.

We used to pass the same Indian restaurant and always wished we had money to buy a couple of bhajis, and maybe more for a curry. One evening we were so arrested by the fine aroma wafting out of the restaurant that one of us went in to check it out. He returned and told us the toilet window was open and possibly big enough for us to scrape through and into the alley behind.

It was a big temptation, we all looked each other in the eye and thought to hell with it, and if we got busted at least we'd fed ourselves in the process. In we piled and found ourselves a table near the toilet. The waiter came waving five menus for our inspection, we didn't waste any time studying and ordered five vindaloos with naan, bhajis and all the trimmings. We were ravenous and devoured the meal in lightning quick time. Tom was so hungry he actually lifted his plate and licked it clean. It was the first square meal we had tasted for months.

Afterwards we exchanged guilty looks. The toilet window was high in the wall and the only way out was to stand on the toilet pan and try and wiggle through. It was a mad scramble to get through that window. It was incredibly narrow but luckily we were all stick thin after starving the previous months and managed to get out.

Performing that caper and getting away with it gave us great heart. We would never have imagined doing that back home in Wales. But it's surprising the lengths you will go to when the chips are down, or you really need to get some chips down you! Sadly, it didn't stop there. A little while later we found ourselves with just enough money to buy a Chinese Special.

The singer Max Bygraves, who was big at the time, had contacted Gordon and asked if the band would record a demo of a song he had written. Gordon promised us a £5 fee, but with the potential of more recording work with Max. We were beside ourselves. At last, some movement and an opportunity to get back on stage and make music: we were chuffed. It was agreed that Max would provide the vocal and we recorded the track at Regent Sound in Denmark Street, in the heart of Soho. Tom was a bit miffed as he couldn't be on the demo, but we softened the blow and gave him an equal share of the fee. After all we were all in it together, at that stage at least.

On a high after the session, we made our way up to Notting Hill Gate, heading for a Chinese restaurant that we had walked past many times and fantasized about eating in. We each of us had about a pound in our pocket, it's hard to believe now, but then that got us a half decent meal. We didn't have to do a runner as we were literally quids in. The waiter gave us a table near the open door, which was much appreciated as the place was packed and it was a very hot evening. There was a nice cool night breeze and we all spent some time poring over the menu.

The waiters produced plate after plate, and we got stuck in. I remember thinking at the time that we had enough money to return the following evening for another blow out. When the bill arrived Tom went white, the colour just drained right out of his face. He seemed really edgy and his foot was beating the floor like he was desperate for the toilet. I grabbed the bill and gave out a long whistle. I had had no idea it would have cost so much. The next moment Tom was out of his chair, and flying for the door as if a wasp had stung him on the arse. Panicking, we all followed suit, hurtling through the open door in pursuit of Tom. The waiters were fast on our tails screaming blue murder.

We were so sluggish after the feast that I was tiring, waddling along and close to vomiting. One of the band grabbed me by the lapels and dragged me behind a high hedge in a front garden. I was surprised to see the rest of the band panting and hiding there too. The waiters and kitchen staff came screaming past waving kitchen knives and machetes. We were terrified. We didn't move from the garden for an age. Eventually they all trooped back, cursing us as they passed.

Every time we went for a curry or Chinese after that we were on tenterhooks, waiting for Tom to do a runner. Nine times out of ten he did. He seemed to have acquired a taste for the excitement of bolting. We got used to making a run for it, and travelled light, in anticipation.

Windswept autumn leaves finally gave way to snow. The two miserable gas fires in the 'Calcutta' gave out as little warmth as the naked light bulbs hanging from the ceilings. We felt old beyond our years and were having serious discussions about Gordon and his plans for the band. At one stage we were so despondent that we decided to return to Wales, but we had no money for petrol and the clapped out van stood idle outside gathering dust. The boys pushed me to get some petrol money from Gordon for a trip home. He must have realised that that would have been the last he'd see of us because he dug in his heels and refused point blank.

Unknown to us at the time, Gordon was like a man possessed. He had been trying everything in the book to get us a record deal. There came a high that summer when he got us a gig supporting the Rolling Stones at the One Hundred Club in Oxford Street.

It really gave us heart after months of kicking our heels.

Bill Wyman, the Stones bassist, describes it better than I ever could: 'The 18th July, hundreds and hundreds of fans jammed the streets around the West End and there were police everywhere when we played the One Hundred Club. Inside the heat was fierce. Tom Jones and his band were our support. The temperature was so high that stewards were throwing buckets of water over us and the audience'. Bill describes it perfectly, my memory is that it was an inferno, it was so hot you felt as if you were melting. We played a forty-five minute set to an audience of six hundred. It was crazy, girls were fainting left, right and centre, and being carried out. After being so long off the stage, we were rocking. The Stones had to drag us off, we didn't want to leave.

Tom got some ribbing from the band later. Wearing white trousers and a white t-shirt he sweated so much that his trousers turned see-through, and the buckets of water flying around didn't help. The audience got a bit more than they bargained for that evening. Even Jagger looked shocked. We shared the same dressing room as the Stones, and we all fell about laughing when Mick Jagger pointed to Tom after we came offstage dripping wet, and said, 'Christ it must be hot out there, look at him and he's only the compere.' I thought Tom was going to stick the head on him but he was too knackered after the set.

It was after that gig that Gordon re-named us 'Tom Jones and The Playboys'. The movie *Tom Jones*, starring Albert Finney, had just won three Oscars. It was about an eighteenth century Jack the lad who shagged his way through society. How prescient! It was a very sharp move by Gordon, the name 'Tom Jones' was so established on the back of the film that everybody associated it instantly with the band: a stroke of genius. It was a formula he was to use for the other acts he'd signed: Engelbert Humperdinck and Gilbert O'Sullivan. Gordon had the knack of coining a name that would capture the public attention.

During that period Gordon was working tirelessly on re-igniting Peter Sullivan's interest in the band. He had thought we had talent, but needed some polishing. Gordon was trying to persuade him to release 'Chills and Fever', the song we had recorded with Joe Meek. He was convinced it would be a massive hit.

We recorded it again, giving it a rhythm and blues feel, and Tom did a fantastic job with the vocal. Then Peter Sullivan ruined the cool arrangement by adding loads of brash-sounding instruments, creating a completely over-produced single. It was released in late August and got nowhere in the charts.

There was bitter disappointment all round. Gordon was at the end of his tether. He was fast running out of money. He finally relented on the gig front and now wanted us back playing live as we all needed the money badly. The only caveat he insisted on was that there would be no gigs performed in London. He wanted all gigs in venues well outside the London area. He must still have been paranoid that we might get poached; he'd invested too much in the band to allow that to happen.

We started gigging regularly again with all the proceeds going directly to Gordon. But it wasn't enough and he had to take out a bank loan to continue developing the band. He received a small amount that kept his head just above water. Eventually he sold his wristwatch for fifty pounds, which was a lot back then, and much later he sold his beloved Ford Zephyr.

7. THE SQUIRES

Gordon changed the name of the band again, this time to 'The Squires'. We were going through so many name changes it was making our heads spin: The Senators, Tommy Woodward, Tommy Scott, Tom Jones, The Playboys and now The Squires. I remember asking Gordon if we were going to hang on to this name a little longer than the previous one and received a scowl in response. Apparently the change had been forced on him. There was already an American group using the name Playboys who had threatened Gordon with legal action.

Another of Gordon's acts, Engelbert Humperdinck, had secured an important booking at one of London's most famous nightclubs, the Astor Club. Engelbert asked a favour of us, he wanted the band to support him. He could have used the house band but he wanted to impress an important person in show business who was coming along that evening to see him perform. Engelbert confided in us his hopes that this person could get him out of the doldrums and off the breadline. Gordon's management had failed to open doors for Engelbert and like us he was disillusioned.

The Astor Club was situated in Berkeley Square and the owner, Bertie Green, was friendly with some shady characters, including underworld figures Reg and Ronnie Kray. They happened to be in the audience that particular evening. Tom had decided to come along even though he wasn't needed for the gig. He was probably checking out the competition, after all he was vying with Engelbert for Gordon's attention. And I don't suppose he particularly relished spending the evening alone at the 'Calcutta'.

The Astor was a massive club. We set up our equipment during the afternoon so we were able to arrive about an hour before we were due on stage. An Italian waiter led us to our dressing room, backstage near the bustling kitchens. It was really no more than a broom cupboard with a black curtain for privacy. You may imagine our surprise when we saw another entertainer already there and snoozing away. The other entertainer was a bloody great python snake.

Bertie Green had booked another supporting act that evening, a belly dancer cum snake charmer. The snake was obviously waiting for his mistress to finish the belly dancing part of her set and collect it for the finale. It was coiled in a hold-all, snoozing away. I prodded it with my finger but it didn't stir which was a great relief to the rest of the band.

There were some heavenly smells emanating from the kitchen and we realised how hungry we were. We'd blown our one pound allowance from Gordon earlier. The dressing room was right next to the waiters' station, where the food trolleys were parked ready for delivery to diners in the cabaret room. As soon as one waiter disappeared through the flexible rubber doors to serve the food, another fully laden trolley would appear from the kitchen for the next waiter to collect. It was a regular assembly line of fine culinary production.

The aromas from the silver tureens made our mouths water. I lifted one of the lids to see what was being served and the boys gathered around too. In the tureen was the largest and most succulent T-bone steak, still sizzling.

'Have a sniff of this then boys,' I practically drooled. Just as

I was about to replace the lid a hand darted out and grabbed the steak. We all stared in amazement as Tom made a dash for the fire exit to make good his escape. Unfortunately for him the door was blocked from the outside and wouldn't open. So there he crouched, devouring the steak like a rabid wolf. We all dragged him back into the dressing room, and then thought what the hell. We shared the steak, passing it around until we had devoured every last morsel. It tasted wonderful.

The commotion woke the snake, which slithered out of the hold-all. Suddenly a waiter appeared screaming half in English and half in Italian, accusing us of stealing the steak. We vehemently denied it but the waiter was almost hysterical. He informed us that the steak had been for Mr. Kray and he was far from happy, the waiter sobbed, 'the bad man he will sleeta my throat!' I pointed to the snake slithering across the floor, 'Tell Mr. Kray the snake ate his steak and prepare him another one.'

The next day a livid Gordon gave us a right dressing down. Bertie Green had been complained about the missing steak. Of course, we all denied it. To be honest we didn't feel any remorse, we were there to do Engelbert a favour and we weren't getting paid for it. We had taken payment in kind. We tried to fob Gordon off with our story about the snake, but he just wasn't buying it.

By now we had made so many friends in Ladbroke Grove that we felt comfortable leaving our equipment in the van. The locals had accepted us, and we all used to look out for each other. Unfortunately one of the tyres on the van had been punctured after the last gig and no-one had volunteered to repair it. We had grown so apathetic that anything that required any effort, other than to do with music, we shied away from.

One rainy afternoon we were hanging around the flat, bored to tears. I was rummaging through the kitchen drawers and came across the envelope containing the Purple Hearts that the woman had dumped on me during the police raid. I remembered what Pete the Greek had said about them perking you up. Sod it, I thought, we all of us need perking up living in this shit hole.

'What's that you've got there Vern?' yawned Tom as I popped one into my mouth.

'One of those pills that Pete the Greek said perks you up. It gives you the stamina to shag anything on two legs,' I said.

'I do that already thank you very much,' said Tom.

'Don't we all know it,' chorused the boys.

Thinking nothing more about it I laid back on my bed and stared at the ceiling before dozing off again. I remember opening my eyes a little while later with the determination that I shouldn't be wasting my time hanging about. I was feeling restless and took to pacing the floor, and wandering from room to room.

'Can't you keep still for five minutes,' moaned Tom looking up from the magazine he was reading. 'I'm trying to bloody concentrate here.'

'It's about time someone sorted out the flat tyre on the van,' I piped up enthusiastically. 'If Gordon comes up with a gig at short notice we'll be in a spot of bother. I'm going to change the wheel.'

'But it's bloody raining,' everyone chorused.

Undeterred, off I went up into the drizzle. Out came the jack and the spare wheel. I was feeling as bright as a button despite getting soaked through to the skin. All our equipment was piled up in the back of the van and it was a miracle that the jack didn't collapse under the weight. Job finished I was back in the flat and decided on giving the place a good clean from top to bottom. I was driving the band barmy. I can't remember quite how long this went on for but much later that day I crashed and became very depressed. It was an awful feeling and seemed to last for ages. I never took a purple heart again, and flushed the rest down the toilet. But I noticed that one of the pills was missing. Tom admitted to taking it but said, 'It did nothing for me. All I did was keep staring at the ceiling.'

The nights were drawing in and the temperature in the flat plummeted. We became ever more reliant on our two miserable little gas rings for warmth. It made a bit of a dent in our food allowance as we had to keep feeding shillings into the meter to keep the heat on. One evening there was a banging at the front door. I opened the door to two women. We recognized them as local prostitutes who worked the corner nearby. They pleaded with us to let them in and warm themselves; the poor girls looked frozen.

In exchange for some piping hot tea they offered us a few cigarettes. They stayed for a while chatting and then were off again to work their patch. The following night they knocked on the door again; this time there were four of them. Soon the kettle was whistling and there was tea and cigarettes all round. This routine continued whenever the weather turned bitterly cold. Over time we got to know all the girls that worked the area quite well. We listened to their stories about abuse and wife beating, and all the terrible events that had befallen them. It was understandable that they had turned their backs on society.

We felt sorry for them and the marginalized lives they were

forced to live. They were lost young souls, vulnerable to the local pimps and drug dealers who exploited them ruthlessly. Many of the girls had come to London from as far afield as Glasgow, Belfast, Cardiff and the north of England. They were putting as much distance as they could between themselves and the traumas they had suffered. London offered the attraction of relative obscurity, but with little or no money they were easy targets for the unscrupulous.

During their visits we tried to persuade them to make a break, and turn their backs on prostitution, but they seemed to be too much under the influence of their pimps. One thing was certain, we never needed to worry about our van or equipment being stolen. The girls informed us that they had put the word around that we were to be left alone, or else.

During our time together it hadn't entirely escaped my notice that Tom's priorities in life seemed concentrated on sex, singing and sinking beer, quite possibly in that order. They were his three favourite subjects of conversation. I got the impression that if a doctor had informed him that he could no longer get an erection he would have headed straight for the nearest railway line or bridge.

Tom certainly liked to check that everything was in fine working order on a regular basis. One bitterly cold evening there was the usual knock at the door and we let the girls in for their regular visit. There was one girl who stood out from the rest. She was a Glasgow lass named Charlotte, mid-twenties with short cropped ginger hair – no oil painting. Short and quite sturdy she was your archetypal tough little Scot. Her accent was so broad we could barely understand a word she said.

At that time the band where forever coining nicknames for

people to keep all our spirits up, Charlotte had unfortunately been saddled with the moniker 'Grotty Lottie', though not in her presence, of course. That particular evening Tom sat her down on his bed for a heartfelt conversation about getting out of the life and getting a regular job. The other girls told us that due to her appearance she wasn't getting much business. She was the most vulnerable and needed to get out of her self-destructive situation.

Tom chatted to her for hours suggesting possible jobs and things she might consider. They were still talking long after the other girls had left and we had all gone to bed. When I woke the next morning Tom was still in bed fast asleep. When he finally roused himself he had a lecherous grin on his face.

'No Tom, you didn't, say you didn't.'

'Sorry Vern, I had too,' he replied.

'You must be joking, you dirty sod,' I said.

'Well a standing cock has no conscience boys.'

Many years later, long after the band had gone their separate ways, I was watching Tom Jones at the London Palladium on television. The show was hosted by Jimmy Tarbuck. When Tom had finished his set and left the stage, Jimmy quipped, 'By the way Tom, Grotty Lottie is waiting for you outside the dressing room. She's gone and lost the other autograph you gave her.' I almost fell out of my chair. No doubt Tom had proudly recounted some of his conquests from his time at the 'Calcutta'.

Every now and again we would get a little homesick. Being totally skint we couldn't afford the petrol money for the van and Gordon continued to refuse to help in case we didn't come back. Our only option was to hitch a lift on one of the many lorries travelling down to Wales on the A40.

We would leave the flat together, then split up as there was more chance of getting a lift alone. Hitching now is a far more fraught experience, but in 1964 it was the 'done' thing. People were far more willing to give a lift to strangers, especially if the weather was bad. We all hitchhiked home a number of times that year. Sometimes I would get a lift as far as High Wycombe and have to walk the ten miles to the next busy spot to catch another ride. Other times one of us might catch a lift from Shepherds Bush all the way down to Cardiff. I got really lucky on one occasion. I managed to flag down a lorry on the A40 near Reading. Climbing up into the cabin I was met with a lilting Welsh accent, 'Get in butt, where are you heading?'

'South Wales,' I replied.

'Well you're in luck that's where I'm heading, whereabouts exactly?'

'Pontypridd,' I told him hoping he'd be able to drop me off somewhere nearby.

'Ponty, I'm heading there myself.'

It was the beginning of a wonderful friendship between John Jones and the band that would continue for many years. Our 'King of the Road' was a real blessing. John was a giant of a man in his thirties with fair hair and a wicked sense of humour. He had a regular run from Pontypridd to different parts of London. From that moment onwards he used to go out of his way to pick us up and drop us off on route to Wales or back to London. He knew we were going hungry trying to catch our big break in London: out would come his sandwich tin crammed full of sandwiches and fresh fruit. 'Here we go boys, get stuck into that lot. I had a big breakfast this morning and I'm full to bursting. It's a long haul back to Ponty and Mam's cooking.'

Tragically John died at a relatively early age.

Chris Ellis was another godsend at that time. He would pay us a visit in London every now and again and come laden with tins of beans, corned beef, soup and other goodies. He knew the dire straits we were in but thankfully kept it to himself. Our local paper back home, *The Observer*, was forever informing its readers about our successful transition to London and how we were on the cusp of great things. They would have had a field day reporting that Tom and The Senators were living like tramps in a doss house in Ladbroke Grove, and wasting away through lack of food. Chris Slade's mother would have hit the roof if she had got wind of the situation we were in. Chris was still only seventeen, and she would have been up like a rocket to London to drag him back home.

On some occasions Chris Ellis would pick up Tom's wife Linda and drive her up for a visit in his white Mini. Tom and Linda would spend the weekend at Gordon's flat in Notting Hill. There was no way she could have stayed in the 'Calcutta'. Having a familiar face like Chris around lifted our spirits. He would fill us in on all the gossip from back home, as he heated up tins of beans on the dodgy gas cooker. Chris was a real diamond, from our first meeting back in the Green Fly, and all his driving us around the clubs and even up to Joe Meek's studio for that first recording, he was a great friend to us all. I don't know what we would have done without his support. Tom has even more to thank him for. Chris did a superb job as his personal manager. Unfortunately he was paid a pittance by the multi-millionaire superstar, but he never complained and performed his highly responsible job with complete professionalism.

The situation had become quite desperate for Gordon and the band during that time. Gordon was in deep trouble with the bank and it felt like everything was falling apart. One morning a member of the band was missing. Tom had risen early and was paying a visit to Gordon's flat. Having the worry of a wife and child to support he was in a bad place psychologically. Linda was suffering a rough time back in Ponty, having to scrape and struggle to make ends meet. She wanted her husband back home and told him so.

Tom had a heart to heart conversation with Gordon. He wanted the manager to slip him a few extra pounds a week to send home to Linda and explained that she was getting restless about how things were going. Tom told us all later that Gordon also unburdened himself at the meeting. He told him that he was fast running out of money. Jo's modelling career was on hold because she had recently given birth to their daughter Tracey. They had been relying on songwriting royalties but they were slow in coming through. His overdraft was rising daily and he was on the verge of selling his car.

'I'm sorry Tom. I can only just about manage to feed you and the boys. You'll have to tell Linda to go out and find a job.'

That cut Tom like a dagger to the heart. Back then housewives never went out to work, they stayed home, washing the laundry, keeping the house tidy and looking after the kids. That was the culture then, particularly in the mining communities of South Wales. Tom must have thought it was the end of the line. After the hard months of struggling it had come to this. He was on the edge staring into an abyss of humiliation and defeat.

'I understand, Gordon.' Tom was a broken man. He left Gordon's flat and headed for Notting Hill Tube Station a few hundred yards away. He bought a ticket and stood on the platform waiting for the next train.

We were all at Pete the Greek's café ordering our usual egg and chips. I finished first and was desperate for a pee so I left the band there and headed back to the 'Calcutta'. I found our troubled singer sitting on the edge of the bed with his head in his hands. I noticed that he was trembling and wondered what the hell had happened.

'You okay Tom?' I asked but he was completely silent so I asked him again. He raised his head and his eyes were red and tearful.

'I nearly topped myself Vern,' he said.

'What?' I asked, shocked.

'At Notting Hill Tube I watched the train coming in and got ready to jump in front of it.'

'Why, for Christ's sake,' I shouted.

He then told me all about the meeting with Gordon. He recounted how Gordon could barely afford to keep the band going. By Tom's reckoning that was it, we'd had it. The dream was all but over.

I told him it was not worth killing himself over. We were all in this together. Things were pretty desperate but we had come this far together. I felt sure Gordon would come up with an answer. I explained to Tom that Gordon was just as desperate as the rest of us for the band to be a success.

'He's not going to throw himself under a train. Neither are the boys and neither are you,' I told him.

I reminded him about our great send off at The White Hart. I wasn't ready to go back home with my tail between my legs. Not while there was still an outside chance that things might work out for us in London.

'That's a laugh,' he said sourly, 'it was supposed to kick off for us when we first came up here. Now Gordon's completely skint. It's a bloody joke. It's pointless staying another minute in this shit hole. You can stay Vern, but I'm going back home.'

I tried to explain that if he did that he'd be letting us all down. I reasoned with him that we might not get another chance, 'You'll regret not wringing it out to the bitter end. You'll curse yourself for not ever knowing if it might have worked out.'

I suggested we do the rounds of all the local pubs that night to see if we might drum up some gigs to help support Gordon and ourselves. As far as I was concerned the 'no playing London' policy was now dead in the water. 'Gordon won't mind us playing anywhere now that he needs every penny he can get hold of. The North Star and The Bush have live music. We'll all go up for a nosy around later, Tom.'

That seemed to cheer him up a little, 'Come on let's get out of this dump. The band is waiting down at Pete's. Let's go and get you some grub.'

It was true that if Tom had crumbled then we would all have been breadcrumbs. But we did manage to secure some gigs in Shepherds Bush later that evening and after that he was okay.

Gordon was down but far from out. He needed every penny to stop the ship from sinking. He got to hear about Tom's Notting Hill incident, which must have left him with many a sleepless night. Really desperate measures were now called for. Gordon's only option was to bring on board some money men in exchange for a stake in the band. Gordon was inherently a greedy man, and he would have been at pains not to go down that particular avenue, but what choice did he have? As luck would have it, when he was exploring potential investors, a much needed royalty cheque arrived. It was enough to get us out of the 'Calcutta' and Ladbroke Grove. I think he'd realised that Tom and the band were close to the edge and the freezing, damp flat wasn't helping matters.

We packed our belongings and headed for Shepherds Bush and Lime Grove. What a change in environment. Lime Grove consisted of elegant bay-windowed Victorian houses set along a wide tree-lined road. The BBC studios were at one end, their massive presence hidden behind two of the houses. It looked ever so ordinary to anyone passing by. The only clue to what was going on behind the scenes was the familiar face of a newsreader rehearsing his script in the window. The studios were situated in the labyrinth deep behind. *Top of the Pops* was filmed there and we all dreamed about appearing on that show one day.

Directly opposite the studios was the Lime Grove Baths where you could have a good scrub for a small fee. Not that we ever used the place, for we now had our own bathroom; we were chuffed to bits.

A friendly Polish family were our landlords. They lived on the ground floor and we had the run of the first floor. The rooms were large, with a spacious lounge and three bedrooms. We split up along similar lines to the 'Calcutta'. Well almost, Tom claimed the smaller bedroom for himself, I doubled up with Dai in one room and Micky Gee and Chris Slade took the other. We even had a black and white television set. There were only two stations then, BBC and ITV, but we weren't complaining. This was a real step up: there was a three-piece-suite to sit on – we felt like kings.

Goodbye dry rot, wall fungus, grubby carpets and dodgy gas

fires. We were still having to get by on our one pound food allowance, but it was bearable now that our spirits had risen. We scoured the area for another greasy spoon as good as Pete's. We had become used to dining on Greek egg and chips and now we got used to Turkish egg and chips. We discovered a Turkish café, and just like Pete the Greek's menu there wasn't a foreign dish in sight!

Things were definitely on the up. One morning Gordon came around banging on the door. He had a song he wanted us to record. I let him in and he came rushing up the stairs carrying a tape recorder, 'I want you all to listen to this song I've written: 'It's Not Unusual'. I've booked a twenty minute slot at Regent Sound Studios for 2:30 p.m. so listen carefully: you'll only have one crack at it.'

Gordon played the new tune; he was accompanying himself on piano and providing the vocal. The melody was quite catchy but the lyrics sounded a little effeminate, 'I wanna cry, I wanna die,' and so on. After playing it through a couple of times we headed for the studios in Denmark Street.

When we arrived at the tiny demo studio there was a guy sitting at the baby grand rehearsing the song. His hands were spread all over the keys. I think he was using every digit and he was producing these almighty chords. It was an early run at the rousing introduction to 'It's Not Unusual'.

It was inspiring. Gordon's piano interpretation back in the flat earlier had sounded more like the comedian Les Dawson's famous *piano lessons*. Suddenly the little tune came magically to life and with a real awe-inspiring driven intensity. In that moment it really struck me how a twee little melody could be transformed into something very special by a gifted musical arranger. In this case his name was Les Reed and he was the co-writer of that now famous song. I learnt a lot from Les, he really enlightened me on what's possible with the right arrangement.

We hurriedly set up our gear. There wasn't even time for Chris Slade to get his drum kit together, so he grabbed a tambourine instead. We had time for one quick run through and I have to admit, Dave Cooper on rhythm guitar and me on bass hadn't paid quite enough attention to the song back at the flat. There was no time to go through it again. The clock was ticking and we only had five minutes of studio time left. It was left to Micky Gee, lead guitar, Chris on tambourine, Les Reed on piano and the voice of Tom.

We were told after that the song had been especially written for Sandie Shaw. We thought nothing more about it: it was just a demo to record. Gordon told us to go and grab a pint in The George around the corner on Shaftesbury Avenue. He wanted to get an acetate of the demo there and then, and told us he would follow us later. Once settled in The George we came to the conclusion that 'It's Not Unusual', was indeed very unusual thanks to Les Reed's deft use of chords and fillings. We convinced ourselves that this could be the breakthrough we had been striving for. By the time Gordon had arrived we had set our hearts on releasing it. We all believed we had a real chance of making a break through with this song.

When Gordon pitched up, we told him our thoughts. It would be crazy to give the song to Sandie Shaw when it could be the making of us and Tom. Disappointingly he told us that his hands were tied. Les Reed had co-written the song and it was his intention that it be presented to Sandie Shaw. He went on to explain that it had been especially written for her. After having a hit with 'Always Something There to Remind Me', Les wanted to present her with a song that had a similar beat. With its laid back Motown feel and 'shuu, shuu, shuu' rhythm they thought this was that song. If she had a hit with it then Gordon explained he'd have more money to invest in developing the band. It all sounded a little near-sighted to me. Why bother having the band under contract if he was going to give away the best songs to other artistes? It didn't make any sense.

Mickey Gee and I were always the most confrontational members of the band, and we ended up having a blazing row with Gordon. All our frustrations of the past year boiled over. Tom took a back seat. When it came to confrontations with Gordon he was a bit of a shrinking violet. He'd stoke us all up beforehand, but he wouldn't say a word in Gordon's presence.

The argument ended in a stalemate with us threatening to pack it all in and head back home, and Gordon promising to do his best to persuade Les Reed to let us release the song. But Tom didn't want to leave it there as he'd set his heart on the song. He took to visiting Gordon two or three times a day trying to coax him into letting him release the song. Tom thought it would be less confrontational if it was just him doing the asking, or so he told us anyway. What we subsequently learnt was that he was lobbying hard for a solo release and was putting some distance between himself and the band. Tom thought he might go for that. But Gordon stuck to his guns and insisted the song was for Sandie Shaw.

Then his hand was forced and he had little choice. A few days later Les and Gordon had a meeting with Sandie Shaw's famously volatile manager, Eve Taylor. Gordon presented Taylor with the acetate of 'It's Not Unusual' telling her it was a sure fire hit. After listening to the track for all of twenty seconds she asked, 'which of my acts is this for?'

'Sandie Shaw,' Les and Gordon answered.

'This record will never be a hit,' Eve Taylor informed them bluntly and turfed them out of her office.

On hearing the news we were jumping with joy. We thought that Gordon had to give it to us now. We were to be sadly disappointed. Gordon informed us that Les Reed had arranged a big-band sound for 'It's Not Unusual'. They both thought this was the best way forward and a tight-knit group sound just wasn't part of the arrangement. 'To put it bluntly,' said Gordon, 'you boys are not going to be on the record.'

Gordon began lining up session musicians for the recording instead. At first we couldn't quite take it in. We had spent years playing with Tom and had our own distinctive sound. Now we were being sidelined, shoved into the background. It was a bitter pill to swallow. Tom and Gordon tried to put a spin on it, saying we would all benefit if the record was a hit. But after all we had been through together it didn't seem right or proper. Whichever way you looked at it just didn't make any sense. In retrospect it was probably his intention all along to ditch us eventually. We were a means to an end. That end being: Tom under contract and settled in London under Gordon's wing.

We were pretty demoralized. But what could we do? Go on strike? Send Tom to Coventry? Tom told us if we had a hit on our hands we'd all be sitting pretty. So we got over our disappointment and all got behind the decision for a 'big band' sound as opposed to ours.

The first recording session was a total waste of money, it was a complete disaster. The arrangement just didn't work. That session was recorded at Decca's studio in West Hampstead and Tom's verdict was that 'It wasn't really happening. The music was all wrong.' So it was back to the drawing board and another session was booked. This time the arrangement was changed from a jazz feel, smooth and silky, to something far funkier and with a more positive beat. There were plenty of brass instruments, trumpets, trombones, saxophones; it was a big raucous dance band sound. I remember thinking at the time that it was pretty meaty and brash.

There were around twenty musicians, gathered around Tom. He was in a small recording booth, no bigger than a shower cubicle, and that helped muffle the awesome sound of the orchestra. I was fascinated by the actions of one particular musician. He'd been booked for the session and paid an equal fee to the others, but all he did for the entire duration was rub a sheet of sandpaper in a circular fashion on a wooden stool. It made a distinctive '*shh, shh, shh*' rasping rhythmic sound into the mike.

Our old friend Peter Sullivan was there, though we still hadn't entirely forgiven him for over-producing our earlier track, 'Chills and Fever'. But he was a good record producer and a complete perfectionist. I remember him giving Tom a really hard time during the session. He wasn't entirely happy with Tom's singing. Time after time he kept pushing him to give a bit more. Take after take, again and again. He saved every single take in case Tom's voice packed in. But it was the final take of the day that nailed it.

It was a real tense evening's work. Back then the singer and the backing had to be in real time. Every take was a fresh combination of both elements. I felt sorry for the brass musicians, their lips must have been red raw the following morning. I'll always remember Peter Sullivan addressing the orchestra from the control room, at the end of the session, via the intercom, 'Thank you gentleman, for your patience and co-operation. I do believe we have a hit record. Good night.'

With Christmas only six weeks away Decca decided not to release the record until the New Year. There was far too much competition with other artistes fighting for that elusive number one slot on Christmas Day. Gordon was coming apart at the seams. No-one knew what the future might yield. It's fair to say that if the record didn't work out it would have almost certainly have been the end of everything; it was the last roll of the dice.

Gordon confided in me that he owed the bank £1000 as it was; this was a huge amount at the time. He had sold off everything of value that he owned and was just getting by on the essentials. Although as I pointed out at the time, so were we. We were starving on a wage of one pound a day and all the revenue from gigs was going directly to him. We agreed that we were all in it together and that when we made it, as we all hoped we would, the spoils would be distributed evenly. It was the first time that Gordon had really opened up to me on an emotional level. He went on to tell me that Jo was having problems with her second pregnancy. She was ill and in hospital at the time it was all very worrying for a young couple. They were still only in their late twenties.

Christmas arrived and everyone was feeling a bit depressed and on tenterhooks. The euphoria of not losing the song to Sandie Shaw had long dissipated. We all realised the chances of having a hit record were still comparatively remote in the grand scheme of things. No one was kidding themselves. Gordon was broke, we were broke, and all our gig money seemed to go into the black hole of keeping the whole venture afloat. Gordon turned up at the flat sheepishly and admitted there would be no Christmas dinner that year, he couldn't even afford boiled rice. There was nothing else for it but to head back home to Wales.

It was a nail-biting time for Gordon, he had put all his eggs in the one basket, and 'It's Not Unusual' simply had to be a hit. The pressure was getting to him and he took me aside before we all broke up for the hitch hike home. He was a little worried that we all might enjoy ourselves a bit too much at home, what with decent regular food and being amongst family and friends. He thought we might not come back. I assured him he didn't have to worry; we had come too far and suffered too much to pack it all in now.

Decision day was fast approaching. What I didn't know back then, but obviously recognise now, was that 'It's Not Unusual' was truly unique. Put in perspective, the charts at the time were strongly biased in favour of pop groups. The whole Liverpool bands scene had fostered a certain climate. The Beatles and The Rolling Stones had spawned a whole generation of artistes and the charts were teeming with them. The public was receptive to something a little bit different.

Suddenly this 'hybrid' song was released into the mix: a blend of Motown and traditional dance band, with cutting rhythm guitar and biting lead guitar. There was a hint of Latin rhythm sexing it up and coupled with Tom's contribution of soul and pop vocal it was really out there. Tom's jarring machismo actually offset the feminine lyrics in a really powerful way adding an extra level of depth. Gordon's wife Jo had composed most of the lyrics with Sandie Shaw in mind but Tom made them his own.

It was one of those happy accidents that strike the right chord at the right time. The lack of macho lyrics became advantageous. Tom's big drawback then was that he didn't fit the typical pop star profile. The press cruelly described him as the bricklayer singer. All the solo singers back then were Elvis and Cliff Richard clones: good looking silky smooth rock 'n' rollers and balladeers. Gordon was no mug. He took this all on board and set about softening Tom's image.

'It's Not Unusual' was released at the end of January 1965. It was promoted on radio and by a couple of appearances on television. Tom's stage wear for those appearances was black leather. Gordon quickly realised that was a big mistake, the audience weren't receptive to that side of Tom. Then came the big one. *Top of the Pops* was the make and break appearance of the time. It was a short hop up the road from our flat in Lime Grove. Tom made his appearance on that all-important show dressed entirely in white: virginal wool sweater, trousers and white patent shoes. He looked so clean and pure it was if the show had cut to a commercial break for Persil washing powder. One of the boys piped up that he was surprised that Gordon hadn't made him get his hair dyed peroxide blonde like Joe Meek's buddy Heinz.

It was around 4 a.m. on the 21st February 1965 when Chris Ellis parked the van at Watford Gap services. There was a gang of tired lorry drivers huddled around a smoky coal burning stove in the car park. They were sipping mugs of tea and scanning the early editions of the morning papers. What they must have made of us mop-haired musicians God only knows. They all rolled their eyes as we trooped past.

We crowded around a table and ordered five sausage sandwiches with five piping hot teas. Chris checked the budget and we had just about enough to fill our faces and fill the van with petrol to get us back to Lime Grove. We ate in silence, we were so tired. We just wanted to get some food in us and then to flop into bed. On the way back to the van Chris cheekily asked one of the truckers if he could borrow his newspaper for a second. The great big bear of a man reluctantly obliged.

Chris hastily flipped through the pages. We all knew exactly what he was searching for: the current record listings. Suddenly he gave out a whoop of joy, 'It's Not Unusual' was at number twenty-one and climbing. Tiredness forgotten we were all running around like maniacs, whooping and hollering. The gang of truckers just stared blankly at us thinking we were nuts. Chris showed them the chart listings and pointed at us and Tom and told them we were on the way to a number one single. The truckers barred our way back to the van and insisted we autograph every newspaper. We all piled back into the van elated. Dawn was breaking when we got back to Lime Grove and suddenly none of us felt like going to bed.

The song hit a chord and went into the charts at number twenty-one. Then it started climbing and by a quirk of fate it got to number one on St David's Day. You couldn't have made it up! It was obviously written that the boy from Wales would smash the charts on our patron saint's day. Gordon was beside himself, having written a number one hit with Les and having it performed by a singer he was managing, he was on a roll. It meant double bubble, he was raking it in and for once his bank manager was a very happy man. It was all such a turnaround from a couple of months before. He rushed down to the flat to show off his new watch – he'd had to sell the previous one to keep the band going.

8. IT'S NOT UNUSUAL

A number one hit record. We all cracked the bubbly at Gordon's flat at Campden Hill Towers. The champagne was flowing, it was a massive relief and a celebration rolled into one. All of Gordon's friends came along to join in: Engelbert Humperdinck, Les Reed and the money men who had helped out Gordon when things were really bad, Mike Bradley and the agent Phil Solomon. Those guys were especially pleased knowing that they'd invested their money wisely. The Welsh singer, Dorothy Squires, was there as well. She'd had quite a bit to drink and was swearing like a docker, turning the air blue.

Tom and the band were knocking back the beer and helping themselves to the buffet. Gordon was walking on air, he was in the clouds. He was wearing a left-over paper hat from a Christmas cracker and wandering the room with a grin plastered across his face, merrily topping up everyone's champagne glasses. His eyes were wild with excitement that he had finally pulled it off.

'It's Not Unusual' was being played over and over again, much to Tom's delight. Though Dorothy Squires wasn't particularly enamoured and told Gordon as much, 'for fuck's sake Gordon, change the fucking record will you. Put one of my fucking songs on.' Up to that point I don't think I'd ever heard a woman swear and here was Dorothy Squires peppering her speech with expletives. I was pretty shocked. Tom told me he'd never heard such foul language coming from the lips of a woman. We both reckoned even the call girls we had befriended down at The Grove would have been shocked. Dorothy was married to the suave and sophisticated film star Roger Moore at that time, and this made it even more shocking somehow. She was certainly a character.

As the evening wore on we all got pretty rowdy, surfing a wave of elation. Quite suddenly Gordon approached me a little the worse for wear and he snapped something with his fingers, directly under my nose. Suddenly I was reeling. I felt as if I'd hit a brick wall at a hundred miles an hour. Momentarily stunned I then felt an incredible rush that sent me soaring. Gordon wagged his finger at me and roared with laughter. My legs were giving out under me and I staggered to a nearby chair. Tom and the boys gathered around fearful that I'd had a heart attack. Gordon slurred drunkenly, 'I bet that blew your bloody head off Vernon. Don't worry, it's only amyl nitrate. You'll soon feel okay.' And with that he wobbled off, tossing the empty phial into an ashtray.

The aftershock left me feeling queasy. On top of all the beer and champagne I'd consumed I felt really nauseous. I just about made it to the toilet before throwing up, and it affected me for the rest of the evening. Amyl nitrate is a powerful stimulant that causes the heart to beat extremely quickly. The veins and arteries dilate and blood rushes through the body at an accelerated rate. This often causes dizziness. Medically it's used in the treatment of angina, where the heart isn't receiving enough blood, due to narrow veins and arteries. Notably it has the same effect on the system as Viagra.

I wish Viagra had been discovered in 1965. Gordon wouldn't have needed to be using amyl nitrate to get his kicks, and I wouldn't have had a bloody bass drum pounding inside my head. Later I told him in no uncertain terms never to pull a trick like that on me again.

At that stage, Chris Ellis, our former roadie from Wales and blessed bringer of food parcels, came to join us in London. He was now enlisted as our permanent official roadie. When 'It's Not Unusual' first appeared in the charts Gordon decided we needed a full time driver to take us to all the gigs that were springing up. We were now very much in demand. Up until that point, Tom and the band had been taking it in turns to drive the van. Looking back it was madness: none of us carried a licence to drive, we were all breaking the law and did so for quite a while.

Gordon had set his mind on hiring an old friend of his as our roadie. But I argued that Chris Ellis had been with the band almost from the outset. In addition to that he had always been there for us in our times of greatest need. Gordon was having none of it. Stubborn as a mule he refused to take Chris on. One evening we were changing into our stage gear in the toilet of a venue. Gordon and I started arguing over the roadie position. Things got heated very quickly. The issue had dragged on for some time at that point. Our voices were echoing off the tiled walls, which seemed to magnify the argument even more. Finally he cracked, which was most unusual as Gordon never gave in. The band were pleased that Chris was now our official roadie and all slapped me on the back. Gordon's face was a picture, he was giving me daggers when he left and cursed me under his breath. I remember thinking at the time that I'd better watch my back.

Tom's arch rival at that time was the American heart throb, P.J. Proby. He was a handsome, black pony-tailed Texan. Proby had decided to try his luck in the United Kingdom and already had three chart hits under his cowboy belt. He was top dog and had become used to hogging the solo-singer limelight. The girls would go crazy for him. They loved his powerful slow vibrato voice and suggestive stage antics. P.J. wore velvet blouses and extremely tight velvet trousers. His trademark was a black velvet bow that held his pony-tail in place.

Proby had landed a plumb spot on a major Cilla Black tour which started at the end of January. The tour was booked into all the major UK cities and the bill included The Fourmost, Sounds Incorporated and the American singer, Tommy Roe.

Things didn't get off to a good start. Within a few performances Proby's tight pants split open from his bum to his thigh. It was a trick for which he had a penchant, especially when he wanted some serious screaming from his female fans. He used to drop suddenly to a squat and the trouser seams just couldn't take the strain. His trousers would split open and Proby would shamelessly milk it for all he was worth.

It happened once too often, however, and the wild American singer was fired. Rules back then were as tight as his pants. Things were pretty stringent and less broad-minded. So there was a gap to be filled and opportunity came knocking. We joined the tour during the first week of February, just as 'It's Not Unusual' was shooting up the charts like a rocket. It was perfect timing for adding the song to our usual set. Tom sang it at every venue in every city and it went down a storm. Gordon balked at the cost of providing an orchestra for the song so there was no big band sound. We pared it back to a four-piece arrangement and made it really tight. The reaction from the audiences was electric, they loved it. I remember mentioning to Gordon at the time, that due to the reaction we were getting from playing it live, what was the reasoning for going with the big band sound in the first place? He just shrugged. Then he dropped the bombshell.

Gordon thought it was best that Tom now moved into his own place, obviously the band would keep Lime Grove, but he thought Tom needed to be in his own space. We were all taken aback; up to that point we'd been a very tight knit bunch of mates looking out for each other. It was a bit of a wrench to suddenly separate with no advance warning. I remember looking at Tom to gauge his reaction and was surprised to see his suitcase already packed and sitting at his feet. Obviously it was a done deal and this was the send-off. Gordon and Tom trotted off to Gordon's blue Jaguar XJ6, turned it over with a roar, and sped off with a little wave.

We felt deflated. It felt odd that Tom was no longer with us twenty-four-seven. We'd all got so used to having each other around through all the turmoil and hard work. It just didn't seem the same after that.

Later Gordon called a band meeting with me, Chris Slade, Dave Cooper and Mickey Gee. He announced that things were on the up and we should all be very happy. Then he soured the mood somewhat by announcing that from now on we were to be paid the princely sum of twenty pounds a week. We all knew that money had been flooding in through the success of 'It's Not Unusual' so we were taken aback. At that time twenty pounds was considerably less than the average weekly wage. I pointed out the fact that we'd been starving up to that point waiting for our break and that surely we should all share a bit in the success of a chart hit. Gordon wasn't having any of it. He went on and on about how he had to reinvest the profits to keep the band moving forward. Gordon pointed out that he'd have to spend an awful lot on a full make-over for Tom. Stardom demanded it, and handmade shirts, suits and stage wear didn't come cheap.

The real sting was in the tail though; we were utterly stunned when Gordon informed us that out of our twenty pounds a week wage he was deducting one pound at source to pay back our food allowance from the time spent at the Calcutta. Not only that, we would now have to pay for our own accommodation on the road, as well as taking on the rent for the flat in Lime Grove. You could have heard a pin drop. We realised that we'd soon have to find cheaper lodgings as there was no way we could finance the flat as well as accommodation on tour. This was a kick in the teeth.

Gordon's parting shot was to inform us that we'd also have to be responsible for our own tax affairs as he didn't have the time to sort out all that out. As for being responsible for paying our own tax, filling in returns and paying stamp, we didn't know where to start.

What was going on? Tom and Gordon were doing very well for themselves and the band had been kicked into touch. We tried to get hold of Tom to see what he thought about all this but he'd decamped to Gordon's flat and moved Linda and his son Mark in with him. He promised a meeting to discuss the issue but kept making excuses as he was house hunting, and viewing potential properties was taking up all his time. He eventually moved into an ultra-modern house in Shepperton, 89 Manygate Lane, for which he paid £7,000 in cash. After Tom failed to show up for yet another meeting the band asked me to go and speak with Gordon. I explained our grievances and asked for a more equitable share in the success of 'It's Not Unusual'. Gordon was his usual charming self and told me, 'If you don't like my terms, you can all piss off back to the valleys.'

Considering that's where both he and Tom came from, this was demeaning to say the least. Go back to Ponty? Go back to what exactly? We had sacrificed our jobs to get this far and struggled through the lean times together. Now there was a chasm opening up with Gordon and Tom on the one side and the band on the other. It caused a hell of a lot of bad feeling. We felt it was an awful way to be treated, especially as Gordon and Tom were on a spending spree, and took delight in showing off their new acquisitions.

Tom's appearance changed dramatically in a short space of time. As that summer rolled on so did his taste for the good life. He took to wearing expensive handmade suits cut by top West End tailor, Dougie Millings. He'd drop by the flat to show off handmade shirts, ties, shoes and jewellery. He had a bunch of gold rings, identity bracelets and neck chains, one of his favourites had a huge chunky gold cross attached. Tom's humble Woodbines had been replaced by expensive Havana cigars. Gordon had also finally sorted out Tom's driving test. Rather than him take it in London, it had been arranged in Bristol, where it was assumed he'd stand a better chance of passing. He duly did and turned up at Lime Grove in a gleaming new white Volvo sports car, the model made famous by Roger Moore in the television series, *The Saint*.

Happily stunned by the success of 'It's Not Unusual', we were now dismayed by the direction in which things were moving. It was great for Tom and Gordon, but not so great for the rest of us. We discussed packing it in, but decided to muddle on in the hope that after another hit we might actually share in the spoils. Looking back, we were young and naive. But on the upside we were certainly getting a lot of attention and there were a lot of amorous distractions along the way that cushioned the blow somewhat. We were certainly really hot at that time and took full advantage.

Around that time we played a visit to our old stomping ground in Ladbroke Grove. Not because we missed the 'Calcutta' but because Gordon had asked us to set up our gear for a session at All Saints Church, close to Clydesdale Road. It was mid-afternoon and Gordon was being all mysterious. He wanted Tom and the band ready on stage for a good jam session. Gordon finally arrived accompanied by one of the world's greatest composers, Burt Bacharach. He was there to audition Tom for the soundtrack to a new Woody Allen comedy. The film was in production at the time – *What's New Pussycat*, starring the great comic actor Peter Sellers.

Even at that time Burt Bacharach was a living legend. He'd had a precarious start to his career, having songs rejected time after time. He finally scored a major hit with Perry Como's 'Magic Moments', and went on to write one hit after another for the cream of American singers, with his lyricist Hal David.

It was a magic moment for us and we belted out a number of songs from our act: 'I Can't Stop Loving You', 'Stand By Me' and 'The Midnight Hour'. Burt Bacharach stood stony faced throughout the audition, and he left as quietly as he had arrived. But he gave the nod to Gordon on his exit, and Tom was in. Later, Gordon played Tom a demo of the music he was to record for the film, and he was less than impressed. He was down to Lime Grove in a shot complaining about it. It was, he said, 'humpty dumpty music, all over the place'. Even the title had put him off, 'What's New Pussycat?'. I had to agree with him: everything about it sounded outside Tom's macho style. Nevertheless Gordon had set his mind on it and would brook no dissent. Tom enlisted our help to dissuade him, but Gordon was adamant and would not budge. He wore Tom down as he always did and Tom took the credit for singing the hugely successful film's title track. It was an enormous hit and Tom had Gordon to thank for his persistence in making him record the song.

The band was still on the road and enjoying the adulation, especially our sizeable, and growing, female following. We were a bunch of kids from the valleys of South Wales: from our teens until now girls had been exotic, foreign creatures, always difficult to score with. Chapel preachers back in home were always warning young people about the perils of copulation and the inherent sins of being – God forbid – loose. Now it felt like we had struck gold, girls were throwing themselves at us, and I admit it was pretty difficult to say no.

We were recognized from television appearances with Tom and from playing venues up and down the country. Scoring with girls quickly became a bit of a sport amongst us and helped take our mind of the fact we were getting shafted on the pay front by Gordon. Tom decided to muck in with the boys. Gordon had bought a new Commer van for the band and booked us into bed and breakfasts (which we had to pay for ourselves). He'd planned for Tom to travel separately and to stay in far more salubrious accommodation. But as soon as Tom realised how much fun we were having he threw in his lot with us. He didn't like being on his own and there was always more fun to be had with the gang, and the copious amount of groupies who were orbiting us. It allowed him the vanity of playing 'top dog', and boy did he enjoy it.

It was at this time that we had our first major appearance on BBC television's *Billy Cotton Bandshow*, on March 13th 1965. That was immediately followed by the BBC's *Beat Room*, alongside The Kinks, John Lee Hooker and Julie Rogers. The phone lines back home to the valleys were red hot, letting everyone know to tune in and watch us. Then we were off to Glasgow to appear on *Scottish Round Up*, and straight on to a converted church in Manchester to record *Top of the Pops*. We were booked to appear on the BBC's successful show *Crackerjack*. We shared the bill with The Animals, and the risqué girls dance troupe, Pan's People. We went straight from that recording to appear on *Blue Peter*.

In between all this crazy exposure the band pulled me aside and showed me a recent newspaper article they weren't particularly happy with. It was an interview with Tom, and he'd said that 'one of the biggest effects is that success gives you more confidence in your work. Before, the group was getting fed up and disillusioned but now we all have a contented feeling.' The boys asked me to pull him up on this statement; it was a case of them and us at this point, with Gordon and Tom raking it in and the rest of us getting squarely shafted.

From the very start in Ponty, even before Tom had teamed up with The Senators, I had always admired the bloke, not only because of his singing voice, but also because of his charismatic 'Jack the lad' street-wise ways. More importantly he knew his music inside out and I always respected him for that. I felt we had a strong bond between us, we had shared an awful lot together, and not just music.

It was evident to me that the friendship and all we had shared had become pretty strained. From that point I felt a little like a Walter Mitty character. I was on the payroll, and I played along with things as best I could, as did the rest of the band. We played our parts musically and socially, but we couldn't entirely mask our disappointment. We all felt let down by Gordon and Tom: we had struggled and scrimped and toughed it out, then two of our number sailed off into the distance with newly made riches, and a casual 'see you boys' flung over the shoulder. Many years later Robin Eggar came to discuss it with me when he was writing a biography of Tom. I remember talking over this time with him and explaining our disappointment. I'll never forget what he said, 'Tom Jones is like a ming vase Vernon, with an ugly crack running down its centre.'

Mid-tour, Gordon dropped another bombshell. He'd decided to add three more musicians to our line-up: trumpeters Tony Mabbett and Australian Frank Chapman, and Doug Firth on tenor sax. Our previous stage gear had been blue Marks and Spencer shirts, black trousers and black leather waistcoats. Now we were all to be measured for dark blue mohair suits. We all waited with bated breath for Gordon to send us a bill for the tailoring, but thankfully it didn't arrive, though that's not to say he didn't take it out of our wages at source.

Our first performance with the new brass section was on April 11th. We were booked to play at the NME Poll Winners' Concert in front of 12,000 screaming fans at the Empire Pool in Wembley. The bill comprised of The Beatles, The Rolling Stones, The Animals, Dusty Springfield and P.J. Proby. What a line up! We could hardly wait to take our place on stage. It was a Sunday afternoon and backstage, seeing all those legends nervously waiting their turn to go on, and fiddling with their appearance and instruments was quite something. The stage was immense, mostly taken up with Vox amplification. It was a real amphitheatre.

We raised our game when we went onstage to compete with the amount of talent around us. Straight after our performance we rushed across London to the Palladium, where we were booked to appear live on *Saturday Night At The Palladium*. It was a real thrill to be standing on the rotating stage for the finale, waving to the audience both in the auditorium and on the television. We all knew our folks and friends back home were glued to the telly waiting for our performance, which gave us a real lift.

That was all but a taste, we would appear regularly on television with Tom, and we loved every minute of it. A real highlight was appearing on the *Royal Command Performance* two years later in November 1967. The line-up included Tommy Cooper, Lulu and Bob Hope, and the show was compered by Jimmy Tarbuck. The band was particularly pleased as finally we were included for the first time on the credits at the end. Up to that point Gordon had managed to get us white-washed out of the credits. We didn't realise at the time, but every we didn't appear he didn't have to pay us; he pocketed all the fees himself. The first I got wind of this was when the tax man came calling. Having not bothered to fill in our tax returns after Gordon cut us loose on that score, I had no invoices, petrol or expenses receipts. They hit me with an almighty bill, way more than was fair or affordable, and then demanded extra on the undeclared fees from all my appearances on television shows. I didn't know what they were talking about as we hadn't been receiving any appearance fees. TV companies were obliged to pay a standard fee for each appearance, if the performer's name appeared or not on the credits. In other words we were being paid the same fee as Tom for each television appearance. I have no idea if Tom was in on this scam, but Gordon was raking it in on our behalf and paying us nothing. It later transpired that he was pulling the same trick with Engelbert Humperdinck, and fiddling him out of all his television appearance fees. I later found out that the money Gordon was raking in from the television fees alone amounted to thousands of pounds.

I remember Tom telling me at the time that, 'Roy Orbison deals with his own financial affairs, something I couldn't handle myself, what with being caught up on the road, singing and stuff'. He would have had a fit if he had known what Gordon was up to.

At that time Gordon had moved into a suite of plush new offices in Bond Street and formed a new company called MAM to oversee operations. He'd made himself and Tom directors of the new enterprise. I told the tax man in no uncertain terms to take his enquiries there, as I didn't have the foggiest idea about any television appearance fees. I was so angry I told him, 'tell those greedy thieving bastards to deal with it.' The Inland Revenue must have taken my advice because they never got back to me.

Gordon had set his sights on the United States as the next target. The band had a brief respite and opportunity to take a break and take stock. 'It's Not Unusual' had climbed to number 10 in the US charts. Gordon had big plans for the American market and had arranged a spot on CBS TV's *The Ed Sullivan Show*. This was the show that Elvis had famously appeared on almost a decade previously. He had only been shown from the

waist up as it was thought his wild movements were too suggestive for the audience tuning in from coast to coast. Gordon was
terrified of flying, but the financial stakes were too high to be
ignored. Gordon and Tom flew to the States on April 28th and
made five appearances on television, earning a whopping £2000
per show.

A week later, upon their return, we were back on the road.
Gordon had organized a month's variety tour of the UK,
supported by Engelbert Humperdinck, comedian Dave Allen and
a stunningly beautiful twenty-year-old singer from Abercrave. Her
name was Mia Lewis, but some considerable time later her
surname would change to Hopkins, on our wedding day.

Mia Lewis was already living in London, with her uncle and
aunt in Crouch End. She had left Wales at about the same time
as The Senators to make it big in the smoke. Mia was under the
same umbrella as the rest of the acts on the tour, the Acuff-Rose
Agency. Its London office was run by Colin Berlin and his
understudy nephew, Alan Field. Mia had recently launched the
first of six releases on a new London label and was getting good
airtime. She was petite and vivacious, and had a lovely singing
voice.

The tour started at the New Theatre in Cardiff and was
followed by concerts at the Theatre Royal and the Hippodrome
Theatre, in Birmingham and Bristol. Each venue was fully
booked and the month tour positively whizzed by. I remember
meeting some of my family in the foyer of the New Theatre
before the start of the show. I was taken aback when I caught
sight of my old headmaster, Mr Railton, amongst the crowd. It
caused me to wince a little as I had an image of him thrashing
me six times with his willow cane. I didn't bother to approach

him and reminisce about my schooldays…. The tour was a great success, then the whole cast went their separate ways, including Mia. It would be almost a year before we would bump into each other again.

Straight after the tour Tom flew back to America for another appearance on *The Ed Sullivan Show*. Whilst he was away Joe Meek came back to haunt us. Joe was annoyed when he found out that Tom and the band had been signed by Decca Records. He released two of the tracks we had recorded with him back in 1963: 'Little Lonely One' and a B-side 'That's What Love Will Do'. This time he had no problem in finding a record company to release the songs. He sold them to Columbia Records (UK) and Tower Records (USA). 'Little Lonely One' reached number forty-two on America's Billboard chart. The UK release coincided with Decca's release of 'Once Upon A Time'. Many fans decided they preferred the Joe Meek recording and 'Once Upon A Time' got stuck at a dismal number thirty in the UK charts.

Gordon was furious and Tom went ballistic, calling Meek a 'thieving swine'. Tom told the media at the time, '"Little Lonely One" is something I could well do without. I made it a long time ago and tastes have changed a lot since then. They were tough days when the group and I made that record. We were called Tommy Scott and The Senators back then, and we really pinned all our hopes on that recording session with Joe Meek. I think it's dated and I want to disassociate myself from it entirely.'

Joe Meek was far from happy and came back with both barrels blazing, 'I have four other tapes which I would like to release. Tom and The Senators auditioned for me and nobody wanted to know about him because it was a time when the group scene was very "in" and everyone said Tom sang too well. I originally did him singing "Chills and Fever", the record Decca finally re-recorded and released. I wouldn't have released "Little Lonely One" if I thought it was poor. I think this is a very good record.'

Gordon and Tom were seething that Joe Meek had beaten them in the charts with the earlier recording, and that they were receiving no payment for the success of 'Little Lonely One'. Joe never released the other tracks. Two years later in 1967 Meek killed his landlady Violet Shenton and then himself with a single barrelled shotgun.

9. WHAT'S NEW PUSSYCAT

The Joe Meek recordings weren't the only ones we made along the way. The band had missed out on recording 'It's Not Unusual' but just prior to the brass section joining us we went into the studio to record four songs for an EP: 'Bama Bama Bama Loo', 'I Can't Stop Loving You', 'Lucille' and 'Little By Little'. The recording was entitled *Tom Jones On Stage*. Actually, there was no stage and all the screaming in the background was added in the studio. But the EP was well received and became a big seller. Naturally the band didn't receive a penny for our contribution, but at least on this occasion Gordon had credited us on the record. The EP went out as 'Tom Jones and The Squires'. Whenever I raised this issue with Gordon he would fob me off with one excuse or another: he was re-investing profits, we were still paying off our food and lodging from 'Calcutta' days, money was tied up in studio time etc. We received the same treatment two years later when we recorded *Live At The Talk Of The Town*.

We played a month there in 1967 and recorded the show for release. It was hugely successful, but again we didn't receive a penny. This was far from equitable, especially as both Tom and Gordon had recently moved to St. George's Hill, in the Weybridge stockbroker belt. They had purchased palatial mansions, with swimming pools and tennis courts.

When Tom returned from his second visit to America he began promoting 'What's New Pussycat?'. By this stage we all knew the position with Gordon and Tom; we were all disillusioned with this state of affairs but just got on with it. We tried to keep our spirits up by having as many laughs as possible and simply riding with the tide. There was talk about touring Australia in the New Year: 'Chills and Fever' had become a big hit there. Our mantra had become, 'sod those miserly bastards, let's make the best of it and see as much of the world as we can'. It was pointless trying to reason with Gordon, he just had no intention of ever paying us properly for our efforts; he was far too busy lining his own pockets.

Around this time our roadie Chris Ellis broke his arm. It was just before we had to move out of Lime Grove. We had a golden rule that if one of the band got lucky and happened to bring a girl back for the evening then the others would move into another room to provide some privacy. One particular evening I got lucky and Chris moved into the room with Dave Cooper.

We were in the back bedroom, which looked onto the yard. To the left of the window was an extension which housed a toilet. I noticed the curtains were half open but thought nothing of it. Pretty soon we had both divested ourselves of our clothes and were locked in a passionate embrace. Suddenly there was an ear-piercing scream followed by a dull thud from outside. I rushed to the window, below in the moonlight was our intrepid roadie. Chris was wailing and crying out in pain. It was around 11 p.m. and suddenly the whole house came alive. Our landlord rushed into the back yard to see what all the commotion was about. Chris was in a bit of a state with a badly broken arm. He seemed badly concussed and kept muttering about having fallen out of the toilet window.

We took him to the nearest hospital and they checked him over and put his arm in plaster. By the time we got him back home and safely tucked up in bed, my girlfriend had upped and left. The following morning in the toilet I wondered how the hell Chris had managed to fall through the window. He would have had to have stood on the toilet seat. I opened the narrow window and looked down. It was quite a drop. If Chris had fallen on his head he would have been a gonner.

When I leaned out the window I could see Chris tucked up in bed, pumped full of painkillers. The dressing table mirror provided a perfect viewpoint. Then it hit me. Our broken armed roadie had positioned the dressing mirror to get the best possible angle on the bed. He must have lost his balance while perched on the toilet and toppled out the window.

Later when he was well on the road to recovery we teased him mercilessly with hilarious one-liners about his escapade. Chris emphatically denied any mischief, insisting that he wanted to get a bit of fresh air. Well he got a little more fresh air than he bargained for that evening. He continued to deny everything, for many years. Our poor roadie drove the Commer van for the next six weeks steering with just the one hand.

Pretty soon we had a little band celebration. Tom and Gordon were not invited. We had finally paid back every penny that Gordon had spent on us at Clydesdale Road. I still think it was especially mean of him to claw back that money, especially as we were under contract and he was making it big. We wondered what Gordon was paying the new brass section. After all they were all members of the Musicians Union, so we assumed they were getting a better deal than us. Unfortunately we never got to the bottom of it as Gordon had instructed them not to tell us, on pain of dismissal.

Soon we were on the move again. This time we took on a ground floor flat in Fulham, which was considerably cheaper than Lime Grove. It was quite shabby, but after the 'Calcutta' we were used to slumming it. With no more deductions we were now earning the princely sum of thirty pounds a week. I even managed to save a few quid. The brass section had really pumped up our sound, and our live shows were eagerly anticipated. We were packing them in up and down the country.

Tony Mabbett had learned to play trumpet as a bandsman in the Army. He was a hell of a nice guy, as was Dougie Firth on tenor sax. The other trumpeter, Frank Chapman, was a bit of a slimy character, and none of us took to him. Tony and Dougie didn't like him either. Gordon had brought them together; they hadn't worked with each other previously. We nicknamed Tony 'The Phone King'. He practically lived in a phone kiosk and must have spent most of his wages in them. If mobile phones had been around then Tony would have had one glued to his ear twenty-four-seven. One moment you'd be having a conversation with him, but if you got distracted for even a second, you'd turn around and he would have disappeared to the phone kiosk. Dougie Firth was the complete opposite. Thin and quietly spoken, he wouldn't say boo to a goose. All three were very talented musicians. Now with the band numbering seven Gordon decided we needed an element of discipline, so he chose Frank Chapman as the new bandleader. The position went to Frank's head and he began to throw his weight around. The first person in the firing line was poor old Tony Mabbett. I'll never forget Frank scolding him with his broad Australian accent, 'You can cut out disappearing round the corner to use the phone every five minutes, Mabbett.'

'What's it got to do with you?' replied Tony.

'Gordon has made me bandleader and he wants to keep a tight ship. I like to know where everyone is at any given time. I don't want to be having to search for you cobber, especially when we're due on stage or whatever.'

'Don't tell me when or not to phone, you Ozzie prick. I was in the army, I don't let people down.'

Things degenerated from there and we had to separate them, or Tony would have knocked his block off. Frank's new position hadn't got off to the best start. The fault lay in his condescending manner. He'd squint his eyes shut and stare narrowly at you as he spoke on any given subject on which he professed be an expert. It was irritating, and it used to drive Tony half up the wall.

Eventually after one altercation too many and a constant tide of verbal challenges from the band, Frank told Gordon to stuff his bandleader position up his arse unless he was paid double for putting up with the abuse from the rest of us. Naturally Gordon refused and that was the end of the matter.

In the meantime Tom's stock in the U.S. was soaring, especially on the back of 'It's Not Unusual'. Right through to the end of 1965 he would fly the Atlantic on numerous occasions. Dick Clark, the host of ABC's long running TV show *American Bandstand* was also involved in running a live tour throughout the States. *The Dick Clark Caravan Show* comprised of a dozen acts touring from coast to coast and taking in over thirty-six cities. Gordon had managed to get Tom on board the Greyhound bus known as the 'Caravan of Stars'. He was squashed in alongside a host of stars: Sonny and Cher, The Turtles, The Shirelles, Peter and Gordon, The Jive Five, Ronnie Dove and Jackie DeShannon.

The Squires were left behind so we went back to Ponty for a month, on a retainer of twenty pounds, while Tom used the tour band which backed all the stars on the bus. It didn't sound like we missed much. On his return Tom told us that, 'it was bloody murder. The bus packed to the seams with uncomfortable seats. We did a show and then got straight on the bus again, travelling through the night. We were sweating like pigs during the long hours' drive through the desert on to the next gig.'

Tom also complained about the tour band as they were unfamiliar with our material. The only highlight of the tour had been meeting Elvis on the set of his new film, *Paradise, Hawaiian Style*. 'It might have been paradise for Elvis,' moaned Tom, 'but it was Paradise Lost for me.' He told Gordon in no uncertain terms that he didn't want to do another tour like that.

After Tom's return we continued playing the clubs, theatres and ballrooms up and down the country. Dave Cooper had found himself a pretty dark-haired girlfriend. The rest of the band nicknamed her 'The Governor'. For the life of me I can't remember why: she wasn't bossy or demanding, she was rather petite, around the same height as him. They looked very comfortable together and Dai could hardly wait to get back off the road and into the Fulham flat to meet up with her. It was quite the reverse for the rest of us: we couldn't wait to get out of the grotty Fulham flat and back on the road gigging.

Dave's new found happiness was about to be cruelly shattered. Gordon, obsessed with money matters as always, felt that having to pay for the new brass section was a burden that would be less costly if there wasn't a rhythm guitar involved. Gordon's reasoning was that the brass filled out the overall sound and made rhythm guitar redundant. In a word, Dave was expendable and was promptly informed of that fact by Frank Chapman. But not before Frank had pleaded with Gordon to sack me instead and have Dave take over bass guitar.

Frank's reasoning for singling me out was pretty apparent. We had recently almost come to blows backstage at a theatre in the north. I'm a bit of a slow burner by nature but Frank wore me down. I found his high and mighty ways really irritating, lording it over the rest of us. He just wouldn't let up and continued his habit of giving everyone an unnecessarily hard time. But his pleas to Gordon fell on deaf ears. Frank wasn't like the rest of us; we were all gutted to see Dave leave the band. Frank was gutted that it wasn't me leaving.

Dave had been with us since taking over from Keith Davies, long before we left for London. We all fondly recalled the days when we'd roll him out into the audience hidden in the drum case and he'd jump out in his gorilla costume. How could Tom stand idly by and watch his loyal guitarist get blown out, without a whimper of protest to Gordon? Dave left without a penny of compensation for his loyal contribution. I felt really angry with both Tom and Gordon; this was merciless. We all knew now that the writing was on the wall, any one of us could be next for the chop. We were all expendable and when there was no further use for us we'd be turfed out without a second thought.

It was heart-breaking to see Dave pack his tatty suitcase with his worldly belongings and leave the flat with his girlfriend. With Christmas just around the corner it would be the last time any of us would see Dave again. He went back to Ponty and tried his hand at a number of different jobs, and eventually emigrated to South Africa. I bumped into a mutual friend many years later who told me Dave, 'couldn't stand being in the same country as Tom and

Gordon, he didn't want to breathe the same air'. He was bitter about the way he had been treated. Wherever he is, I hope that he's safe and well and doing fine. Dave was a loveable character and a great musician. We all lost a good friend when he went. He deserved far better treatment from Tom and Gordon. Not long after Dave was sacked Gordon had another bright idea. In January 1966 he decided to get rid of the brass section.

Gordon had settled on a cheaper alternative. Vic Cooper (no relation to the recently sacked Dave) was keyboard player with Johnny Kidd and The Pirates. Vic was a lean, fair-haired twenty-three-year-old, and just like Tom his hero was Jerry Lee Lewis. Born in Battersea, south London, Vic went to school with the legendary lead guitarist, Mick Green, who also played with Johnny Kidd and The Pirates.

Gordon had been pestering Vic for weeks and weeks to join Tom and The Squires. At first Vic declined as he was happy with The Pirates and hadn't even considered leaving. But Gordon being Gordon refused to take no for an answer and kept hounding him. Gordon offered him the opportunity to tour Australia with us in the spring, and dangled a forty pounds a week fee in front of his nose. Vic duly took the bait, and thanks to him we all got an extra ten pounds a week in our pay packet. Gordon realised he wouldn't be able to keep that one quiet for long.

Vic Cooper had a typical south London accent, flavoured with a touch of cockney. He was the original Mr. Smooth, sharp in dress and wit. He'd recently passed his advanced driving test and was swanning around in a powerful blue Austin Healey sports car. Vic was an expert in chatting up the women, a real smooth talker just like Tom. Both were rampant pursuers of the opposite sex. Being from Wales we were all partial to beer, and a lot of it. Vic on the other hand preferred Bacardi and Coke and was partial to smoking a lot of pot.

So we had come full circle and were a four piece band again. With a great keyboard player and singer we were rocking and we belted out our set with gusto. Tom loved the new Jerry Lee piano sound supplied by Vic and was in his element. We went back to knocking out rock and soul numbers: Joe Tex's 'Show Me', Wilson Pickett's 'Land of a Thousand Dances', and 'Midnight Hour'. It was great moral boost having Vic around.

One of Vic's first appearances with The Squires was on TV's *Ready Steady Go!*, followed by *The David Nixon Show*. Vic hadn't appeared on TV with Johnny Kidd and The Pirates and was initially taken aback by the change, but after clocking up a few appearances he acclimatized and really took to it.

A few weeks after Vic joined the band, we were booked to appear at De Montfort Hall in Leicester. On the supporting bill were The Who and skiffle king, Lonnie Donegan. While Lonnie was firing up the audience with 'My Old Man's a Dustman' and 'Rock Island Line', The Who were backstage fretting about their bass guitarist. He hadn't shown up and they were almost due on stage. I was in our dressing room with the rest of the band getting changed into our stage suits. Suddenly there was an urgent knocking at the door. I opened it and was confronted by an agitated Roger Daltrey: 'Can I have a word with your bass player?'

'Sure, that's me,' I said.

'Do us a favour mate, our bass player hasn't turned up. Would you fill in for him?'

'What, you mean go on stage with The Who?'

'Yeah, mate, you must know 'My Generation' surely?'

'Well yeah, but I don't know all your songs Roger.'

'Nah, well they're a doddle. Townshend will shout out the chords if you get stuck. We can't go on without a bass player, will you do it?'

It didn't take me long to chew it over, 'Christ, yeah okay.'

'Great,' and with that Daltrey turned and disappeared back to his dressing room. I was glassy-eyed and my heart was thumping. What had I let myself in for? The Who were down for a forty minute spot. I spent the remainder of Lonnie's set feverishly practicing the bass solos from 'My Generation' and trying to remember all The Who's hits.

Standing in the wings watching Lonnie and his band take their final bows, my heart was going like the clappers and I was in a cold sweat. I ran my sweating hands up and down the neck of my Epiphone bass guitar to ready myself. Then I felt a tap on my shoulder. It was a beaming Roger Daltrey; he told me that Entwistle had arrived in the nick of time. I gave a huge sigh of relief, but watching them perform a few moments later I did feel my moment of glory had been snatched away. They were electric, and Townshend smashed his guitar to pieces at the end of the set. We were also amused to see them hurling their amplifiers and speakers down the fire stairs when they left the hall. It wasn't difficult to imagine Gordon's reaction if we had ever tried something similar.

Vic was partial to rolling a joint before going on stage. It didn't seem to affect his ability to perform; he used to play great piano, or in this case Hammond organ. Vic had always been a complete wind-up merchant, the 'Gotcha' type. It was all harmless fun, although once his humour went a little too far. Not long before we were due to depart for the month's tour of Australia we played a nightclub in Stoke-on-Trent. It was quite a mediocre club with a small stage and packed to bursting point. We were playing the Bailey circuit of small nightclubs all over the north of England. Each club included a casino and on arrival Tom and the boys would make a beeline for the croupiers. They were always attractive young girls. I think it was part of the job description that they had to be stunners. We'd lay on the patter with a trowel and try to line up some fun post gig.

Tom would be booked into a small hotel and we would be in the nearest bed and breakfast. We were normally booked to appear for a week in each nightclub before moving on to the next town. It was often quite a hectic schedule, playing an early spot at one club and then racing across country to another, sometimes over thirty miles away. It could wear you down.

'What's New Pussycat' had been released by then along with a number of other songs, but none of them had taken off like 'It's Not Unusual'. Tom was still riding on the success of that particular hit, and it was always our most eagerly anticipated song at all our gigs. Tom had also released 'Thunderball' at that time for the James Bond film, but it had bombed. It reached a dismal thirty-five in the UK charts and then sank without trace.

Still, we were playing to packed houses, performing heavily produced and orchestrated songs as a four piece band. Gordon had hit on the idea of getting Vic to play Hammond organ instead of piano. This filled out the sound and replicated the records to a degree. It worked a treat and everyone, including Tom felt very comfortable with the new arrangement.

Tom would be out centre front of stage with us nestling behind him. We were all so well rehearsed at that stage of our careers that we could have performed the set blindfolded if required. But then came the crunch. I have no idea what Stoke-on-Trent is like today but back then I recall it being a very depressing and drab town. On the winter's day of Vic's prank there was a steady icy drizzle. It was pretty bleak. We weren't due on stage at 10 p.m. and were getting ready after finishing booking into our bed and breakfast earlier. Just before we left Vic collared me and offered a drag on his monster-sized spliff. I'd never tried it before, and really didn't fancy trying it then, so I declined. But Vic being Vic was insistent: 'Go on Vern, you look on a bit of a downer, this will cheer you up.'

'It's hardly surprising Vic, what with the weather and this town being a dump and all. But it's not for me,' I remember telling him.

'Come on, take a drag or two,' I shook my head, 'It'll make you play better Vern, honest. Go on, take a pull.'

Vic went on and on at me: he was relentless, and finally I gave in. 'Go on then, pass it over.'

I took a tentative puff and felt nothing unusual, so I took a longer pull and handed it back. We all climbed into the van and headed for the club. We had sound checked earlier that afternoon so we had only to change into our stage gear.

Making our way toward the club entrance, I began feeling a little light-headed. Then Vic started getting up to his tricks, he told me we were being followed by a policeman, it was starting to make me feel really paranoid. By the time we were due on stage I was feeling wave after wave of light-headedness. I felt as though I was on a boat rocking on a turbulent sea. I told Vic I was feeling really strange. He had a devilish glint in his eyes and told me that two puffs wouldn't have much effect and not to worry.

On we went, performing a couple of openers before Tom sprang on stage. Everything was going smoothly until about half way through the set. We were mid-way through 'What's New Pussycat'. We used to provide the backing vocals to the chorus. Tom would sing, 'What's New Pussycat' and we would reply, 'Whow, whow, whow, whow'. That was when I lost it. I came in well behind the rest of the boys. Everything seemed to be going slow in my head; it was as if time had stopped. Tom turned to stare at me with an incredulous look on his face. The band never made mistakes, everything was second nature, and he was shocked.

I turned to Vic behind me. I was panicking and so was he. I didn't make another mistake during the number. But as soon as the song ended I began to walk offstage. I thought the show was over. I'd only got a couple of yards before Vic grabbed me and walked me back to my microphone stand. Tom hadn't seen it happen; he was busy introducing the next number.

I got through the rest of the set in a cold sweat. By the end of the set my head was more or less back together. Nothing was said about my strange behaviour. But when we got back to London, Gordon went ballistic. He confronted Vic and gave him a huge dressing down: 'I know you're on it. But don't you dare let any of the boys try it again.'

That was the last time I saw Vic smoke a joint before we went on stage. I was under no illusions, Vic was a seasoned smoker and could handle it, but two puffs had almost sent me into orbit. I was never stupid enough to be tempted again. I fully understood Gordon's concern, though it was a bit ironic that not long before he had snapped that phial of amyl nitrate under my nose.

We continued playing the Bailey Clubs right up until the

Australia tour. It was essential that we had all the relevant jabs against tropical diseases. Our first stop on the tour was to be Darwin in the Northern Territory. We finished the UK tour in Blackburn and one afternoon traipsed down to the local hospital for our jabs. The five of us mop-headed musicians caused a bit of a stir. We were dressed in leather jackets and jeans, and were immediately recognized from our TV appearances. The male nurse preparing to inject us made quite a fuss and told us he was a big fan. Job done, we were preparing to leave when the nurse pressed a clutch of disposable needles into our hands, 'Don't tell a soul boys,' he whispered, 'they may come in handy.' We stared at him blankly as we filed out. Later the penny dropped. As we climbed into the van Chris Ellis piped up, 'I told you to get your bloody hair cut,' he moaned, 'that nurse thinks you're a bunch of drug addicts.' We got shot of the needles, but we didn't get our hair cut.

10. AUSTRALIA

The flight from Heathrow to Australia took at least forty-eight hours in 1966. We climbed aboard the notorious Boeing 707 anxiously. I can't recall the amount of times those particular aeroplanes had crashed during the Sixties, but it was a lot. We stopped over in Berne for an hour while the Swiss passengers left the plane: that was first of eight stops on the journey. With nothing else to relieve the boredom and tension we got thoroughly pissed. By the time we arrived in Australia we fell out of the plane drawn and shattered.

After landing in Darwin, Tom told us we were going on to Sydney to start the tour instead. The Boeing re-fuelled and we carried onto Sydney, where we had to circle the airport for ages waiting for a slot to land. Our pilot informed us that the delay was caused by another Boeing having lost its wheels on landing.

For the month long tour we shared the bill with Herman's Hermits, a lightweight group from Manchester. They had been blessed with a string of hits including, 'No Milk Today,' and 'Henry the Eighth I Am'. We were riding high at the time thanks to the success of 'Chills and Fever' Down Under. There was a great deal of squabbling as to who would close the shows. It didn't come to a fist fight, but it wasn't far off.

Tom stayed at the Sydney Hilton and, surprisingly, The Squires landed a very nice hotel too. It was courtesy of the Australian promoter, who had also paid for our air fare. Throughout the tour, which included a New Zealand leg, we stayed in respectable hotels. It was a real turn-about from the way we were used to being treated by Gordon.

I remember playing a massive venue in Sydney on a revolving stage. We performed bang in the centre and the stage revolved 360 degrees so that all the audience would have the opportunity of seeing us play. The place was packed to the rafters with thousands and thousands of fans. On that particular evening we appeared with The Four Tops, with not a Hermit in sight. The evening ended farcically. Tom and the band were signing autographs from the stage. Suddenly Beryl Evans jumped up and joined me on stage. Beryl was the gorgeous elder sister of my ex-girlfriend Jean from Ponty. She had emigrated to Australia with her footballer husband, Colin Gale. We were happily chatting away when I noticed Tom staring daggers at me. He was busily signing autographs as loads of attractive girls swarmed around him, but he had eyes for just me and Beryl.

The band was aware that Tom had a jealous streak. Back in Wales he had lusted after Beryl from way back. Now here she was the other side of the world, married, chatting away to me, ignoring him completely. Tom shouted over, 'Hey Vernon, stop farting around over there and put your fucking guitar away.'

My jaw dropped and so did Beryl's. 'I'm just having a little chat with Beryl, you do remember Beryl from back home?' I replied.

'Yeah well hurry up, they want to clear the stage. Let's get out of here, me and the boys are off in a minute.'

The rest of the band looked away, smiling. It was obvious that Tom was turning green with jealously. He didn't like to be ignored and he could never disguise it. Just then Beryl's husband joined us on stage and Tom sheepishly went back to signing autographs.

Gordon was back in London and had decided not to accompany us on the tour. But he was busy scanning the daily newspapers back home. Virtually every day there was a news report about Tom's antics Down Under. He was rubbing his hands with glee at all the publicity. The Australian authorities were rather prudish about Tom's suggestive antics on stage. They didn't care for his tight trousers, and his thrusting pelvis was causing consternation. The British press reported that the Australian police had been ordered to mingle with the audiences to form an opinion as to whether he was breaking any laws with his performance.

On one occasion a theatre threatened to close the show when Tom took his shirt off and began swinging it around his head. Tom later joked to a *Daily Mail* reporter, 'I only took my shirt off because it was too hot.' The police didn't take too kindly to such flippancy. The next performance was filmed by the Sydney police and handed over to a magistrate for inspection. It's my guess that it was a female magistrate who studied the film, as the report was that it just looked like Tom was dancing, and the magistrate was looking forward to seeing his next performance.

We had nights off during our dates in Sydney, so we went down town to have a nosy around. On one occasion we found ourselves in a basement club in the Chinese district. Celebrations for Chinese New Year were underway, and we settled down to watch the colourful entertainment. There were huge dragons, animated from within by crouching Chinese dancers. They circled and twisted around the dance floor to a deafening cacophony of Oriental music. We sat mesmerised by it – we'd never seen anything like it back home.

Later three guys appeared on the small stage, one of whom

was far taller than the others. They started singing three-part harmonies and playing guitars. Along with us they must have been the only other non-Orientals in the club. They were mostly singing Everly Brothers songs and other harmonious melodies. One song particularly stood out, as it didn't fit with the rest of their set. They knocked out Lonnie Donegan's classic, 'My Old Man's A Dustman'. The roomful of Chinese didn't know what to make of it at first, but soon got into clapping along.

I thought they were quite entertaining, although it was pretty non-adventurous music. After they'd finished their set they came over and introduced themselves. They were the Gibb brothers, later to find worldwide fame as the Bee Gees.

Barry Gibb recognised us, 'Hey you're The Squires, where's Tom?'

'Probably back at the Hilton, chatting up some bird,' I replied.

'We've got some demos back in the dressing room Vernon, a few songs that my brothers and I have written. I wonder if you could pass them on to Tom's manager when you get back to London?'

I told them how difficult it was to get a break, having already been through the mill myself. Our 'Calcutta' days were still fresh in my mind. But we went back to the dressing room to get the demos, chatting about how to get on in the business. They were a nice bunch of lads and I wished them well.

I returned to join the boys and showed them the three demos and some black and white publicity photos. I'd promised the Gibb Brothers I'd pass them to Gordon upon our return to London. I did exactly that and told Gordon they were a talented trio. But Gordon being Gordon dismissed them out of hand;

'they'd never amount to anything' he said. He tossed the demos in the rubbish bin. But it was his loss and their gain as they achieved super stardom. The following year, in 1967, the Bee Gees released the first of their number one hits, 'New York Mining Disaster'. It was all legend status after that and the hits kept coming.

I bumped into them again at Elstree TV Studios in late 1967. I told them about Gordon's reaction to the original demos. Whether they believed me or not, I don't know. But they were three very happy guys; everything was on the up and the Chinese basement club in Sydney was a very long way behind them.

Many years later I was clearing out my attic in Shepperton and came across one of the publicity shots Barry had given me in Sydney. I remember keeping it back as a memento before passing on the rest along with the demos to Gordon. It's a good job I did or Gordon would have binned that as well.

Our Australian tour took in Brisbane, Adelaide, Melbourne and Perth, and then moved to New Zealand. Looking back it was a wonderful time which we thoroughly enjoyed. We were made to feel like superstars and the attention we received was like a drug. I have very fond memories. But it was soon time to head back to the UK.

Tom took the Pacific route back to London via Los Angeles and across to New York where he was to promote his latest single. Chris Slade and Mickey Gee stopped off in Singapore to sample the delights of that particular city. Vic headed straight home to London. Chris Ellis and I plumped for staying in Perth a couple of extra days. It was bliss, lazing on the beach. After we had soaked up as much sun as we could possibly take we followed Slade and Mickey to Singapore. We arrived there to find that we had just missed them, but they had left us a message at Singapore International Airport. It read: *'Vernon, Chris, look out for tall thin Oriental bloke. He's got horn-rimmed glasses, can't miss him. Gave us a great time but conned us. Be careful. Best, Mickey and Chris.'*

Sure enough as we walked out of the airport to hail a taxi, up steps Mr Horn-Rims. He promised us a ride into the city and a cosy cheap hotel. After reading the note we were on high alert but accepted his offer. We drove to a decent hotel; Chris checked out the price for a three night stay, and it looked pretty reasonable, being just a few Singapore Dollars each. Mr Horn-Rims had promised us it would be cheap and it was. He didn't even charge us much for the drive from the airport.

Chris and I had spacious rooms with a single bed in each, mosquito nets and massive rotating fans hanging from the ceiling. The hotel had a laundry service and we deposited our spent tour clothes there. They were returned washed and ironed to perfection. All for the price of a couple of pints back home in London.

We went out that night to sample the nightlife. Hung over the next morning I swept back the mosquito net and almost jumped out of my skin. The bare white washed walls were alive with millions of bright green lizards, each about six inches long. I let out a croaky yell and they all scattered, disappearing into narrow cracks in the wall. I checked in on Chris and found him sitting on the edge of his bed, holding one of the lizards. He'd found they were harmless, and great at keeping mosquitoes at bay.

Later Mr Horn-Rims came a calling and suggested we take a 'nice cool bath and massage with honourable geisha girl, who work in public relations'. Considering the temperature was in

Tom Jones and the Squires, with two new members on the right, Bill Parkinson and Vic Cooper, who replaced Dave Wendels and Dai Cooper.

The Bee Gees publicity shot I kept as a souvenir in 1966, before presenting their photos and demos to Gordon Mills. He wasn't interested in them: boy, did he rue the day!

The Squires augmented by a brass section. Left to right: Dougie Firth (saxophone), Frank Chapman and Tony Mabbett (trumpets). Chapman was suppposedly band leader.

Top. Singapore 1966: Mr Horn-Rims leading Chris Ellis and I into temptation on the way back from the Australian tour.

Bottom. Taking over from Brian Auger, Rod Stewart and Julie Driscoll in a bar at Juan les Pins. Our new guitarist, Dave Wendels looks tanned.

Top. Las Vegas airport. Flamingo Hotel manager Vince Silvestri, a powerful figure in Vegas, sees us off on our trip to the Grand Canyon.

Bottom. Chris Ellis looking cold at the top of the Empire State Building.

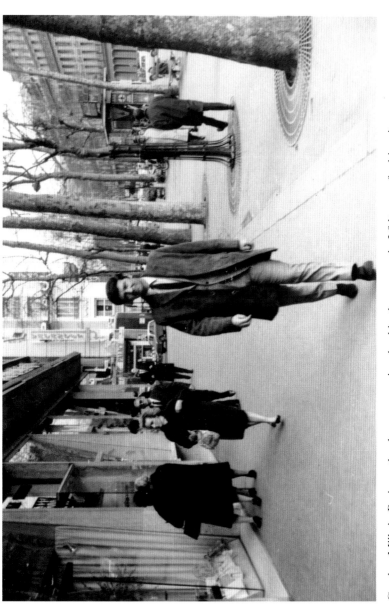

Gordon Mills in Paris on the day we were involved in the car crash. I felt sorry for his suit.

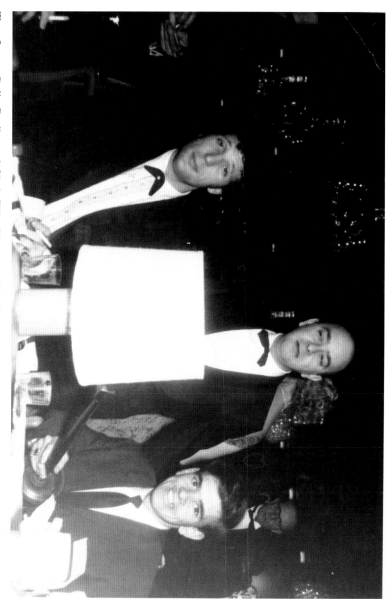

Tom Jones, Colin Berlin and Chris Ellis. Tom and The Squires were appearing at the Dorchester Hotel.

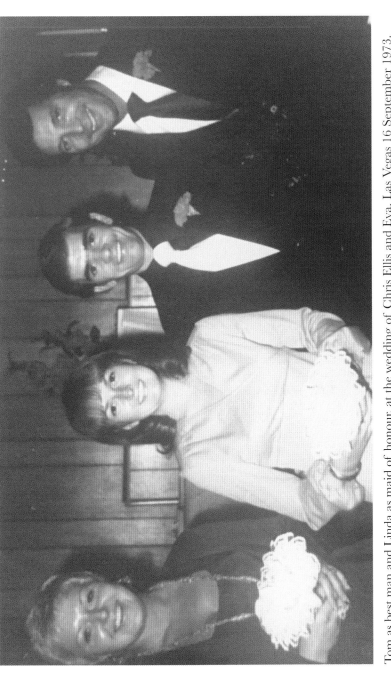

Tom as best man and Linda as maid of honour, at the wedding of Chris Ellis and Eva, Las Vegas 16 September 1973.

the high nineties, it was as humid as hell and we were nursing hangovers, I looked at Chris and asked if he was up for it. We were both sweating buckets so we readily agreed.

'How much for the massage?' I asked.

'Very cheap, just five pound each, include cool bath and fragrant oils massage. Very refreshing, you enjoy,' he said.

'Where,' asked Chris.

'Not far, just little way. You ride in white Mercedes, same car as airport drive.'

Chris and I hopped in the Mercedes expecting a short drive. Instead we were driven far out of the city and over the border into the dense Malaysian jungle. 'Not far' was obviously an understatement. The locals appeared from mud and straw huts to peer at us as we drove deeper and deeper into the jungle along a dirt track. After about an hour the car finally stopped in a clearing next to a white bungalow, with a noisy generator humming beside it.

Mr Horn-Rims led us into a clinically white room and sat us down at a table. The jungle was steaming hot and there was vapour rising from our clothes. He suggested we have a few ice-cold beers to chill out. We both readily agreed and a very old, feeble Malaysian woman brought us a tray of beers. I asked Mr Horn-Rims why we had to cross over to Malaysia for a massage and bath. He told us the clinic was not licensed to operate in Singapore, which made us uncomfortable.

Pretty soon our masseurs entered the room. They were two stunningly beautiful Malaysian girls, one petite and one slightly taller. The shorter girl took me into a small room containing a single bed and a tin bath. On a shelf next to the bath was a line of small bottles of oil in various colours. She pointed to the ridiculously tiny bath and motioned for me to get undressed. I crammed myself into it and she poured a jug of cooling water over me: then handed me a bar of soap. After washing away the jungle sweat I got the full massage treatment, and it relieved the tensions of months spent on the road on tour. This was followed with the oil treatment which had me dozing, it was so incredibly relaxing.

We were there for about an hour and a half, I remember thinking, not bad for a fiver. After lining up the bottles of oil back on the shelf, she undid her white housecoat and let it fall to the floor, standing naked. She was absolutely stunning, and being young and carefree the inevitable happened.

Afterwards back in the main room I waited for Chris to appear. He was certainly taking his time. I was then presented with the bill: £5 massage, £10 extra services, £20 four beers, £5 taxi ride. In total £40 each. I broke out in a cold sweat as we'd blown a whole week's wages in one afternoon. We protested to no avail. Mr Horn-Rims threatened that if we didn't pay, he'd leave us stranded in the jungle. We both paid up and chalked it up to experience. Slade and Mickey had tried to warn us after all.

We flew out of Singapore back to London. Our flat in Fulham had been kicked into touch and we'd rented a small detached house in West Hounslow, directly opposite the tube station. It had worked out cheaper to rent a small house than the four of us paying the same rent on the flat in Fulham. It was sparsely furnished and needed a good make over, but you couldn't argue with the rent. I took the front box room and the rest of the boys fought over the other two bedrooms. The back garden was overgrown and had been left unattended for years, but who cared – none of us ever went out there. In an echo of earlier 'Calcutta' days, when we first moved in we spent days trying to catch a mouse that had taken up residence rent-free. In the end we didn't have the heart to set traps and it quickly became tame and was adopted as band mascot.

Chris and I were the first to arrive, as Slade and Mickey had gone straight back to Wales on returning from Australia. London was freezing, especially as we had become acclimatised to the temperate southern hemisphere. Shattered after our long flight from Singapore we let ourselves in the front door and were confronted by a mass of icicles hanging from the ceiling. Some of the icicles were six feet long and stretched the entire length of the hallway. The pipes had burst in the bathroom due to the extreme cold. The hall was like an ice rink. We turned on our heel and jumped in the van. Unfortunately the battery was flat as it had been parked unused for over a month. A local garage charged the van, and we booked into a bed and breakfast until our landlord sorted out the leak.

Pretty soon we were back on the road again, playing gigs the length and breadth of the UK. We had also regular TV appearances which ensured the venues were all booked out well in advance. Tom, though, was a bit down as he was finding it difficult to produce another number one single. Although, really, he didn't have much to moan about as there was an enormous amount of money flooding in from the venues, and some of them were cash-in-hand jobs.

Mickey Gee was becoming increasingly disenchanted with the way Gordon and Tom were treating us financially. Mickey had joined the band days before leaving for London, almost two years earlier. He'd struggled through the early days when we were scrimping to get by, and now the money was flooding in we weren't in any real better shape. On the other hand Gordon and Tom were living like millionaires. Matters were brought to a head by our being back on the road again, which was costing us whatever we made in wages. We were running to stand still. With the cost of digs, rent on the house back in London, petrol for the van, meals up and down the country, and all the expense involved in touring, we were flat broke. Mickey decided that we should make a stand and ask for a tenner more a week to cover tour expenses.

We were playing in Southampton when Gordon made a rare appearance. Increasingly he'd been spending more and more time in his plush new offices in Bond Street, directing the MAM Empire. Gordon was in conference with Tom, in his dressing room. Mickey elected himself spokesman, with our backing, and went to discuss matters. We had agreed that Mickey would ask both Gordon and Tom for a ten pounds raise and our tax paid, or a twenty pound raise and we'd sort out our own tax and stamps. Mickey was gone some time and upon his return he reported, 'Tom was stood next to Gordon, wearing sunglasses with his arms folded, and Gordon was all stern and business-like. It was like a scene from a Humphrey Bogart gangster film. I thought I was going to get whacked!'

After considering our request for a small rise and help with our tax and stamps: Gordon had sent Mickey back to get the rest of us. He wanted us all in Tom's dressing room pronto. In we filed and Gordon produced one of his big pronouncements. He was relishing it, 'I was in a band once. We were called The Viscounts, and when I didn't like being in the band anymore, do you know what I did? Well let me tell you, I left. You can forget about this money you're asking for, you're not getting it, and if you don't like it, then you can all piss off back to Wales.'

Tom just stood there expressionless behind his sunglasses, puffing on a big cigar. He didn't utter a word of protest to Gordon for cutting us down so coldly. What we were asking for was a minuscule amount compared to the money they were making on a daily basis. They wouldn't have even noticed such a small amount, and yet it meant a great deal to us. After all, we were doing all the donkey work promoting and gigging, and we were the ones paying for it too. Tom had come up on the hard rail with us; he really should have said something to support us. But he didn't.

Gordon issued an ultimatum, 'Mickey, what are you doing, are you staying or going?' Mickey looked at Gordon and then Tom. Then ignoring Gordon he said to Tom, 'I'm going Tom, I'm not going to leave you in the lurch. I'll back you on tonight's gig and I'll stay on until you find a replacement. That's what friends do for each other. After all we've been through together Tom, have you got nothing to say?' Tom Jones didn't say a word, and we left the dressing room, as Gordon slapped him on the back.

Mickey was disgusted, more with Tom than Gordon. I thought it was very brave of Mickey, and noble of him to stay on until they found another lead guitarist. The rest of us decided to stay on, we could see which way the wind was blowing, but thought we'd stay for now and start looking for new opportunities. I couldn't bring myself to leave at that stage. I was the founder member of The Senators; I'd been the one to enlist Tom. I'd put an enormous amount of my life and soul into the band since its inception six years before. I just couldn't walk away from it now; it would have broken my heart. Though that's what did happen, eventually.

Mickey later told Stafford Hildred and David Gritten for their biography, *Tom Jones*, that, 'the only reason we went up to forty pounds a week was because we had started to work with session musicians and found out what the proper rates were. Even then the other guys in the band were pretty easy-going about the session men getting more than us. I kept saying, "for God's sake, they never starved with you, or went on the road to all those awful places. Tom and Gordon are paying them session rates, let them pay us session rates". Of course Tom and Gordon got rid of the rest of the band in the end, as I knew they would. But the thing that really pissed me off was that after I left them they did all get to tour America and meet Elvis. It was always my dream to meet Elvis, so I missed out in that way.'

The episode in Southampton was a watershed moment. We saw a very different side of Tom that day. Prior to the confrontation with Gordon whenever we asked Tom why we were being treated so badly, he had put it down to Gordon, and told us he was fighting our corner. Now we had seen him in his true colours. In the midst of the argument he had stood stony-faced puffing on a big cigar, and had taken Gordon's side. And to not even say a word to Mickey was pretty rotten behaviour. It was hard to believe that less than a year previously we had been holed up together in the 'Calcutta', sharing two sausage rolls between the five of us.

The whole situation was very sad. I remember thinking about an occasion back in Wales before we left for London. Tom was going on and on about how much he hated the police, and how they were the scum of the earth. It probably had something to do with him being clobbered for thieving or fighting. He was ranting and raving when I reminded him that my brother, Norman, was a copper. Tom instantly quipped back, 'I'm more like a brother to you than he is'. We were certainly very close back then, but now we were oceans apart and I didn't understand how he could treat us as he did. After all these years I'm no closer to understanding. Tom lost a fine musician and a good, loyal friend when Mickey left. He also lost the respect of the rest of the band. Mickey went on to appear in a lot of great bands.

The effects of the Australian tour, coupled with his liking for Woodbines and cigars, had put a major strain on Tom's voice. It was decided that he should have his tonsils removed. The surgeons checked his throat at the same time and the prognosis was not good. If he didn't stop smoking Woodbines immediately his voice would crack. Gordon suggested that he cut out the Woodbines and just smoke cigars, but not inhale. As for drinking alcohol, the specialist recommended that beer and spirits be completely avoided at all costs. Gordon had the perfect solution: champagne. Tom took some convincing to give up the pints, but Gordon played on his vanity, telling him that he didn't want to end up with a big beer belly – after all who would pay to see him then?

Tom gave an interview at the time in which he said, 'I've always smoked Woodbines and drunk beer. My manager told me that one day I'd be smoking cigars and drinking champagne. I told him at the time 'I love Woodbines and beer, and that's that.' So what am I doing today? Drinking champagne and smoking cigars, when you can afford to do that, what the hell. Lots of people say I've changed. The only change in me is that the real person has come out.'

Tom had changed and not for the better, the band would all testify to that, those of us left anyway. Mickey's departure also had the knock on effect of us losing our rented house. With only Chris Slade, Chris Ellis and me living there, we couldn't afford the rent. The only option was to split up and look for our own accommodation. Chris Slade's girlfriend Lynne packed in her job in Ponty, and she and Chris rented a small flat in London. Chris Ellis and I went looking for somewhere near Tom and Gordon. Gordon wanted us to be within a few miles of his home to be available when needed. We both settled on Shepperton, near the River Thames, an up-market area of West London, a few miles from each other.

I had Tony Cartwright to thank for helping me find digs. The band had befriended Tony when we lived at Ladbroke Grove. He was the singer and rhythm guitarist of a young Liverpool band that had migrated to London on their quest for fame, like us. Tony was a bit of a character. Like many Scousers he had the gift of the gab, and was the spit image of the movie star, Tom Hanks. His Liverpool accent was sometimes impenetrable and he was seriously streetwise. Having grown up in the poorer part of Liverpool he had elevated 'blagging' to an art form.

Sadly we had lost touch after leaving the 'Calcutta' at Ladbroke Grove, but amazingly when I went back to Ponty while Tom was in hospital having his tonsils out my sister said he had been in touch. Actually it was more than just getting in touch. Tony being Tony had got his band put up at my Dad's house. They had been on tour playing all the dance halls in the Valleys. Tony remembered me mentioning my address, and along with his fifteen-year-old drummer, who had absconded from school to take part in the tour, knocked on my Dad's door.

The cheeky bugger talked Dad into putting the band up for a few nights. Tony told him they were too skint to afford accommodation. My kindly father duly obliged and they slept in the front parlour, where Tom and The Senators used to rehearse. The diminutive drummer, truanting from school, would go on to great things. He became one of the most famous and celebrated musicians in the world. His name was Mitch Mitchell and he became the drummer with The Jimi Hendrix Experience.

Tony had heard on the grapevine that Chris Ellis and I were looking for lodgings, and got in contact. He was holed up in West Molesley, three miles from Shepperton, lodging with a family in a council house on a small new estate in Tonbridge Road. Tony told me he was lodging there illegally as council red tape banned the taking in of lodgers. It was a four bedroom house and there was a room going spare for five pounds a week, with an extra couple of quid for laundry and joining the family for evening meals. I jumped at the offer and Chris Ellis found lodgings with my new landlady's sister in nearby Thames Ditton.

It would turn out to be the best move for both of us. After all the dumps we had previously bedded down in, this was a real step up, and we were made to feel part of the family. Muriel McKenna and her ten year old daughter Jill, lived there with Mu's elderly mother, Nancy. There was also a yappy little Jack Russell, called Julie. The house was cosy and spotless. Tony and I went back a way so we got on like a house on fire. His Liverpool humour always used to crack me up. It was a manic laugh a minute with him: you never knew what he was going to come out with next, and he had the whole family in fits of giggles.

Tony was out on a limb at the time. He'd finished playing

with the band and was on the dole, but he was always on the make, looking for opportunities to make a bob or two. Gordon took him on eventually, getting Tony to drive him around and do the occasional odd job.

I really took to my new family. Muriel was about forty, tiny in stature, thin and a little old for her age. She had short fair hair and could produce a cackle that could haunt a house. Mu was always stressed and her language could be quite ripe at times, as could her considerable bark. But it was all very theatrical; she was one hell of a character, with a heart of gold. Mu's daughter Jill was a love child. Her black American father had been stationed at an American army base nearby and Mu had met him at a dance hall in Walton-on-Thames. When he was drafted back to America, Mu and her daughter had moved back in with Nancy, and subsequently they had managed to secure the tenancy on the council house. Mu had a job as a house cleaner in nearby Weybridge. Her most famous client was the pop singer, Adam Faith.

At that time Gordon had arranged for a new band member to join us. Lead guitarist Dave Wendels was a former member of Lulu's band, The Luvvers. Dave was a tall good-looking twenty-four year-old and lived with his mother in Central Hounslow. Dave's house is ingrained in my memory. I had passed my driving test (at last) and had bought a clapped out Ford Anglia, the very same model made famous in the Harry Potter movies. I'd driven over to Dave's house to catch up and have a cup of tea or two. Leaving the house I was dismayed to find that the offside front wing of my car had been bashed by another car, which hadn't stopped. After surveying the damage, my attention was caught by a nearby news stand. The headline on the bill board read:

South Wales Tip Tragedy. Over 100 Schoolchildren Buried Alive. It was the day of the Aberfan tragedy in October 1966 and it stopped me dead in my tracks. The damaged front wing was forgotten. I was shocked and numbed by the terrible news, and went to find a phone kiosk to call home to Wales.

11. SHEPPERTON

Earlier that year, on the 15th May Tom and The Squires were booked to appear at a charity concert at Blackpool Opera House, with Dusty Springfield, and The Mindbenders. Immediately after the concert we boarded a plane for Brussels to make a television appearance. Then we went by train to Paris to appear on a television show filmed at the famous Paris Olympia.

Gordon was there to meet us. He had arranged to meet Tom at a Paris nightclub after the show and asked me if I'd like to come along. We were offered a lift there by a journalist and hopped into his battered old Citroen 2CV. It was a tight squeeze with Gordon and I both being six-footers. We felt every bump in the road rattling across town in that tin can. Stopping at some traffic lights, a powerful red sports car pulled up alongside us, a convertible with the hood up. At the wheel was a stunningly beautiful brunette who gave Gordon 'the eye'.

Gordon wound down his window and smiled. He asked if she would mind giving us a lift, 'of course,' she purred in a smouldering French accent. We squeezed out of the Citroen and hopped into the sports car. Gordon took the passenger seat and I sat in the back. We explained where we were heading and invited her to join us for the evening. The convertible sped off with the tyres screeching.

Curled up in the back I was barely able to move. We shot across Paris at breakneck speed. Gordon seemed to be enjoying the thrill of it, but I was beginning to wish I'd stuck with the 2CV. I could see some traffic lights up ahead turning red. The woman put her foot to the floor and drove straight through. Suddenly she lost control of the car and it smashed into the side of another vehicle. I blacked out.

When I came around I was hanging out of the front passenger door with my head resting on the tarmac. Dazed and confused I struggled to my feet. Lights were flashing, there was hissing steam everywhere and the unmistakable smell of petrol. The car we had hit was overturned, resting on its roof, a complete write-off. The red sports car wasn't in any better condition, it was smashed to bits.

I saw Gordon standing on the pavement nearby, his clothes were torn and he was bleeding from the face. He was yelling at some gendames, 'But I'm British, I'm British'. He seemed very animated, and a little concussed. The beautiful brunette was lying at Gordon's feet, out cold. He had placed his jacket under her head as a pillow. Moments later an ambulance arrived and Gordon helped lift the woman into it.

I stumbled over. I was very unsteady on my feet and my vision was swimming in and out of focus. Gordon turned to me with a look of utter disdain on his bloodied face. He was livid and snarled, 'where the fuck was you when I needed you?' I explained that I had been knocked out but he just scowled at me.

After giving our details to the police and explaining as best we could what had happened, they let us go. We found our own way back to the hotel. I helped Gordon to his room as the full effects of the accident started to show on him. I inspected his wounds. His trousers were ripped revealing a nasty gash on his shin. He looked pretty shook up as I bathed the wound with a flannel. I seemed to have got off quite lightly with just a few cuts, bruises and a pounding headache.

It was gone midnight by now when the phone rang. Gordon reached over and answered it. He seemed to turn an even whiter shade of pale. It was his wife calling from Shepperton, apologizing for waking him up. Gordon instantly recovered his cool, 'That's okay Jo. I was just about to turn the light off. I've been tucked up in bed reading a novel. Yes, everything's fine… What!'

Jo had decided she wanted to join Gordon in Paris and enjoy a little of the Parisian highlife. She promptly informed him she would be arriving in about twelve hours' time. He was in a right old panic. Only the night porter was on duty at that hour and Gordon's only suit was the one he had been wearing. He'd left his jacket at the scene of the accident. His white shirt was covered in blood and the trousers were torn.

Putting down the phone he threw his shirt at me and begged me to have a go at cleaning the blood off. There I was, in the bathroom, attempting the impossible while Gordon paced the bedroom.

'How am I going to explain this one Vernon?'

'Well Gordon, you shouldn't have told her you was tucked up in bed with a book,' I said.

'You're right. I'm in a bit of a pickle here.'

'Why not tell her you fell down the hotel lift shaft,' I cracked.

'No, she'd never believe that. What if I tell her I was mugged and I didn't want to upset her at this time of night?'

I left him to it and crawled back to my own bed down the corridor. When I woke my entire body ached. God only knows how Gordon must have felt. As for the beautiful brunette, we made some enquiries and were informed that she had survived, but was in intensive care.

We returned to France not long after for a month's tour of concerts along the south coast. Gordon had decided to make the long journey in his new blue Jaguar XJ6. He didn't want to drive across France on his own so asked me if I would accompany him on the journey over. Tom and the rest of the band had already flown down to the south of France. Chris Ellis was driving the van down to the Riviera with all the equipment in back.

Gordon and I boarded the ferry from Dover to Calais and practically raced through Paris. We caught up with Chris not far from the city. He'd pulled the van into a lay-by and was cooking some food on a portable stove. The poor guy look completely knackered and yet he was hardly half way there. I told Gordon I should share the driving with Chris, but he was having none of it and told me I needed to share the driving with him. Forget Chris, he was doing what he was paid for.

I really started to regret not joining Chris and the equipment when I had the chance. Gordon was overbearing for the whole journey. About half way there Gordon got bored with driving, tossed me the keys and stretched out in the back. Up until that point I'd been navigating. I couldn't drive and read the map at the same time but Gordon just told me to get on with it and fell fast asleep. He woke to demand that we pull over at the next restaurant. Luckily I was carrying some French currency because when it came time to settle the bill, Gordon threw a couple of francs on the table, and strolled out. 'See you back at the car,' he tossed over his shoulder.

I fumbled with the money to pay my part of the bill. Of course, Gordon had woefully underpaid and left me to make up the difference. This was a man who had just become a million-aire. I fully expected him to ask me for petrol money next.

JUST HELP YOURSELF

The mountain roads leading down to the south were baking hot and quite treacherous. This was long before motorways in France. Gordon asked me to pull over as he was bursting for a pee. He had polished off a good few beers at the restaurant and I'd had a couple too. We pulled over and both went for a pee. I was blissfully relieving myself when I heard the throaty roar as the Jag's engine sprang into life. Gordon roared off, shouting, 'You're taking too long Vernon. You can hitch a ride.' He disappeared around the side of the mountain in a cloud of dust, leaving me standing with my flies open and my mouth gaping. I had figured out a long time earlier that Gordon was a bit of a joker. But this was taking the piss, quite literally. I was convinced that he would return after a few minutes of winding me up. I waited. The sun blazed overhead and I was dehydrated, the beers at the restaurant hadn't helped. I started walking along the mountain road. A couple of cars went by but no-one offered me a ride.

I walked for what seemed like hours cursing Gordon to kingdom come. Finally I saw the Jag pulled over at the side of the road. Gordon was fast asleep in the back. I shook him awake and had a real go at him, calling him every name under the blazing sun. Typically, Gordon just smiled and yawned. He told me he was going to come back, it was just a wind up, but he'd fallen asleep. He tossed me the keys and said, 'You drive Vernon those continental beers have knocked me for six.' I could have strangled him.

Arriving in Nice we teamed up with Tom and the boys. They had been waiting patiently for Chris Ellis to arrive with the equipment, but there was no sign of him. We were beginning to worry. It was impossible to get in contact to check if he was all right. Finally, to our immense relief, he arrived looking like death warmed up. He had big shadows under his glazed eyes and was walking in a trance. Chris always carried a bag of Dexedrine tablets in the van, so that he wouldn't fall asleep on our long hauls up and down the M1. But driving through France had been another kettle of fish entirely. Chris was pumped to the eyebrows with uppers. He hadn't slept a wink since leaving London. He was flying but at the same time he could hardly stand!

Chris mumbled something to Gordon about being held up in traffic. Then he staggered like a zombie and disappeared into a crowd of tourists. Before we knew it we had lost him entirely. The sun was setting so we organized ourselves into two search parties. Thankfully we eventually found him wandering the streets, bumping into people and cars and mumbling incoherently. He didn't even know he was in France, but thought he was in London. Gently we led him to the hotel and put him to bed, where he slept for eighteen hours straight.

At the end of the tour Gordon and Tom drove back to London in the Jag. I was thankful that I hadn't been enlisted for the drive back with Gordon and hoped Tom fared better than me. There was no need for The Squires to return for a few days so we decided to explore the coast. We drove to Juan les Pins, not far from St Tropez, Brigitte Bardot's home town. There we found some cheap accommodation, which we later learned was infested with ants, and spruced ourselves up to hit the town.

Juan les Pins was a quaint little fishing village at that time. It was unassuming by day, but once the sun set it exploded. Live music resonated along the seafront. We went on a bar crawl and came across The Brian Auger Trinity and their lead singer Rod

Stewart, an unknown at that time. Brian Auger played Hammond organ and they also had a female vocalist, Julie Driscoll. They were on the cusp of stardom and we visited the bar every night, really enjoying the music. One evening the band quarrelled with the owner and moved to another venue close by. With no band to take their place at short notice the owner asked us if we would fill in.

That night we belted out rock 'n' roll classics and Rod Stewart's audience drifted back from their new venue to watch us. The Brian Auger Trinity weren't very happy with that state of affairs. After the gig they challenged us to a drinking contest. We nominated our new lead guitarist, Dave Wendels to uphold the band's honour. Dave could consume a lot of alcohol without feeling many effects. The choice of liquor was a bottle of vodka each, to be consumed within half an hour. The duel take place at the new Trinity venue. The bands gathered around a table and faced off.

It's no easy task sinking a bottle of neat vodka in such a short time. A good twenty minutes in and Auger's lead guitarist was swaying like a pendulum. Dave seemed to be holding his own, glassy-eyed and poker faced. A little while later, with both bands cheering them on, Auger's guitarist fell off his chair and was counted out. It was a great shame as he only had to finish a couple more tumblers and he would have won.

We congratulated our champion. He was looking a little the worse for wear and, cross-eyed, he staggered across the bar in search of the toilet. We all settled in with Rod and Auger's band and got down to some serious drinking. Dave Wendels was nowhere to be seen for the rest of the evening and we assumed he'd gone back to the hotel to sleep it off. The bar finally closed and we stumbled out for a moonlight wander down to the beach. Walking along the sea front we dimly made out a figure, sixty yards away, leaning against the seafront wall.

I remember saying 'Isn't that Dave?' but before anyone could answer a gendarme van pulled up, tossed him in the back and sped away. He had been whisked off to the cells. Rod said, 'They'll let him out in the morning after he's slept it off.'

Chris and I staggered back to the hotel the worse for wear to find our beds swarming with ants. They were everywhere, in the beds, under the beds and scampering all over the walls. There were millions of the little buggers. We were too drunk to deal with it so we turned on our heels and slept on the beach.

The following morning there was still no sign of Dave. The day wore on and we were due on stage at the bar in a couple of hours. Vic could speak a little French so he made enquiries at the police station. He explained that Dave had been arrested the previous evening for being drunk and incapable. A few minutes later the gendarmes escorted Dave from the cells. He was still completely smashed. They released him to Vic and, miraculously, he managed to play that night .

When we got back to London we were booked to appear on Bruce Forsyth's new show on ITV. Directly afterwards we were off on our travels again, this time to record a TV special in Madrid. Dave Wendels behaved himself on this occasion; he'd sworn off the alcohol, and just the sight of a bottle of vodka was enough to make him turn green.

Tom had decided to buy himself a new car. He became the proud owner of a gleaming red Jaguar. It was the same shape as the revived S-Type, very sleek and powerful. On our return from Madrid, Tom, Tony Cartwright, Chris Ellis and myself met at

The Cromwellian Club, one of our favourite haunts. The club was on the Cromwell Road, opposite the Natural History Museum. Eric Clapton, Ginger Baker, Jimmy Page and a host of other 'yet-to-be-discovered' musicians used to play in the club's basement, and we enjoyed their company and the general vibe. It was also a great place for pulling girls and later that year I would bump into Mia Lewis again there.

This particular evening, Tom and Tony had latched onto a couple of air hostesses. Everyone was in fine spirits and it was turning into a raucous time. We decided to head to The Bag o Nails in the West End. This was the pub where Paul McCartney met Linda Eastman. I followed Tom in my little Ford Anglia and was finding it increasingly difficult to keep up with him. He was driving like a lunatic up Park Lane. One of the air hostesses in the back was giving Tom directions and told him to make a sudden right turn into an opening in the dual carriageway. Chris and I watched the whole scenario unfold.

It was obvious that there was no chance the Jag was going to be able to cut through at speed. Tom crashed into a wall on the reservation at considerable speed. The car was a write off. Chris and I pulled over and leaped out. Tom and Tony were both in a bit of a mess, crumpled up in the front seats. Tom had a nasty gash above his left eye, and there was blood everywhere. They stumbled out of the wrecked Jag. Tom mumbled that he was in the shit big time. He was drunk and he had two air hostesses in the back. We could all imagine the headlines in the morning newspapers.

I went to check on the girls; both seemed fine if a little shaken. Tom and Tony decided to make a run for it and sprinted up the road. Unfortunately their escape attempt was foiled when a police car and ambulance arrived with lights flashing. They were all bundled into the back of the ambulance and taken to St. George's Hospital at Hyde Park Corner, two minutes away.

Tony was stretchered out of the ambulance, moaning and groaning and probably concussed. But after being checked over it turned out there was nothing wrong with him. Tom on the other hand had fourteen stitches above his eye and was kept in for observation until dawn the following morning. Tom got off very lightly. Luckily the newspapers never caught a sniff of the accident and it went unreported.

Tony Cartwright and I were being spoiled rotten at Tonbridge Road. Mu was like a mother hen fussing over us. She fed us, washed and ironed our clothes; we had our own keys and came and went as we wished. Mu used to make the biggest Sunday dinners on the planet. A lot of fellow musicians got wind of this and took to calling in at all hours of day and night to visit. Mu and her mum, Nancy, were so easy going they didn't mind a bit.

One of our most regular visitors was Mick Avory, The Kinks drummer. We had performed on the same TV show in 1964, BBC's *Beat Room*, and been friends ever since. At that time he was living close by in West Molesley. We used to meet at The Cannon in the village, and Mick would invite himself back to Mu's for a cup of tea when he wasn't touring. He was a lovely guy and a very talented musician.

Another regular visitor was Noel Redding, who would become famous as the bass guitarist with The Jimi Hendrix Experience. He had joined the band along with my old friend, the drummer Mitch Mitchell, who had crashed at my Dad's house in Wales. Noel used to stay over at Mu's when he was out on a limb work-wise. We'd put him on the couch and he was happy dossing there. However whenever we had him to stay it was a necessity that every downstairs window and door be left open. Noel had the smelliest socks imaginable, enough to bring tears to your eyes. Even Julie the Jack Russell used to beat it out the back door to get some fresh air. Sadly both Noel and Mitch died at a relatively young age. They were a great loss to the music business: they were both incredibly talented musicians. I have very fond memories of the times I shared with them both.

Another regular visitor was Adam Faith and his wife Jackie, a beautiful ex-dancer. Mu was their cleaner but had been adopted as one of the family. Looking back on those days at Tonbridge Road it's amazing the people that used to drop in for a cup of tea and a chat. As well as Tom, Engelbert Humperdinck and Gilbert O'Sullivan a host of fellow musicians would rock up unannounced because they knew they'd always be welcome. They were certainly very happy days.

Tony was earning a few bob as Gordon's 'gopher'. As Tony explained to me at the time, he was using the opportunity to pick up as many business tips as possible. He had his sights set on becoming a successful manager, like Gordon. One day he would realise his ambition, and he went onto manage the comedian Freddie Starr, the singer Malcolm Roberts and eventually took over the management of Engelbert Humperdinck from Gordon.

But during that lean spell he hardly had a shilling to his name. Gordon was notoriously tight with money and was paying him practically nothing. Tony would probably have been better off on the dole, but he was biding his time and learning the business. His favourite drink was Guinness and bitter mix and he was always on the scrounge for a pint, pleading poverty. He was such a colourful character no-one could refuse him. I knew what it meant to be skint and always helped him out when I could.

Tony used to wind up Mu something chronic. When Julie the Jack Russell came into season, Mu gave strict instructions not to let her out of the house. She didn't want to have to be dealing with a litter of puppies. We gave her our solemn promise. I remember being up in my bedroom and I happened to look out the window. There was Julie across the road surrounded by a pack of five panting dogs. They were all taking turns to try to mount her. Tony, of course, had left the door open after collecting a parcel from the postman.

I rushed downstairs where Tony was reading the newspaper, the door wide open. Mu's mum Nancy was fast asleep in the chair opposite. I shook him, so as not to disturb the old girl, and urgently beckoned him outside. It was too late. The Jack Russell was being mounted by a flea-bitten mongrel and they were stuck together, bum to bum. Poor little Julie was yelping whenever the larger dog swung her around, desperately trying to get herself unstuck.

We were in trouble now. Net curtains were rustling up and down the street to see what the commotion was all about. By the time we threw a bucket of cold water over them, Mu's neighbours had all come out to see the show. The water did the trick and we shooed Julie back into the house and put her in the bath. Thankfully Nancy slept through the entire incident: we thought we'd got away with it. But when Jill came home from school she went out to play with her friends and a few moments later came back clecking to her Mum. Predictably Mu hit the roof. I used to think Dorothy Squires had a bit of a mouth on her, but she wasn't a patch on Mu. The air turned blue, 'Okay own up. Which one of you bleedin' tossers let my Julie get raped by a pack of mongrels? The poor little fucker, she's in bleedin' shock. Mum, did you see any of it?'

'No Mu. I must have been kipping. Didn't hear a thing,' said her Mum.

'Tony I bet it was you. You never remember to shut the fuckin' front door. You're the worst lodger I've ever 'ad. I know it was you that poured half a bottle of bleedin aftershave over the dog because she was niffin. All dogs smell after they've been in the rain you pillock. The poor little fucker went bald because of you. She looked like a piglet for months after.'

'Calm down Mu. I paid for the vet to have a look at her didn't I?' squirmed Tony.

'Yeah, I know you did, Cartwright. But who had to pay for all the fuckin' ointment. Not you, you're always fucking skint. I know it was you Tony, cos you haven't denied it,' she raged. 'You can't put the blame on Vernon this time, like you did when you set the fuckin' chimney on fire.'

That was news to me, and I stared narrowly at Tony. 'I told you Mu, I had nothing to do with that,' he piped up in his Scouse accent.

'Course you did, when the bleedin fire brigade turned up you was the only one in the bleedin house. Our next door neighbour told me Mick Avory and Vernon was up at The Cannon for a pint at the time.'

Tony was backpedalling furiously and realised he was going to have to come clean, 'I'm really sorry Mu. There was a bloody great bee hovering around Nancy while she was having her kip. Her mouth was wide open like, and the bee was buzzing, so I chased it out the front door. That must have been when Julie slipped out,' lied Tony convincingly. Even I started to believe him and I'd witnessed him nonchalantly reading the paper.

'Bee, fuckin' slipped out. You can slip your bleedin 'and in your pocket, the one with the imaginary hole in it rent time. You 'is paying for the bleedin abortion let me tell you.'

I don't know how I kept a straight face. It was all true: Tony Cartwright did cause the Jack Russell to go bald, and it was him who had set the chimney on fire. It was just his luck that Julie must have been sterile because to his great relief she never did have a litter of puppies. As for Mu, although it was all soon forgotten, she never usually swore like that.

Although Tom and The Squires were now a million miles apart in financial terms, Tom still sought out our company socially. We were most of us based in and around Shepperton so it was easy to meet up. He still considered himself 'one of the boys'. Tom had an aversion to being cooped up in his mansion. He didn't like being indoors with Linda and Mark, when he could be out on the town. We used to meet regularly in the village, knock back a few pints and go on the pull. Chris Ellis and I would frequent The Anchor, one of four pubs located in Shepperton Village Square. Many years later my daughter Tara would be married in St Nicholas's Church directly opposite. The whole area was steeped in history; the church was over a thousand years old. The oldest pub in the area was The Kings Head, built during the reign of Henry VIII. One of his many mistresses was reputed to have stayed there to be close to Hampton Court Palace.

The Anchor was a bit of a celebrity hangout and was often frequented by film stars. It was within shooting distance of

Shepperton Studios and many a famous actor would stroll over for some refreshment. Some of the more memorable people we met there were Peter Sellers, Richard Burton and Elizabeth Taylor. The film star John Gregson was a regular. John had played the leading role in the classic film *Genevieve*, about the London to Brighton car race. He had a house close to the Square in a lovely riverside setting. John would often prop up the bar with his great actor pal, Ian Hendry. Ian was famous at the time for being the villain chased by Michael Caine at the end of the gangster movie *Get Carter*. Tom and the band would stay drinking to the early hours with them both. They were great raconteurs and would have us in fits of giggles listening to all the tales about their film careers and personal lives.

John Gregson was a real character. After a few whiskeys he'd start complaining about his wife. According to John she spent all of her time at the bottom of the garden worshiping at a shrine. We never did find out which deity the shrine was dedicated to. But when he started whining about the situation it was pure comedy gold. Ian Hendry, on the other hand, was a raucous alcoholic and sometimes our small company of after-hours drinkers would have to suffer his boorish behaviour. Ian would get paralytic and insult everyone within earshot. When he got really bad his long suffering wife, the actress Janet Munro, a reformed alcoholic herself, would collect him and cart him off. She would come for him in a rowing boat from the other side of the Thames and coax him back home.

One particular evening in The Anchor, Tony Cartwright, Chris Ellis, Tom and I were propping up the bar until the early hours. Parked outside was Tom's white Volvo, Chris's Commer van and my clapped out Anglia. Everyone was well oiled and nobody had any intention of turning in anytime soon. Then I remembered that my driving test was arranged for 9 a.m. the following morning. The boys had been nagging me for ages to take it and get it over with, and I'd finally relented. I didn't fancy driving my old motor so I asked Tom if I could borrow the Volvo. Stumbling out of The Anchor much the worse for wear, Tom told me to collect it from his garage in the morning; he'd leave the keys in the ignition.

I managed to get in a couple of hours sleep and Tony accompanied me to pick up the Volvo. We transferred the L-plates from the Anglia and drove to the test centre in nearby Weybridge. I had never driven the Volvo before and it was a real beast, very slick and fast. I'd made sure I had familiarized myself with the test route through Weybridge town centre and the surrounding area. I had my fingers crossed that it would all go well, although it didn't get off to the best of starts when I accidently collided with my examiner and caused him to stumble into the gutter.

One thing was for sure, he was very impressed with the gleaming sports car, and said as much. I was still feeling a little tipsy from the previous night. But everything seemed to go very well. My hill start, reversing and emergency stop all passed without comment. But the examiner wasn't very happy with my gear changing. He kept asking if I was in the correct gear. I assured him that I was, but the Volvo felt sluggish, as though I was in top gear and yet driving at around 20mph. He seemed puzzled and when we got out of the 30mph limit asked me to open it up and give it some stick. I felt a little paranoid about the way the car was behaving, it made me hesitant, and I told him it wasn't advisable to be giving the car some welly on a provisional licence. He remained silent and jotted down some notes in his pad.

Back at the test centre I sat the theoretical test and the Highway Code. I got all the questions correct until the very last, which threw me a bit. What's the first thing to do after being involved in a road accident with another vehicle? I rattled off a number of replies: exchange insurance details, check for injuries, and phone for an ambulance. The examiner kept shaking his head to all my answers. I thought well that's it, better luck next time.

Tony was waiting for me outside. He took one look at my face and patted me on the back, 'Well done Vernon, first time and all.' I'd passed. Whilst ripping off the L-plates I asked the examiner about the answer was to the last question. He gnomically told me to consult the Highway Code when I got home. I did and there it was, just one word… Stop!

I returned the Volvo to Tom and thanked him. He piped up that I must have bribed the examiner. I advised him to get the car checked as it seemed a little sluggish at 30mph, and the examiner had commented on it. Tom checked the gears and told me I'd been driving the Volvo in 'overdrive'. Back then 'overdrive' was completely alien to me, I'd never come across it in a car before, having only driven old bangers.

Tom was acquiring a real taste for cars at that time. Not long after he had an olive-green Rolls Continental delivered to Manygate Lane. It was a monster of a car, a real status symbol number. Tom swung by the Arches to show it off and our jaws hit the floor. It was pretty impressive. I remember him complaining later that Linda had burst into tears when he showed it to her. He told me she had preferred the red Jag, the one he wrote off in Park Lane, and pleaded with him to ditch the Rolls and get another one of those instead. Tom couldn't understand it; the Rolls status seemed to mean nothing to her. Naturally he refused. I pointed out that with the money he was now making he could afford to buy her a fleet of Jags, one for every colour of the spectrum. He looked at me as though I'd taken leave of my senses.

12. THE GREEN, GREEN GRASS OF HOME

Toward the end of 1966 we were working the club circuit in the North of England. Playing in Leeds, we discovered that Tom's idol, Jerry Lee Lewis, was performing at another venue there. It wasn't just Tom who idolized Jerry Lee, we were all great admirers and loved the man and his music. There was hardly any discussion: we decided to descend on 'The Killer' and take in his show.

Vic Cooper was pressed into service to drive Tom to the gig in his new Rolls. He wanted to make an entrance. The rest of us piled into the van and were chauffeured by Chris Ellis. The hall was packed to the rafters so we stood at the back. Jerry Lee made his entrance backed by his four musicians and launched into a cracking set; he went down a storm.

Some of the audience noticed Tom standing with the band at the back of the venue, and heads started to turn as the message rippled through the audience. Pretty soon they began chanting for Tom to get up and sing. This didn't pass unnoticed by Jerry Lee Lewis; he wasn't called 'The Killer' for nothing. Not only could he beat a piano to death, it was well documented his wild streak ran deep. He was reputed to have a vile temper and at that moment his face was like thunder. But the chanting just got louder and louder.

Finishing 'Great Balls Of Fire' midway through the song, he kicked over his chair and glared at the audience, staring them down. It looked as if he was going to reach into the front row, grab someone and throttle them. Jerry Lee told the audience they were welcome to Tom Jones and then he stormed off the stage.

That was the cue for the audience to push and hustle Tom up on stage. Tom, being Tom, was basking in the attention, and allowed himself to be manhandled up on to Jerry's recently vacated stage. We were all shocked, and even more shocked when he grabbed the mike and called for us to join him onstage. I was cringing and when I turned to the rest of the band and I could see they were mortified too. Jerry Lee Lewis was our hero for goodness sake. I motioned to the exit and we all started edging toward it.

So Tom asked the audience to help get The Squires up on stage, and they duly started chanting and hustling us forward. We had no choice but to join him. It was even more embarrassing when Jerry's band handed over their instruments to us and left the stage to join Jerry in the dressing room. I remember thinking that you just don't do that sort of thing to a fellow artiste. I think in Tom's case he wanted to prove that he could outshine his hero.

We launched into some rock 'n' roll songs ending with 'It's Not Unusual', and left the stage to thunderous applause. The audience stayed rooted to the spot waiting for Jerry to come back on, but they would have a long wait. The venue manager had to eventually inform them that Jerry would not be finishing his act. There were loud catcalls and boos all around. But you could hardly blame him after he'd been undermined big-time.

We felt incredibly guilty and traipsed backstage, and knocked on Jerry's dressing room door. He called us in. He was sitting in a chair looking utterly miserable. Tom apologized for being 'forced to override Jerry' and went on to gush about how he was such a massive fan, and how Jerry had been his inspiration. 'The Killer' responded with a glare that could have peeled paint. Needless to say our visit to the dressing room was very short, some of Jerry's band could see which way the wind was blowing and hustled us out. Jerry obviously never forgot the experience because many years later he confronted Tom and they almost came to blows.

Tom and Gordon were down in the dumps during that period. There was no sign of another chart hit on the horizon. To make matters worse, Wilson Pickett had berated Tom both personally and through the press, telling him to, 'stop recording the crap he's bringing out and be a soul brother'. Tom's voice was as soulful as any black singer and if he had taken Pickett's advice he might have found a real rich niche at the time. Gordon wasn't convinced and wanted to keep chopping and changing: blues, soul, country and western, rock 'n' roll, jazz, folk and a mixture of mainstream pop. It was pretty dizzying for us, God only knows what it was like for Tom.

Funnily enough, in the end it was Jerry Lee Lewis he had to thank. In the autumn Tom was going through his record collection and came across an album of country songs by Jerry Lee. He was really taken with one of the tracks and played it over and over. He told me later that he'd played it so many times that the grooves on the vinyl were almost worn through. The track was 'The Green, Green Grass of Home'. I remembered that back in Wales Tom had a yearning for country music, almost as much as he loved rock 'n' roll. The culture of the Welsh valleys identified with that whole mid-west American sound, the open scenery, the psyche, the whole ambience struck a real resonant chord.

'The Green, Green Grass of Home' was a track from an album entitled *Country Songs for City Folks*. It had already been covered by a host of stars in America, as well as Jerry Lee Lewis. Most of the earlier arrangements were mild, toned down instrumental affairs. Les Reed on the other hand gave Tom's version a much lusher sound, complete with a string section and vocal backing. Tom said at the time, 'it was the right song. Some numbers are so personal they can hardly fail. There is an immediate bond between the singer, the lyrics and the audience. What makes me especially proud is that it was chosen by me alone. I knew instinctively that it was right for me.'

The song had been written by Claude Curly Putnam Jnr., inspired by a film called *The Asphalt Jungle*. The film starred Marilyn Monroe and one memorable scene depicts a gangster who wants to return home to his farm before he dies. At the end of the movie he collapses, bleeding and shot through with bullet holes, onto the green, green grass of home.

Tom's version was released in November 1966 and went to number one in the charts in December. It sold over one million copies in the UK alone and went onto to eclipse that figure when it was released in America. The song appealed to a far broader audience than his previous hits and as a result Gordon decided to 'spruce up' Tom's image. Now he was to wear beautifully handmade suits and large bow ties. Colourful shirts, jeans and black trousers were banned. The Squires were also smartened up with dark blue suits. The jackets had high collars, which was my idea, based on the coats that seventeenth century squires would have worn. Elvis commented on the suits when we met him in Las Vegas in 1968, he told us he was going to get himself some jumpsuits made with similar collars. He certainly did. I remember seeing his white rhinestone encrusted jump suit and the collar was enormous, dwarfing ours.

Tom and Gordon were back on a roll. With two number one hits under their belts, things were definitely on the up. This hadn't gone entirely unnoticed by the ex-editor of the *New Musical Express*, Chris Hutchins. Chris was in his mid-twenties, slightly-built and fair haired, he was quick minded and softly spoken. He had a comprehensive knowledge of show business from his time at the *Express* and had recently set up his own public relations company. Chris was on the prowl for stars to represent and had Tom in his sights.

Gordon had employed a PR man, John Rowlands, when 'It's Not Unusual' went to number one. John represented Tom for some time after but Gordon felt he was getting Tom's image wrong. John was thin and tall and looked a bit geeky with his heavily framed spectacles. He'd set up a series of publicity shots with Tom washing the dishes in the kitchen at Manygate Lane. Gordon thought this cut across the grain of Tom's macho image. So he replaced him with a new guy called, Max Clifford.

Max was a good-looking man in his mid-twenties. He was the polar opposite to John Rowlands. Whereas John was a bit of a snob, Max was really down to earth with a fantastic sense of humour. The band warmed to him, especially as for the first time he started to bring us into the limelight a little. We weren't invisible to Max and whenever he thought it would benefit his duties as Tom's PR man, he'd include us in interviews and TV spots. He was very professional and diligent, and would advise us beforehand on just what to say.

None of us knew what happened, but there must have been a falling-out between Gordon and Max, as suddenly he was replaced by Chris Hutchins, who was a different kettle of fish entirely. Chris came across as a very good manipulator, which is essential in the PR business. He eventually went on to represent a host of stars including Engelbert Humperdinck, The Bee Gees, Eric Clapton and many others.

With Tom now firmly established and with Chris running his PR, Gordon had more time to devote to another of his acts, Engelbert Humperdinck. I can still remember when Gordon first told me that Gerry's stage name was going to be Engelbert Humperdinck. I thought he had lost the plot. It was a ridiculous name for a tall, dark and handsome pop singer. It sounded like something from a children's story book. But hats off to Gordon, it certainly seemed to work.

Gordon asked me to take a listen to a track on a portable tape recorder. We were setting up for a gig in Birmingham at the time. He played me a very pleasant country song, not unlike Ray Charles's 'I Can't Stop Loving You'. Being a bit of a country fan I told Gordon about the similarities, especially the female backing singing one line in the chorus and the lead in the other.

Gordon went back and changed the arrangement and 'Release Me' was released in March 1967. It went straight to number one and became the biggest selling single of that year. Gordon was beside himself, he had the Midas touch. Engelbert was ecstatic after so many years of struggling.

It's fair to say that Dickie Valentine was partly responsible for the song's meteoric rise. Dicky Valentine was a major heartthrob of that era, who was sadly to die in a car crash a few years later. He was due to appear on *Sunday Night at the London Palladium*, which had a TV audience of over twenty million viewers. It was every artiste's dream to appear, the exposure was invaluable. As luck would have it, for Engelbert, Dickie had to cancel his spot due to a throat infection. Gordon got wind of this and managed to get the virtually unknown Engelbert Humperdinck to replace him.

I remember watching the show on television. Engelbert looked a million dollars and was groomed to perfection. Gordon had learnt his lessons with Tom, and put Engelbert in exactly the same stage wear: tuxedo, low cut waistcoat, white frilled shirt and a large bow tie. Before Tom had started the fashion, bow ties used to be small and narrow, now they were like bloody great black butterflies.

Gordon was grooming Engelbert to follow in Tom's shoes, quite literally, right down to the same kind of material. He had seen Tom's success with an older audience and wanted Engelbert to plough the same furrow. As singers they were poles apart vocally, but they became intertwined through Gordon's management. He had hit on the right formula for Tom and now wanted to replicate it with the new kid on the block. Tom didn't seem entirely happy with this arrangement but he didn't protest to Gordon. They had many similarities, Gordon saw to that, but their personalities were like chalk and cheese. Engelbert was like a Chardonnay, smooth with delicate undertones, sweet yet crisp. Tom on the other hand was more your full bodied Tarragona, a wine trampled by wild Spanish gypsies.

I have backed them both on stage and to my mind; Tom was by far the better star, both vocally and visually. Performing on stage with Tom was always a thrill. Right from the very first day he joined The Senators I got a kick out of working with him. He had a phenomenal stage presence. Engelbert on the other hand was full of insecurities. He was a very sensitive man and always seemed concerned about something or other. I guess everyone has a bit of that in their makeup but Engelbert took it to extremes. He was a real worrier, if he had any nails left they would have been bitten to the quick.

Engelbert was very proud of his sideburns, which he considered his trademark. Not long after 'Release Me' was launched I bumped into him leaving the Acuff-Rose Agency, close to Bond Street. Both Tom and Engelbert were represented by them. We had a little chat and caught up on all the latest news. Suddenly he pointed to his sideburns and asked me what I thought of the new look he had given them. To be entirely honest they looked dreadful. They were grown down below the earlobe, which wasn't unusual as Elvis had done something similar. But Engelbert had sliced a gap halfway down exposing about an inch of bare skin. It looked absolutely ridiculous. I told him I didn't think it was a very good idea and the sooner he grew them back together again, the better. He didn't seem impressed with my honesty and sloped off.

That was the last I saw of him for about a year. Tony Cartwright had taken over from Gordon as Engelbert's manager and asked for me to meet him at The London Palladium. I turned up ahead of time and was taken to wait for him in Engelbert's dressing room. It was a bit uncomfortable as I sat waiting for Tony to arrive while Engelbert ignored me completely. Talk about the cold shoulder, he just turned his back on me and my greetings went unanswered.

I stayed put in the dressing room in silence wondering if Engelbert would eventually acknowledge my presence. He never did. I made my excuses and left him staring blankly into his dressing room mirror. I've often wondered what this childish behaviour was about. We went back a considerable way together, I used to visit him and his wife at their flat in Hammersmith, and we had both come up together through Gordon's management. Maybe he saw me as being in the opposition camp after leaving Gordon on bad terms. I'd hate to think it was over the fact I hadn't liked his sideburns. I guess I'll never really know because that was the last time we would ever meet. Thankfully cooler heads had prevailed there because that look was never launched on the British public.

After the success of 'Green Grass' Tom decided on a house move. He put Manygate Lane on the market and moved Linda and Mark into a larger mansion in nearby Sunbury-on-Thames. The property was at the end of a posh cul-de-sac and had excellent privacy. Springfield House was a sprawling palace with five bedrooms, two bathrooms, four toilets, countless lounges and a study. Tom also had a den, where he set up a screen and film projector to watch his favourite films: mostly Cowboy and Indian movies with the odd American Civil War adventure thrown in.

Tom would invite the band over to watch some of the movies. We were always in awe to see the luxurious furnishings. Ivory coloured calfskin sofas and easy chairs, expensive paintings in ornate frames, a monumental colour television – the technology was still in its infancy and it was a rare sight. There was every kind of luxury imaginable. Meanwhile we were still living in digs, and were mesmerised by all the trappings of stardom.

At that time we were performing regularly on *Sunday Night at the Palladium*, and Tom had become very friendly with the compere, Jimmy Tarbuck. Every time we called in at Springfield House Jimmy would be there, he'd become a bit of a permanent fixture. He was desperate to raise his profile at the time and having Tom as a close pal certainly helped in that regard. Jimmy was a shameless name dropper, and littered his conversation at every opportunity, letting you know he was a friend to the stars. It could be tiresome after a while and the band thought he was overly cocky, self-opinioned and a loudmouth. He could be very boorish. It was as though he was always on stage, and he just couldn't switch off.

Around that time our guitarist, Dave Wendels, was in Gordon's bad books. Dave had become a bit too laid back for Gordon's taste. I got on great with Dave, but admittedly he was a bit of a dreamer and sometimes his attention wandered. Whenever I visited Dave, at his mother's house in Central Hounslow, the front room would be chock-a-block with models of Count Dracula. There were even toy bats dangling from the ceiling. Every surface was covered in models of Frankenstein, ghouls, zombies and every imaginable character related to horror movies. The walls were decorated with voodoo masks and witches' brooms. Although his mother had managed to retain the upper hand with one particular wall which was decorated with three innocent flying ducks, a Sixties style classic. They looked quite bizarre surrounded by all that horror. When Gordon fired him we were all sorry to see him go.

Gordon began looking for Dave's replacement. We arranged to meet a potential new lead guitarist, Bill Parkinson, a north-erner from Morecambe Bay. I remember the venue was a rickety building, a hotel-cum-nightclub somewhere on the banks of the Thames, on the way to Hampton Court. Bill was a six foot, muscular guy, with a broad Lancashire accent. Gordon intro-duced us and we got straight down to business, running through

Tom's stage act and getting a feel for our new lead guitarist. Bill fitted in great and he could read music to boot, which was always handy.

Bill settled into the band very quickly. He was married to a lovely girl, Jenny, and they had two beautiful daughters. The family was living in Muswell Hill, North London, at the time. Bill had completed his National Service in the army, where he did a bit of boxing for his regiment. He was a keep fit fanatic which was very unusual then. Most musicians were into booze, fags and sleeping in until noon.

It was during this period that I met up with Mia Lewis again. We bumped into each other at The Cromwellian Club one evening. Mia was still staying with her aunt and uncle in Muswell Hill. Her uncle Vivian was headmaster of Muswell Hill Senior School, and his wife Margaret taught there. We got talking and it went from there.

Mia had got her first break with a singing residency at Swansea's Townsman dance hall, fronting a local band. She was one of eight children. Arthur, her father, was a coal miner and Razzie, her mother, a very busy housewife. The family lived high up the Swansea Valley in Abercrave, a stunning part of the Brecon Beacons. Mia had been spotted by Welsh pop singer, Larry Page, who was also involved in artiste management. Larry had persuaded her to make the move to London, the only way to make it in the business at the time. Mia had packed in her job at a watch and clock assembly factory and made the move. She was immediately signed to Decca Records.

Stunningly pretty, she made the front cover of the *New Musical Express* on the release of her first single 'Wish I Didn't Love Him'. With her voice and striking look, the eighteen-year-old blonde bombshell was in constant demand for TV appearances. She released a further four singles, 'It's Goodbye Now', 'Nothing Lasts Forever', 'No Time For Lovin', and 'Woman's Love'. They didn't make the top 10 but her TV work really picked up. Mia appeared on the panel of *Juke Box Jury*, and her down-to-earth honesty struck a real chord with viewers and won her many plaudits.

Mia also appeared on *The Simon Dee Show* with Ken Dodd, singer Vince Hill, and Roy Hudd. The ratings for the popular show were averaging over twenty million viewers at the time but that all-important hit single still eluded her. The problem was with the record company. She had no say in what songs were released. The only voice she was allowed to project was her singing voice. It was a real shame because some of the B-sides were far more commercial than the A-sides.

The Acuff-Rose Agency, part of the American organization that represented a massive slice of country and western stars, kept her very busy with work. She was booked into venues from one end of the UK to the other. It was crazy for a young girl to be constantly on the road alone, travelling from city to city by train and coach. Our drummer, Chris Slade, married his long term girlfriend, Lynne, at the time. It would be another five years before Mia and I tied the knot. We saw each other whenever possible, most of the time passing like ships in the night. I'd be travelling up the M1 for a gig and she'd be on her way back to London for another gig.

Tom had been booked to appear in London's famous Talk of the Town. The Hippodrome nightclub now occupies the site of this famous venue. At the time, The Talk of the Town was the jewel in the crown of the capital's nightspots. It's plush decor was legendary. The cabaret room was absolutely massive and the colour scheme was all red and gold, with huge glittering chandeliers. The vast majority of the clientele was very well-heeled and would enjoy a sumptuous meal followed by the cream of international talent. The house orchestra would top off the evening, providing dance music into the early hours.

Talk of the Town was managed by Bernard Delfont, a close relation of Lew Grade. They were two of the most powerful men in show business. Lew would watch the acts and then decide whether they were good enough to appear on television. The lucky ones would then go onto become household names. Simon Cowell is doing a very similar thing with *X-Factor* and *Britain's Got Talent*. Give them plenty of TV exposure, turn them into stars and smile all the way to the bank.

Tom was booked to appear at The Talk for a month and we were booked to augment the orchestra. On the opening night the place was jam-packed with celebrities. There was a real buzz in the air and everyone was looking forward to Tom's appearance. But you could have heard a pin drop when Ava Gardner swept in with her entourage, and took a table in front of the stage.

Ava Gardner was Hollywood royalty. She was considered a legend along with Marilyn Monroe, Barbara Stanwyck, and Bette Davis; at one time she had been married to Frank Sinatra. She had appeared in numerous movies: *55 Days at Peking* with Charlton Heston, *The Night of the Iguana* with Richard Burton, *The Life and Times of Judge Roy Bean* with Paul Newman, *The Barefoot Contessa* with Humphrey Bogart, the list is endless: she was a real superstar. Ava would have been in her mid-forties at the time and the whole place was in awe of her fame and beauty.

Word soon reached the dressing rooms, and Tom and Gordon were delighted by her attendance. 'It's great copy for the morning papers,' said Gordon.

The orchestra struck up and the resident troupe of dancers appeared on stage, complete with legs up to their armpits, skimpy rhinestone costumes and ostrich-feather head-dresses. They went through their high-kicking routine and eye-watering splits to warm up the audience. The curtains closed and The Squires took up our positions as the rhythm section of the orchestra. The resident bass player, guitarist, keyboard player and drummer all gave us beaming smiles as they disappeared across the road to the pub for an hour.

The curtain swished open and a clearly nervous Tom charged onto the stage to thunderous applause. He went into his opening number and the audience really responded. Lew Grade was sitting at the back of the room watching Tom, and Gordon was in turn watching Lew intently, trying to gauge his reaction. There was a lot riding on it. Gordon was convinced that if Tom went down a storm Lew might offer him his own TV show.

After the performance we went back to our dressing room, next door to Tom, and changed out of our stage gear. Tom had invited us to join him for some champagne. We knocked on the door and were ushered in. The room was full of dense cigar smoke and tinkling champagne glasses. Lew Grade was amongst the guests, puffing on a large Havana. Cliff Richard and The Shadows were there also, but all eyes were drawn toward Ava Gardner. She was dressed in a slinky black gown, and was chain smoking and knocking back the booze.

Ava tottered toward me, giving me the once over with her alluring green eyes. I stood rooted to the spot, mesmerised.

'Don't feel nervous honey,' she quipped, 'I won't eat you.' I thought about what to say back, but my mouth was dry and my throat had seized up. 'I'm staying at The Dorchester, room 101,' she smiled and winked at me. Then squeezed my arm and moved on.

The raven-haired beauty had left me speechless. I watched her make her way through the room and re-join her entourage. A few minutes later and they all swept out, probably back to The Dorchester. After knocking back a few drinks I thought about heading over and knocking on room 101, but imagined 'Ole Blue Eyes' opening the door and demanding an explanation. Somehow the thought of one of Hollywood's hottest stars and a 'boyo' from an obscure mining town, illegally renting a bedroom in a council house and driving around in an old banger, didn't quite cut the mustard. Besides I'd recently started getting serious about Mia, who was less than half Ava's age and far prettier!

Tom's stint at The Talk proved a huge success. Gordon had also used the opportunity to record an album, *Live At The Talk Of The Town*. I think this was Tom at his best both vocally and physically. That year he managed to get five hit singles under his belt. 'The Green, Green Grass' had been the catalyst and had undoubtedly sealed his reputation as a superstar.

13. LENNON

My good friend and housemate Tony Cartwright had taken his first steps to becoming a 'manager to the stars'. He'd learned as much as he could from Gordon and now set out on his own path. One of the first artistes on his books was Freddie Lennon, John Lennon's estranged father. My first proper meeting with the old rascal was marked by a funny turn of events.

My landlady, Mu, was under the impression that I would be on the road with Tom and the band for over a month. Mu always liked the idea of me being away on tour, she still got her rent money but it was one less mouth to feed and no washing and ironing chores. On this occasion I returned to Tonbridge Road earlier than expected as some of the venues had been taken off the tour due to Tom's television commitments.

I arrived at the front door, only to find I had misplaced my keys. This was unusual for me – it was normally something that happened to Cartwright, the bane of Mu's life. I didn't want to wake everyone up as it was the early hours of the morning. I noticed that my front bedroom window was open and decided to shimmy up the drainpipe and climb in. My bed was directly under the window and with my legs half hanging out I flopped in, landing on the bed. There was an almighty scream, piercing enough to wake the neighbours. I was so startled I scrambled over the bed and switched on the light. Sitting bolt upright in bed, her hands wrapped around her nightie was Mu. I should have been the one screaming. She had a thick white pancake of night cream on her face and her hair was a mass of pink curlers.

What a bloody sight, she looked like a vampire!

Mu's eyes were shut tight and she had no idea it was me in the room, she just kept hollering for her mother. Before I had a chance to say anything and calm her down, the door burst open and little old Nancy staggered in brandishing a poker. One of the neighbours was banging on the front door enough to break it down. Then Cartwright arrived wiping the sleep from his eyes. Mu finally stopped screaming and began calling me all the foul names under the sun.

After she had calmed down and everyone else had gone back to bed Mu told me she hadn't expected me back for another week and had moved into my bed to give her daughter Jill and mum Nancy a bit more space in the other room. Mu also informed me we had another unexpected visitor, 'Freddie bleedin Lennon's downstairs sleeping one off on the settee. Cartwright's aiming to manage the scruffy bugger and turn 'im into a star. He'll be bleedin lucky. The old scrote's only got about three teeth in his head, e's as fat as a pudding, 'ardly any hair and he's got a bloody nose like Fagin.'

The following morning I woke early and found Freddie still asleep. Mu and I stood over his slumbering form, and I had to admit Mu hadn't been exaggerating; he was certainly no oil painting. Mu gave him a shake to wake him up. His clothes were dishevelled and a bit whiffy.

Lennon had deserted his young family and run away to sea. He had joined the Merchant Navy when his son, John, was just a young kid. John never forgave his father for deserting him. Freddie had returned to England and was living like a vagrant, sweeping floors and collecting glasses in a pub in Surbiton, in exchange for lodgings. At closing time he'd empty all the ashtrays looking for dog-ends to smoke. Tony Cartwright had heard that his fellow Scouser had come back home and signed him up. Tony had big plans, what with Freddie being John's dad and all. He made him lose weight until his clothes were practically hanging off him, dabbed some self-raising flour on his face and roughed him up a bit. When Tony was satisfied that Freddie looked the part, he marched him up to John Lennon's front door. At that time Lennon was living in a sprawling house at St Georges' Hill in Weybridge.

John Lennon answered the door and Tony laid on the sympathy. After exhausting his fiddle, he asked John if he'd help his father out financially. The three Scousers became involved in a proper Liverpool conversation and it ended with Lennon telling the pair of them to piss off or he'd set the dogs on them. Tony took Freddie back to the local pub to drown their sorrows and it was there they hatched their next plan.

Tony accompanied Freddie to a local dentist and had the last of his rotten teeth removed leaving him completely gummy. Then he had him fitted with a set of false teeth, big shiny tombstones. God only knows how Tony paid for it as he was always skint. I'll never know how he managed it, sheer blag more than likely, but Tony then managed to get Freddie a recording contract with a German record label. Not only that, but Freddie's first single with the label was a massive hit in Germany. It never made it outside that country, but Tony and Freddie were over the moon.

Of course Freddie's new career as a pop star didn't last very long. He was a bit too fond of lazing around and smoking and drinking himself to death. But at least Tony had made enough money out of the venture to continue his management company and set up Winterfold Music, a publishing company. Poor Freddie Lennon passed away aged sixty-two, a victim of cancer, and sadly his relationship with his son was never resolved.

At that time Tom and The Squires were booked to appear at The London Palladium for a four week stint. The comedians Mike and Bernie Winters were the supporting act. We played six nights a week, also a matinee performance on Saturday afternoon. Sunday was normally our day off and The Palladium would book a top-flight star to fill the gap. One particular booking was the legendary comedian George Burns. George was famous for his dry wit and used to wise-crack his way through his set smoking cigar after cigar. Every visiting performer would be given the number one dressing room, the star's room. This was Tom's room for the duration of our stay at The Palladium.

Monday night came around and Tom rocked up with Chris Ellis. He was just about to change into his stage gear when he did a double take, 'some bugger's nicked my bloody cigars. I left a full box here on the dressing table.' Chris picked up the empty Monte Christo box and a note floated out which he handed to Tom. Scribbled on the note was, 'Nice dressing room Tom. Thanks for the cigars. Keep the change. George.' Tom was spluttering with fury, 'What does he mean keep the bloody change?' Chris picked up a pound note which had fallen out of the empty cigar box and handed it to Tom, 'Is he bloody joking or what, he's nicked all my Monte Cristos, a pound won't buy one of the buggers.' Chris pointed out to Tom that George was a comedian after all, but Tom cursed him for days afterwards.

With two shows a night and three on Saturdays, there was a good deal of hanging around between sets, so we took to nipping across the road for a pint to kill time. The pub was about twenty yards from the backstage door. One evening we were all sat there enjoying a pint. Chris Slade and Vic Cooper finished their drinks in double quick time and sauntered off back to the dressing room. I glanced at my watch and noticed that Bill Parkinson and I had plenty of time to get back before the curtain went up. We were both sat there chatting away and I happened to glance at my watch again to see what time we should make a move. The bloody thing had stopped. I looked around desperately and asked someone the time. We had about three minutes until we were due on stage.

Panicking we dashed across the road, oblivious to the traffic and honking horns. We charged through the stage door and hurtled up the endless flights of stairs. Back in the dressing room we quickly changed into our suits, grabbed our instruments and literally threw ourselves back down the stairs and into the wings. The curtains were closed and Mike and Bernie Winters were out in front going through one of their routines. They had been quickly summoned back from their dressing room to fill in, whilst Chris Ellis had gone searching for us. The pair of us were sweating buckets and quietly crept across the stage. We got to our stage positions and plugged in our guitars. Every eye in the orchestra watched us with disdain. The conductor practically had steam coming out of his nostrils, he looked livid. It was all very embarrassing; I just wanted the earth to open and swallow me.

Receiving animated signals from the wings, Mike and Bernie wound up their routine and introduced Tom. The curtain went up and Tom leapt on stage as if nothing was amiss. The audience seemed unaware of the delay and thought Mike and Bernie were part of the second half of the show. Bill and I called in on Tom afterwards and apologised for not being on time. Naturally my wristwatch took the blame for the whole lousy episode. I cursed that watch: during my eight years in the band with Tom it was the only time I was ever late on stage.

With five hit records, Tom and Gordon were now seriously rich men. The rest of us were still slumming it, but at least we had regular work. Tom felt he had enough new cars and decided he wanted a new nose. He had always been obsessed about the state of his nose. Before joining The Senators it had taken quite a bashing. Back in the dance halls and clubs in and around Ponty, Tom was forever getting into fights and his nose was misshapen after being 'nutted' so often. Gordon agreed that he was overdue a make-over and arrangements were made for him to enter hospital. Gordon also came up with a fabrication to bamboozle the press, 'troublesome sinuses', and after the operation Tom duly reported, 'I had an operation for sinus trouble. When I came out I noticed the nose was shorter. They must have cut something out of it.'

Pinocchio would have been amused. Tom later came clean and admitted to the *Evening Standard* that, 'I don't think I could have done so well if I hadn't had my nose altered. I think it doesn't look as offensive as it did beforehand. Some people might have thought, "well I quite like his voice but I don't like his nose", so you have to eliminate all those things that put people off.' Tom also took the opportunity to get his crooked teeth capped.

Autumn had set in and The Squires found themselves augmented again with a full blown orchestra. This time it was the Ted Heath Orchestra, as Gordon had arranged a British tour also taking in Ireland. Ted Heath had passed away but the orchestra played on, keeping his name alive. Some of the musicians were stars in their own right. Drummer Ronnie Veral and trumpeter Stan Reynolds were legends in that field of music. The orchestra comprised of the cream of big band musicians performing in the UK at that time.

We soon discovered that they all liked to knock back the booze in copious amounts. Some of them carried hip flasks of their tipple of choice. I remember playing a theatre in Dublin where we had a break between shows. The Squires followed the orchestra into a pub near the theatre, with a very long narrow bar with barrel after barrel of Guinness on tap. Being in Ireland this was the real deal, black as tar and smooth as a fermenting swamp. The seasoned musicians got stuck in and they were knocking back pint after pint, just as quickly as the bar staff could fill them. The average age of the orchestra was around fifty and we youngsters could hardly keep pace with them.

Pretty soon it was time to get back to the theatre for the second show. Stan Reynolds, who also fronted his own band when not on the road with the orchestra, was a bit of a character. Slightly built and balding, with a pencil-thin moustache, he was one of the old troupers, and had seen it all and done it all. Positioned at the rear with three other trumpeters and the brass section, Stan sat directly behind me. He always had a mischievous twinkle in his eye and whenever I happened to glance over my shoulder, he would be pulling funny faces and that sort of thing.

On that particular night Stan was feeling the after effects of all the Guinness he'd knocked back at the pub. Midway through Tom's act and Stan's eyelids began to flutter, his head sagging during the gaps in the musical arrangement. The musician next to him had to keep giving him a dig in the ribs whenever they were due to come in again. Toward the end of the show Tom sailed into 'It's Not Unusual' and Stan was almost out for the count. Suddenly I heard a muffled crash. Stan had fallen backwards off his chair and straight off the back of the stage dais. He had fallen a good five feet to the floor below. I turned around and watched incredulously as he rolled into the curtain backdrop. I looked around me, my mouth flapping open, but no one had noticed, not Tom or the audience. Stan lay there sleeping it off, we finished the set and Tom took his bows. The following evening Stan Reynolds was propping up the bar as if nothing had happened. He was knocking back the Guinness as usual, although we were now in Belfast.

I was using a new bass guitar during that tour. When we had toured Australia one of our support acts was an Australian band. The bass player fell in love with my Epiphone. Apparently you couldn't get hold of one for love nor money Down Under. America didn't export the model there. He was using a white Fender Precision Bass, and he begged me to make a straight swap.

Gordon had been on at me for some time to ditch the Epiphone and get myself a Fender, as he thought it had a better quality. Gordon thought the sound was 'chunkier' and fitted better with the material Tom was performing.

I made the swap but what I wasn't aware of at the time, was that this Fender had been rebuilt using some parts that weren't designed for that model. I was playing a hybrid and not a genuine model. I wasn't really happy with this state of affairs and wanted to get rid of it. Tom was due to travel to America at the end of the Irish leg of the tour and as every musician knew at the time, guitars were much cheaper over there than in the UK, due to import duty. I asked Tom if he would bring me back a Fender Bass, and I'd sell my dodgy hybrid to pay for the new one. He readily agreed as it was also in his interest that the band sounded the best it could.

I was chuffed to bits when he returned with a beautiful Sunburst Fender Precision. Tom told me I could pick it up from the Acuff-Rose Agency whenever I liked. But before I could get my hands on it we were off to Birmingham, booked for a week at The Castaways nightclub. This was an amazing venue. The club was a life size model of a wrecked pirate ship with a huge cannon hole shot in the side. The audience would enter through the cannon hole and walk into a cabaret room with all the fixtures and furnishings connected with seafaring. Tom always looked forward to playing there. It was a very special place and the owner was a real gem, he would always give us a hearty welcome and really looked after us.

Before the gig at The Castaways I'd traded in my battered old Anglia for a green Austin Cambridge. It had a lot of mileage on the clock but the engine seemed sound. I'd taken advantage of Tom being away in America and driven it home to Wales to visit Mia and her family in the Swansea Valley. I felt refreshed and a little in love when I said my goodbyes and pointed the car toward Birmingham. The drive was faultless and the Cambridge behaved admirably, even though the suspension seemed to be stiffening up the closer I got to Birmingham.

I have always found Birmingham a bit of a nightmare to drive around. I kept getting lost and the radiator began to boil over. I recognised I was a little over a mile away from The Castaway. Suddenly the car started making a hell of a racket and then stopped dead in its tracks. I raised the bonnet, steam and hot water was spurting out of the radiator and the smell of burning oil stung my nostrils. The engine was searing hot and there was a mess of ruptured hoses hissing steam.

Stranded on a main road I was fortunate enough to find a telephone kiosk. I phoned the club and spoke to Chris Ellis, who collected me in the van. I arranged for a garage to pick up the Cambridge. Later that day I was informed that the engine had completely seized up and I would need a replacement. Parts and labour would amount to £175 including towing charge, or four weeks wages! The evening wasn't any better. I shared a bedroom in a flea-bitten bed and breakfast with a grizzled ex-seaman down on his luck, just like me. The old tar stank to high heaven and like Freddie Lennon had breath like a constipated crocodile. I was now in no position to be able to afford a regular bed and breakfast and had to cut my cloth accordingly.

Along with my wages and Mia sending me the rest I was just about able to settle the garage bill. I took Tom aside and explained I was in a tricky spot and would have to tighten my belt. I asked him if he would let me have the Fender on spec and I'd pay him back out my future wages. But he refused to release it until I coughed up all the money.

The Fender was propped up in the corner of Acuff-Rose Agency whenever I called in for a cup of tea, tantalisingly close but out of reach. It just sat there gathering dust. But it was pointless trying to convince Tom to relent and let me use it. When his mind was made up, that was the end of the matter. In a way he was shooting himself in the foot. Surely it would have been to his advantage to have his band sounding the best that they could. But he obviously didn't see it that way.

When we had some free time in between tours and gigs the band would hop in the van and Chris Ellis would take us for a wander around Denmark Street in Soho. We'd always visit the Gioconda café in Tin Pan Alley where musicians gathered to exchange gossip about the London music scene. There was a clutch of music shops in the immediate area, and we called in at one of our regular stops, a music shop run by Mike, a charming Jewish guy who used to cater to all our musical needs. He knew about the story of my hybrid Fender and the new Sunburst 'in custody' at the Acuff-Rose Agency on Tom's orders. Just like the rest of the band he couldn't understand the logic behind it. He asked me, 'Vern has Jonesy let you have that guitar from the States yet?' I shook my head and told him about my money troubles. 'Look Vern, me and the wife watch you guys on TV all the time, give me the crap Fender and you can have whatever you want from the shop.' I was too shocked to speak and swear I felt my eyes filling up. Mike reached up, took down a pristine Fender Precision Bass and handed it over to me. It was snow white, with a tortoiseshell scratch plate, and the beast felt nice and heavy hanging from my shoulder. I objected to Mike that it wasn't a fair swap, but he wouldn't hear any more about it and shooed us out of the shop, complaining he had other customers to serve. What a wonderful gesture and what a wonderful man.

Poor old Tom was spitting feathers when I told him I wouldn't need that bass after all. It's probably still propped up in a corner of the Acuff-Rose Agency, for all I know.

It took me awhile to clear my debts for the Cambridge's new engine. But finally I got back on my feet again. Everything was going along fine, I was motoring and my new Fender was a real treat to play. Gordon called us into his office for a band meeting around that time, and we went with some trepidation wondering who was next for the chop. As it happened it was really good news.

Gordon informed us that Tom had been chosen to appear before the Queen and the Duke of Edinburgh at the Royal Variety Performance. It was a real signifier that you had arrived. Gordon saved the best for last: we were going to appear too!

We were elated but also a little shocked. This was a very sudden about turn,and a lot to take in. Up until that point there hadn't been an awful lot that Gordon had wanted to include us in. Quite the reverse, he'd gone out of his way to put us down and treat us like the hired help. We had come to terms with that a long time ago. Now he was offering us a royal performance: this wasn't just any run of the mill TV programme, at that time it was the TV programme. We were all a little baffled about this sudden 'hand of friendship' gesture.

We were very excited to be appearing at such a prestigious event with Tom. The band discussed amongst ourselves why Gordon hadn't booked session musicians for the performance or relied on The Palladium's orchestra, as he had done so many times before. It was very unusual to offer us any of the limelight. The only reason we could come up with was that Tom was nervous about the occasion and didn't want to be on stage on his own.

On the evening of the performance we were backstage rubbing shoulders with all the stars of the show. Everyone was a bag of nerves, Tom more than anyone. The only person, who seemed remotely calm, was the American comedian, Bob Hope. There was a great line up including Rolf Harris, Lulu, Sandie Shaw, Val Doonican, Tommy Cooper, Harry Secombe, The

Rockin' Berries, Ken Dodd, Vikki Carr, Mireille Mathieu and of course Tom Jones and The Squires. Everyone had butterflies. Easily the most nervous was Lulu. She couldn't stand still for a moment and was nibbling her fingernails to the quick. Every once in a while she'd blurt out, 'Oh my God'.

If Lulu had been wearing hobnail boots, the poor girl would have worn a deep furrow in the backstage floor. She was enormously relieved to get her five minute spot out of the way. There was a variety act on directly after her, Tanya the baby elephant. Tanya had the audience in fits of laughter, even the Queen was tittering, especially when the elephant dropped a few dollops on stage. Stage hands were nearby to clear it all up, but Tanya wasn't the only performer feeling nervous. There was a queue for the backstage toilet a mile long.

We enjoyed our moment in the limelight. Sadly it was to be our only Royal Performance. Tom got over his nerves and was happy to go it alone for all future royal performances.

With New Year bells still ringing in our ears, 1968 saw Tom and The Squires really pushing ourselves. On a hectic European tour, taking in Scandinavia and Germany, we hardly paused for breath. Toward the end of January we were booked to appear at the Bambi Awards in Munich. At that time the Bambis were Europe's version of the Oscars. We were performing alongside The Supremes. Our eyes were out on stalks; we had never seen so many movie stars in one place and were a little nervous about performing to such a glittering crowd.

Sitting directly in the front row were Clint Eastwood, Richard Burton and Elizabeth Taylor. Eastwood and Burton were making *Where Eagles Dare* and had taken a break from filming to attend. Eastwood was sitting at a different table to Richard and Elizabeth and it was clear to see why. They were going at each other hammer and tongs, knocking back the champagne and doing their best to out curse each other. They were certainly a tempestuous couple alright. Eastwood looked very bored by the whole event, but we were all very excited to see him in the flesh.

Backstage in the dressing room we started getting ready for the show. Just along the corridor we could hear The Supremes, laughing and giggling. Tom winked at us and decided to introduce himself. He had a glint in his eye that we all recognised, and the band started a sweepstake on which Supreme he was going to have a crack at. Tom knocked on their dressing room door and Mary Wilson answered and ushered him in. It was the beginning of a serious love affair.

After the performance we let our hair down at the after show party. The place was jammed with A-list movie stars and celebrities; it was pretty breath-taking being in such exalted company. We were introduced to Henry Mancini, who had recently composed the music for the smash Peter Sellers movie, *The Pink Panther*. The Supremes hung out with us and were delightful, very shy and modest, but a lot of fun. We were sorry to part company with them, but we had to push on to our next gig.

We stayed at a reputed 'haunted hotel' on the next leg of the German tour. I was shacked up with Vic Cooper while Bill Parkinson and Chris Slade shared a bedroom along the creepy, creaking corridor. Vic, as the band's wind-up merchant, was forever playing pranks on the rest of us. Although on this occasion things got a little hairy.

After finishing our gig we headed back to the haunted hotel

for a couple of beers, and Vic suggested we hold a séance. The hotel was said to be full of wandering spirits and Vic thought it would be 'a bit of harmless fun' to make contact with some of them. He marched us up to our room, which he felt had the best 'vibrations' for making contact. He had held a number of séances in the past, he told us, and seemed to know all about it. Vic had us sitting around a table with our hands out flat, and asked us to concentrate. Then he switched off the room lights and draped a hand towel over a bedside lamp, to create the right atmosphere. Soon he was ready to begin and hollered, 'Is there anybody there? If there is anyone there give us a sign.' Suddenly there was a sharp clanging sound a few feet behind Vic, and we all jumped out of our skin. 'Are you a friendly spirit?' said Vic. 'Knock once for yes and twice for no.' There was a single sharp metallic clang, and it cut across the silence. We were all feeling very uncomfortable.

Within ten minutes Vic had managed to connect each band member in turn with a long lost relative. It was very convincing, especially as we were all knocking back the beers to steady our nerves. The following night we settled down to another séance. Vic had let me in on his secret. He had tied a piece of string to his cigarette lighter and placed it in a chamber pot under his bed. The other end was tied to his ankle, and with both hands flat on the table he would give his ankle a little shake to produce the spirit world's answers to his questions. The band fell for it hook, line and sinker. Vic went through the same ritual for the rest of the tour and poor Bill and Chris were convinced they'd made contact with lost relatives.

Back in London we hardly had time to pause for breath before Gordon was busy planning our assault on America. It was around then that I made the mistake of telling him I had some early recordings of Tom and The Senators. During the early years when we rehearsed at 2 Glyndwr Avenue, we were lucky enough to be able to listen to a playback of our repertoire to help iron out the creases. My Uncle Billy had been the proud owner of a portable Phillips tape recorder. It was not much bigger than a loaf of bread and had twin reels on top with a detachable lid to protect it in transit. They were very rare at the time. When my father persuaded Billy to part with it for £10 and presented it to me, the band were over the moon. I loved playing around with it, and also used it to record family and friends. Gordon's ears pricked up and he said, 'next time you're back in Ponty, bring the tape recorder back with you, we may be able to do something with the tapes.'

The day came around and I plugged in the tape recorder at Gordon's place. Jo was there and they both seemed fascinated with this little piece of 'pop history'. Afterwards Gordon asked me to leave the recording with him. He wanted to listen to them through a few more times. 'Call in tomorrow afternoon and pick them up,' he said. I returned the following afternoon and Gordon made an appearance with two of his Siamese cats in tow, one of whom had been christened, Elvis. Gordon looked a little apprehensive, 'Come in Vernon, bit of bad news I'm afraid. Elvis has been a very naughty boy.' I was devastated to see my tape recorder in the corner of the room, surrounded by yards and yards of twisted tape, and two empty spools. 'I trusted you Gordon,' I cried, 'the only recording of my mother's voice was on those tapes, and my father playing the piano, how can a bloody cat do all this damage?'

Gordon just shrugged, 'That's Siamese cats for you, they're

very clever,' he replied without a hint of remorse. I could have cried. It looked as if both tapes had been crushed together and there wasn't an inch that was salvageable. They were destroyed beyond repair. I couldn't bring myself to pick up the recorder. I just left in a daze suspecting that Gordon had deliberately destroyed the tapes. Those tapes were a little piece of history.

They captured all the banter between Tom and the band in between songs. They were priceless to me, but far more important than the band rehearsing was my mother's voice and my father knocking out Charlie Kunz and Winifred Atwell numbers on the piano. Sometimes you completely lose faith in human nature and that was certainly one of those days.

14. AMERICA

Gordon was determined to crack America. He hired a new musical director and arranger, Johnny Harris, to accompany us on tour. Johnny was a fantastic musician and one hell of a character. He was around thirty-five, average height, thin as a rake and as mad as a hatter. He was affectionately known in musical circles as 'Johnny the Boot', having been born with a club foot. Gordon sometimes had to tell him to ease up on the acrobatics. On stage, conducting the orchestra, he would get carried away, stamping his boot and swinging his arms around wildly; baton in one hand he would leap around like a man possessed. Tom didn't like it because Johnny got more attention from the audience than he did.

Arriving at Heathrow Airport, The Squires and Chris Ellis teamed up with Johnny, while Gordon and Tom flew business class. Our plane landed in Miami and there was a black Lincoln Continental waiting for us at the airport. We were chauffeur driven to a two star hotel close to a beautiful sandy beach. I was the last out of the car and following the band into the hotel I happened to glance back and noticed the chauffeur cursing us for not giving him a tip. We were fresh off the plane and hadn't caught up with the American custom of tipping yet. I grabbed the band to see if we could club something together, but we all had empty pockets. The chauffeur gave us a dark look and sped off.

We caught up with Gordon later and he reluctantly agreed to pay us £80 a week for the duration of the tour, insisting that it would go back to £40 a week when we returned to the UK. But there was always a catch with Gordon and he told us we would have to pay our own way for hotel accommodation and all other expenses, including meals, taxis and transport. We were playing Miami, New York, Los Angeles and Las Vegas on the tour and none of those cities were cheap. Johnny Harris thought we were crazy and should have held out for more. He was getting £250 a week plus expenses. We had to explain Gordon's modus operandi to him: we would have been on the first plane home if we tried to get any extra. Johnny thought Gordon was a right cheapskate.

We performed for three nights at the exclusive Deauville Hotel on Miami's famous coastal strip and then headed for New York and a two week stint at the famous Copacabana nightclub. The Copa was the equivalent of The Palladium back home. In the States performing there signified that you had made it in show business. Every major star had played there: Frank Sinatra, Ben E. King, Ray Charles, Dionne Warwick and our friends The Supremes. The stage there was tiny because the room was so small and the tables were lit by dreaded candlelight. The flickering candles gave the room a certain ambience, but their fumes stung the vocal chords: they were the bane of every performer.

It was no use complaining. The guy who managed the Copa, Jules Bodell, was not only a friend of the stars, he was an even greater 'friend' of the New York Mafia. The Mafia frequented the club on a regular basis. It was notorious in that respect, and no one argued with Bodell, if they knew what was good for them. It was said at the time that if the police had raided the Copa, the streets of New York would have been clean of crime.

The Copa was an intimate venue and only held about one

hundred and fifty customers. We were booked for three shows a night, the first kicked-off at 9 p.m. followed by another spot at midnight and the closing set at 3 a.m. in the morning. On Tom's opening night we attracted a crowd of celebrities, some whom stopped off backstage afterwards for drinks. I didn't know where to look there were so many famous faces. We were introduced to Dionne Warwick, Gladys Knight and The Pips, Roger Moore, and the Country singer Jerry Reed, who looked as if he was on something as he was completely spaced out. It was an eye-opener regarding Tom's popularity in the States, he was really making in-roads.

The booze at the club was very expensive, far too expensive for us to afford. One evening thinking we were really clever, we got Chris Ellis to smuggle in some beers from the local liquor store. But Jules Bodell had eagle eyes and spotted we were drink-ing a different brand from that sold at the club. He ordered one of the bouncers to confiscate the lot and warned us about trying a similar stunt again. Naturally we didn't argue.

We worked with a small orchestra at the club, which was crammed in behind us on the tiny stage. Tom had no option but to stand teetering over the audience at the edge; he was so close to the tables he could have shaken hands without getting off the stage. We all felt a little sorry for the front rows as when Tom really got into his act he'd drench them with sweat. The orches-tra we worked with was red hot at the time. They had recorded the soundtrack for the *Mission Impossible* television series, with Lalo Schifrin, and it was a real pleasure to work with them.

During the midnight performance one evening, Tom had the audience in the palm of his hand. Every night was sold out and the word was spreading like wildfire that Tom Jones was hot.

There was one particular song in the set that used to have all the Mob guys weeping into their silk handkerchiefs. 'Danny Boy', would ring out and the room would go completely silent. All you could hear was the constrained sobs of these big tough guys – it was hilarious.

That evening there was a huge bear of a man seated at a table with a blonde woman. They were directly in front of Tom. The woman had her arms draped around the man's thick neck, and she was yapping in a high screech, like a spoiled poodle craving attention. Tom was tenderly singing 'Danny Boy' and every verse was tarnished by this unwelcome high-pitched intrusion. All the musicians glared at her. I could see that Tom was being knocked out of his stride by this boorish behaviour. But he let things ride, probably with the intention of saying something to her after he had finished the song. The lyrics at the end of the song went, 'I...love...you...so,' a soaring climax to end on. The woman was oblivious and kept on screeching and caterwauling. Tom leapt down off the stage and shoved the microphone under her nose. 'Hey,' he barked, eyes blazing, 'are you going to finish this song or what, huh?' The woman sat there in stunned silence and Tom jumped back on stage to finish the song. The response from the audience was deafening, and the big guy and his lady friend slunk out enduring a cacophony of cat calls.

I always thought it took a lot of guts for Tom to do what he did that evening. Considering the clientele of that particular establishment, he had no idea who he was dealing with. The guy could have been a high-ranking mobster for all he knew. It was a little rash of him to deal with the situation so dramatically. I certainly admired him for doing it.

During our stint at the Copa we made the best of our time in New York and took in all the sights. Gordon had flown back to London after watching Tom's opening night at the famous venue. Tom was booked into one of New York's finest hotels, and he reported that he was being waited on hand and foot. We asked Gordon to recommend somewhere we could afford and he suggested the Goram Hotel. It was housed halfway up a skyscraper, and you walked straight out of the lift into a classic 'film noir' dark and gloomy reception. The desk clerk tossed us some keys from a row on the wall and that was the last we saw of him.

There were three single beds in one room and two next door. The rooms had massive heating pipes sweeping around the skirting. They threw off so much heat that we couldn't sleep. The windows were bolted shut, so we were unable to cool the room down. It was bizarre, like living in an oven while the temperature outside was well below zero. After a couple of days the heating broke down and we found ourselves freezing. Then it was miraculously fixed and we were back to living in an oven, unbearably hot.

We found a cosy little bar about five blocks from the Goram and trudged through the snow to enjoy a couple of beers. Vic began rolling his lucky dice on the table, and for a bit of fun we started gambling for loose change. Suddenly a massive hand cracked down on the table and scooped up the dice and coins. The owner of the bar had a face like thunder and bawled at us, 'You're going to cost me my license, you crazy limeys!' We hadn't realised that gambling in public was illegal in America at that time. Atlantic City and Las Vegas were the only cities licensed for gambling. The owner sent us on our way with a right earful.

Outside the snow was about three feet deep, and rising steadily, with a blizzard raging. We thought about taking a cab but all the roads were closed. Returning to the Goram was like Scott's Antarctic expedition; luckily we were well fortified from our time spent in the bar.

In between shows the band would retire to the lounge bar at the Copa to get our second wind. It was situated in the bowels of the club, and was always full of Mafia characters, ironically gathered underground. One evening we were relaxing between sets and there were about half a dozen tough-looking and heavy-set guys staring in our direction. It was a bit unnerving. They were seated across from us, near the far wall and kept muttering amongst themselves and glaring over. Finally one of them beckoned us to join them. Tom nervously looked at the band, and we all piped up, 'it's you they want Tom'.

'Jesus,' he moaned, 'why me?' We urged him not to keep them waiting, so he slowly rose to his feet and padded over to join them.

Tom found himself squeezed in between them. He was no shrinking violet, but he looked horribly nervous as they gave him a grilling about his rise to fame and how much money he was raking in. Tom turned whiter than a sheet, it looked as if they were about to put the squeeze on him for some protection money. Luckily we were due back on stage and hustled him away, making our apologies as we sidled out.

As it turned out, they never got around to asking him for protection money, and by the end of our stint at the Copa we had become great pals and they kept buying us drinks. We were quite sad to say goodbye to them, but they promised to come and see us play in Vegas. We were even sadder when we later read in the *LA Times* that two of them had been killed in a hail of bullets. It was unnerving to see the photograph on the front page of the paper and realise that they had died in the Copa, in their usual spot. The wall behind them was riddled with bullet holes and splattered with blood. We felt a long way from home right then.

Los Angeles was on the cusp of spring when we landed. Blue skies and balmy breezes were quite a contrast to New York. Everyone had been looking forward to arriving in the Golden State. After the gruelling three shows a night stint at the Copa we had a relatively relaxed schedule. Tom was lined up to appear on a number of chat shows and Gordon had organized lots of Hollywood meetings for Tom, to discuss potential movie business. The best surprise of all was our hotel; it had a swimming pool on the roof.

One day we were sunbathing beside the pool and a bit part Hollywood actor, Lance LeGault, introduced himself. He was a handsome, rugged guy with a growling voice in his early thirties. *Knight Rider* creator Glen Larson would later describe him as having, 'a voice that was four octaves lower than God's'. Lance later appeared in numerous films and TV shows including *The A Team*, *Dallas*, *The Incredible Hulk*, and *The Dukes of Hazzard*, and was Elvis's stunt double in all his movies. He was, he told us, on a 'covert operation', which we all took with a pinch of salt.

Lance was a friendly and charismatic guy, and he seemed over the moon to have bumped into Tom Jones' band. He told us he was a big fan and showed us around LA. We visited the recording studio where the Everly Brothers laid down all their hits, and he introduced us to Mexican food, insisting on picking up the bill at some wonderful restaurants. We visited his up-market apartment complex. The walls of his lounge were adorned with sporting handguns, rifles and memorabilia from the American Civil War. The whole time we were with him he never let up asking questions about Tom. He came across as a fanatical fan and by the time we left for Las Vegas he knew everything about Tom's life story.

When we arrived at LA international Airport, on our way to Las Vegas, we ran into quite a commotion. A crowd had gathered to see Liberace. He was incredibly tanned, all teeth and dimples, and the most exaggerated smile in show business. The flamboyant, classically-trained pianist was returning from playing a stint in Vegas. Liberace had been booked by the Flamingo Hotel, which was the same venue that Tom and the band were due to play for a four week residency. Tom piped up, 'I hope you left my dressing room in good order?' Liberace flashed him a dazzling smile.

When we arrived in Vegas, Tom was whisked away to the penthouse suite at the Flamingo. The band and Johnny Harris found a motel, just a few hundred yards from the hotel. Empey's Desert Inn was an updated version of the motel made famous in Alfred Hitchcock's film, *Psycho*. It was a wooden structure. One row of rooms stretched for about fifty yards and running parallel was a two-storey row with a narrow landing running the length of the first floor. There were two beds in each room and it was cheap and cheerful. Chris Ellis and Johnny Harris stayed in the two-storey row, with Johnny directly above Chris's ground floor room.

Gordon had been working up to Vegas for months. He believed it could be the making of Tom in America. If he could win over the Vegas audiences, then America would really open up for him and his status as an international star would be sealed. Tom was being paid twelve thousand pounds for the month, which was a bit of a pay cut. The bosses of the Flamingo were taking a bit of a gamble booking first-time artistes, and were only willing to pay a rock bottom fee. For once Gordon didn't argue, which was very unlike him. I think he recognized that a successful stint with Tom commanding the main theatre was worth more than money on this occasion. Gordon arrived in Vegas with Tom's wife, Linda. They were both there for the opening night. Gordon had bitten his fingernails to the quick. I'd never seen him so nervous. It was unusual to see Linda as she rarely came to see Tom perform. The adulation from Tom's female fan base used to really put her off, and at heart she was still a Valleys girl and didn't like mixing with theatrical agents, promoters and all the assorted hangers-on. Linda was extremely shy and having known her for over eight years I liked her immensely. She just let Tom get on with it, as long as he came home after playing away.

The first thing we all noticed in Vegas was the massive public-ity drive surrounding Tom's appearance at the Flamingo. There were billboards, banners and posters just about everywhere. The marketing was all geared to promote 'Tom Jones Fever'. The radio stations aired commercials at the end of their weather reports informing the listeners, 'what the Tom Jones fever temperature was,' at any given time.

Sadly The Squires were missing our keyboard player for the Vegas performance. Vic Cooper had been asked to audition for a new group called, Toomorrow. He had been approached by Don Kirshner, the creator of the The Monkees and The Archies, the cartoon characters who had a massive hit with

AMERICA

'Sugar, Sugar'. The other person involved in the new group was Harry Saltzman, producer of the James Bond movies. It was an incredible opportunity and one that Vic couldn't really turn down; we were sad to see him go and wished him every success.

Don Kirshner and Harry Saltzman were about to shoot a science fiction movie, a tongue-in-cheek comedy, and they wanted a great soundtrack. They had cast Olivia Newton-John, and wanted a cheeky Cockney type character for the group. Vic was prefect for the part. He had originally been approached in New York, but had sworn us all to secrecy; he didn't want Gordon or Tom getting wind of it until he was sure he had got the part. Harry Saltzman had flown Vic to London for an audition. Tom was busy making TV appearances and interviews so it was easy for us to cover for his absence.

Vic had finally heard that the part was his while we were in LA. We all congratulated him and threw him a going away party. Vic packed his suitcase and was on his way to the airport, but not before sending Gordon a telegram, informing him of his decision to leave the band. Gordon naturally went ballistic and made all sorts of threats about blackening his name. He told Vic he'd never work in show business again and he'd make it his life's work to make him pay for doing this. Vic wasn't overly bothered. He phoned us in Vegas to let us know he'd been picked up from Heathrow Airport by a chauffered white Rolls Royce and had five hundred pounds handed him. They were to be his weekly expenses and didn't even include his wages. It was quite a turnaround from the forty pounds a week he was used to from Gordon.

There were plenty of musicians to take Vic's place, but what upset Tom and Gordon most was that Vic had left them, and not the other way around. They were both incensed, but the rest of us were walking around with smiles plastered across our faces. Good old Vic, he'd certainly punctured their over inflated egos. Gordon hastily recruited a new keyboard player from Cardiff, Mark Stevens. He was an accomplished musician, but he was a bit of a square peg in a round hole and never quite fitted in. It was too late for Mark to join the Vegas tour at that stage, so Johnny Harris filled in by playing piano at the Flamingo.

The bosses at the Flamingo didn't want to try us out during high season, so we were playing before the season began and the venue wasn't exactly buzzing. The showroom held an audience of around five hundred. Our supporting act was the American comedienne, Kaye Ballard. She was a veteran in show business and, importantly for Gordon, relatively inexpensive. Kaye had established herself as a musical comedienne in the 1940s with the Spike Jones revue of entertainers. She played broad physical comedy and stand-up, and was familiar with audiences through her many television and stage productions. Her famous catch phrase was, 'Good luck with your mouth!', and she was the first person to record the song 'In Other Words', which was later retitled 'Fly Me To The Moon'.

One date on the tour, 6th April 1968, is forever ingrained in my memory. We were midway through our month's residency at the Flamingo and the shows had been going really well. All the publicity about 'Tom Jones Fever' had done the trick and our two shows each night were packed to capacity. The first show started at 8 p.m. and the second followed at 10 p.m. Tom was in terrific form, despite his complaints that the dry Nevada desert air was playing havoc with his voice. He had packed his penthouse suite with humidifiers and refused to join the band at poolside, when we were taking our breaks.

That evening we were killing a little time in between shows. I was near the foyer of the Flamingo chancing my luck on the slot machines. The area was mostly deserted, as everyone had filed into the main showroom ahead of the second show. There were row upon row of slot machines and I happened to be playing the one next to the passage that led from the foyer to the showroom. I had pushed my last dime in the slot and yanked down the arm. I glanced over my shoulder and was dumbstruck. Heading right toward me was Elvis Presley and Priscilla, closely followed by their entourage, the Memphis Mafia. Elvis spotted the shocked look on my face and gave me a devilish wink as he swept on by. He was met by one of the casino bosses and ushered into the showroom.

I rushed backstage to Tom's dressing room and instead of the customary knock, practically broke down the door. Tom was seated at his dressing table, applying his stage make-up, and wearing his favourite white towelling bath robe. He was startled by my entrance and said, 'Bloody hell Vernon, you're meant to knock. You almost gave me a heart attack'. I told him I was glad he was sitting down, 'Elvis and Priscilla are here with the Memphis Mafia, to watch the show.'

'Vernon, stop winding me up,' he said.

'I'm deadly serious, Elvis is in the building.' At last it struck home and in a flash Tom leapt out of his seat. He flung open the dressing room door and started calling down the corridor for Chris Ellis. I dashed back to the band's dressing room to let them all know the news. You could feel excitement backstage. We took up our positions, with Johnny Harris at the grand piano, ready for our big moment. Tom was pacing up and down in the wings. The curtains opened and the orchestra steamed into Sam Cooke's belter, 'Ain't That Good News'. Tom leapt across the stage, grabbing the mike from the stand. He was immaculate in a dark blue tuxedo, with white frilled shirt and bow tie. The room was pitch-black, with the only light coming from the stage.

I was desperately trying to locate Elvis in the audience. I finally saw him, directly below me, sitting at a massive table with Priscilla and his entourage. Elvis was puffing away on a cheroot. They had quietly seated themselves as soon as the house lights had dimmed and hardly anyone in the audience was aware of their presence.

It was mind-boggling performing in front of The King. Elvis hardly ever went along to see other artistes perform. When Tom had met him a year earlier on the set of one of his movies, it had made a huge impression on him. Now we were performing for him. We gave it our all that evening. Before we had got on stage, Tom had nervously coughed into his hand and said, 'We got to make a good job of it tonight boys, for Elvis'.

Chris Slade's drums almost crashed off the podium, he was giving them so much stick. Johnny Harris, looked a little frustrated sitting at the piano, you could tell he wanted to be out in front of the orchestra, conducting for all he was worth. Bill Parkinson and I tucked in behind Tom and gave everything we had. Tom belted out every hit in his armoury. He discarded his jacket and bow tie and his white shirt was clinging to him like a wet *Pontypridd Observer*. The audience went wild at the end of the show, and Tom waited for the applause to die down and thanked the audience. Then he introduced Elvis: 'Ladies and gentlemen, the moment has come to introduce you to a man I have long admired, and who has been an inspiration to me for many years.

When I was starting out back in South Wales, where I come from, he was my guiding light, and he's here tonight. Mr. Elvis Presley!'

The audience exploded with five hundred hysterical voices practically taking the roof off. The room was in darkness and no-one knew where to look. A spotlight beamed around the audience, pretending to frantically search for The King. The audience played along, turning wildly around to follow the spot and search out Elvis. Finally the powerful beam came to rest on Elvis and he stood up, sending the place into meltdown. It was an unforgettable moment.

The audience was in raptures and there was no end to the cheering and applauding. I caught Tom's eye and made a subtle finger slash across my throat. He read it and shouted over the PA system, 'Okay, settle down, everyone settle down'. At last things started to calm and Tom thumped his chest, 'Hey, don't forget I'm the star tonight!' The audience roared with laughter and Elvis got back to his feet to applaud Tom, and that set everyone off again.

Johnny Harris took the initiative and counted the orchestra in. We all steamed into 'It's Not Unusual' followed by Wilson Pickett's 'Midnight Hour'. Tom then introduced his new single, 'Delilah', which was flying up the UK charts at that time, and finished off with the explosive 'Land of a Thousand Dances.' We left the stage to a standing ovation led by Elvis. It was magical.

Backstage in our dressing room we changed out of our stage gear. We had made Tom promise to introduce us to Elvis on pain of death. True to his word, Chris Ellis came to take us to Tom's room. We entered to find over a dozen people crammed in. Tom was in the corner in animated conversation with Elvis. Priscilla was seated near the door chatting to Linda. All the Memphis Mafia was present: Sonny West, Lamar Fike, Jerry Schilling, Red West and Charlie Hodge. They were very friendly, if a little guarded. They all had their individual jobs. Red and Sonny West were Elvis's bodyguards, although Red also had a talent for writing songs, some of which Elvis recorded, like 'If Every Day Was Like Christmas' and 'Separate Ways'. Charlie Hodge used to harmonize with Elvis and specced out each stage before a concert. Lamar Fike handled all Elvis's stage lighting, and Jerry Schilling gave advice about what other groups were using for audio equipment.

Red West introduced me to Priscilla and I shook her hand. Her skin was almost alabaster white and was off-set by her intricate black beehive. She looked absolutely stunning; Elvis was a very lucky guy. Everyone was smoking like chimneys and before very long the room was enveloped in a blue haze. Tom caught my eye and called me over. The rest of the boys watched as I excused myself from Priscilla and Linda, and eased my way through the guests. Elvis was wearing a black seaman's reefer jacket, white polo-neck and black trousers. I had planned to ask him if he had any intention of touring the UK, but that thought flew out of my head the moment he shook my hand. Tom introduced me, 'Elvis this is my bass player, Vernon. He's been with me right from the beginning.' I told him it was pleasure and an honour to meet him, and he replied, 'You guys certainly laid it down out there. That was a great bass intro to "Land of a Thousand Dances", really cool.' I thanked him and told him that meant a great deal coming from him.

He smiled and said, 'You know I just can't win. I had this

here outfit flown in from Carnaby Street, knowing I was going to meet you guys, and here's you guys dressed all American in T-shirts and jeans and all.' We all laughed and he shook my hand again, 'It was real good to meet you, Vernon'. I turned, elated and almost bumped into Chris Slade. The rest of the band had formed an orderly queue behind me, waiting patiently to be introduced to The King. It was hard to believe that only a few years earlier, whilst working at the *Pontypridd Observer*, I'd been typesetting Elvis's name in numerous articles.

Red West gave each of us an large colour photograph of Elvis and Priscilla. It was a beautiful portrait of them on their wedding day, cutting the cake. Elvis signed each of the photographs for the band, a personal keepsake from The King. Pretty soon it was time for him to head back to Los Angeles. Elvis invited us to take a look inside his Lincoln Continental limousine. It was as wide as a truck and capable of seating the whole entourage. Elvis was very proud of the Lincoln and took delight in showing us the built-in TV, mini-bar and telephone. Watching the black beast speed away into the night, I turned to Chris Ellis and said, 'C'mon lets go and celebrate.'

Tom had gone back to the dressing room, but Linda overheard us making plans to visit the Aladdin Casino, where Little Richard was booked for the month. Linda had had a bit too much champagne and was a little glassy eyed. Quite suddenly she launched into a verbal tirade about us idolizing Elvis in front of Tom. She scolded us and said we shouldn't have behaved like that, making Tom feel small in front of Elvis; he was ten times a better singer. We tried to calm her down and explain we were more than loyal to Tom, but we had all just met one of our heroes, a once in a lifetime opportunity. The usually shy Linda Woodward could be incredibly protective of her husband.

A short walk from the Flamingo, and Chris and I were propping up the bar in the Aladdin. We had missed the end of Little Richard's set, though we had caught it a few days earlier and even been introduced to the living legend by Tom's PR man, Chris Hutchins. It was way past midnight at this point and the bar was almost empty. A smartly dressed lady, accompanied by a teenage girl, came and sat quite near us. After ordering drinks the elegant women turned to us both and said, 'You guys look like you've hit the million dollar jackpot'. We explained we were celebrating after meeting our hero, Elvis Presley, that evening. The women asked where we had met him, and we explained we were Tom Jones' band and Elvis had come along to watch us play. The women smiled and said the Memphis Mafia were no doubt tagging along, we asked her if she was an Elvis fan and she said: 'You could say that. I'm Priscilla's mom, Mrs. Beaulieu. Elvis is my son-in-law.' She introduced Priscilla's younger sister and said, 'We've been to The Sands to see Jerry Lewis. He's doing just fine without Dean Martin. The man is hilarious. Are you guys from England?'

Mrs. Beaulieu said that Elvis must be a big fan of Tom's, as he never went to watch anyone perform live. She said she'd mention running into us when she met Elvis back at the suite. We were confused and said we'd just waved him off on his way back to L.A. Mrs. Beaulieu explained that Elvis wasn't due back on the set of his latest movie (*Live A Little, Love A Little*), until the morning. He was staying in his regular suite on the top floor of The Aladdin; it was where he had married Priscilla the previous year. Chris Ellis piped up, 'you're telling us that Elvis is staying here tonight?' We were both gobsmacked. We had a great evening chatting with them. Mrs. Beaulieu told us all about Elvis's new song, 'A Little Less Conversation', which we couldn't wait to get our hands on. Finally they made their excuses, and we watched mother and daughter disappear into the lift heading for Elvis's penthouse suite. What an evening it had been, we were too wired to head off to bed and carried on celebrating. A good few hours later we were practically seeing double. A cowboy rancher had joined the party and was telling us all about rattlesnakes and desert critters.

The last I remember was staggering back to Empey's Desert Inn. I made it as far as the deserted swimming pool and collapsed into a sun lounger. I awoke the next morning, squinting up at a cloudless sky, with the mother of all hangovers. Around me was the sound of splashing water, happy chattering voices, and music blaring from portable radios. I was stretched out fully clothed on the lounger, my face redder than a lobster. I glanced at my watch and realised I only had two hours before we were due to rehearse our new song, 'Delilah'. It was in the UK charts and Gordon wanted to include it in our set, especially after it had been so well received the previous evening.

When we met for rehearsals, we heard Gordon was rubbing his hands with glee in London. Chris Hutchins had contacted the British press about Elvis attending our gig. The story was splashed across all the newspapers. Gordon told Tom that the all-important American tour was a huge success and would make them both multi-millionaires. However, it wasn't such great news for the rest of us. Elvis had been knocked out with our drummer, Chris Slade, the previous evening and had approached Gordon with the offer of a substantial amount of cash to let Chris join his band. He thought Chris would fit in really well with James Burton and Glen Hardin. Gordon refused point-blank, and Chris was mortified. It was the chance of a lifetime. Gordon told Chris he was under contract, and that was the end of the matter. It was a disappointment which stayed with Chris for the rest of his life.

I was also to be disappointed. A young producer had acquired the rights to a book, *The Gospel Singer,* and approached Gordon before he left with the idea of Tom appearing in the movie. I remember walking through the floor of the casino with Gordon when the producer made his pitch. Gordon didn't go for it; he didn't think it was the right vehicle for Tom at the time. The producer wasn't discouraged and suggested me for the part instead. Gordon wasn't impressed with this idea at all and went out of his way to put me down. He told the producer that my broad Welsh accent would be a hindrance, and I was a little too green yet to be appearing in movies. We both stood there open mouthed as Gordon sauntered off, he tossed over his shoulder as a parting shot, 'Make sure you're not late for rehearsals Vernon, you don't want to keep Tom waiting.'

Lucy Ellis and Bryony Sutherland, the authors of *Tom Jones Close Up*, capture this behaviour better than I can: 'Gordon thought he had the capacity to make an infinite number of stars. Nevertheless he was curiously reluctant to further the careers of The Squires, whether collectively or individually, regardless of the profit potential. In March 1968 a film producer approached Gordon with the idea of featuring Tom in a movie called *The Gospel Singer*, and suggested also that The Squires' bass player Vernon Hopkins should do a screen test. Taller and more classically handsome than Tom, Vernon was blessed with typical

Hollywood looks, and perhaps better suited to the big screen than the singer's rugged profile. Gordon did not hesitate to block the move in order to protect his protégé's interests, and Vernon was sworn to secrecy "for the good of the band".'

It was very kind of them to describe me like that. I don't think for one moment that the film producer was thinking of me as an option to replace Tom, but I believe he would have liked me to have played a role in *The Gospel Singer* had it come to fruition. He also mentioned a screen test for another film that he was involved in. Naturally I was very keen, who wouldn't be? But Gordon refused and offered me a decision between staying in the band or taking a gamble with the screen tests. There was no reasoning with him. I stuck with the band. Looking back who knows what may have happened if I'd walked out then and taken a chance in Hollywood?

Tom also had another brush with the movie business. He told us he had missed out on playing James Bond by a whisker. Harry Saltzman, the producer of the Bond films, had considered giving Tom the 007 role in the next movie. Tom duly reported through the press that he was up for it. But Saltzman had second thoughts, saying that Tom was too well-known as a singer. If it had come off I couldn't have imagined Gordon telling Harry Saltzman that Tom's accent was thicker than leek soup. The band had a chuckle about that one and the skits were flying fast and furious for weeks after. My favourite was: 'Watch it butt. Put that knuckle-duster away or I'll stick the nut on yew so 'ard, you'll be in 'ospital 'till the 'earse arrives! Now then, place ewer 'ands against the wall an spread ewer legs. Any nonsense butt, an' I'll squeeze ewer balls so 'ard, you'll sound like Mary 'opkin, yew bastud! Ow was that Mr. Saltzman?'

During our stay at the Flamingo we made lots of friends. But one in particular stood out. Vince Silvestri was one of the 'suits' in charge of the casino. Vince was in his thirties, recently divorced, and in charge of emptying the masses of slot machines. He was fairly stocky and always wore a cowboy hat with his impeccable Italian-cut suits. Apart from when we were performing he thought we were a pretty miserable lot, mooching around the casino on our time off. In Vince's eyes we ought to be high-rollers living it large and having a ball. He was as sharp as a cut-throat razor and sensed that something wasn't right in our world. Vince pumped us for information: he wanted to know what was wrong. We told him our troubles and he was speechless, 'our resident musicians are on more bread than you guys, and they get to go home every night'. Vince told us to leave it with him, we were going to have a fun time from now on. True to his word we were waited on hand and foot: if we were having a bite to eat in the restaurant, a word from Vince and the bill was lost. In between shows a waitress would rock up with a tray full of beers: 'On the house. Vince says Hi'.

He even arranged for a four-seater plane to fly us to the Grand Canyon. There we were one morning climbing into this tiny Cessna parked on the apron of Las Vegas airport. It was so warm Chris Ellis was padding about in his flip-flops. Off we went into the wide blue yonder. It was an amazing experience flying above the barren desert. The pilot started to climb so high, we found it hard to breathe as the air thinned out. We approached a landing strip on the Canyon's upper lip and were surprised to see pine trees heavy with snow. Although the temperature at the bottom is desert hot, it's Alpine at the top and Chris was soon regretting his choice of foot wear. The

Grand Canyon is often referred to as one of the eight wonders of the world. As far as I'm concerned it's the first. Awesome! On the return journey the pilot took us on a helter-skelter ride through the canyon, diving right to the bottom and skimming the waters of the Colorado River. A good hour later we were back in Vegas and eternally indebted to our great friend, Vince Silvestri.

With our residency at the Flamingo drawing to a close there was one final surprise in store. Johnny 'The Boot' Harris was a randy old sod who never looked a gift horse in the mouth. Skinny as a beanpole, his 'boot' weighed in at more than he did. Bill Parkinson and I were practicing some chords for a new song that Tom wanted to include in the act. Suddenly Chris Ellis burst into our room and told us to follow him. When we arrived at Chris's room we could hear one hell of a banging, and wondered where on earth it was coming from. Chris Ellis pointed to the ceiling. There was a maze of hairline cracks running through the plaster, caused by a consistent hammering on the floor above. Every so often the constant thudding would be accompanied by rapturous moaning.

We stood rooted to the spot watching the cracks get wider and wider. We heard bed springs squeaking and bits of plaster started dropping from the ceiling onto Chris's bed below. The motel was ancient and I guess the unrelenting desert sun had done its work; the place was falling apart under Johnny's onslaught. Suddenly the thudding stopped and, giggling, we started to help Chris clear the debris from his bed. Then it started off again and we were covered in plaster from the ceiling as the thumping resumed.

By this stage we were in hysterics and practically holding

each other up. Chris piped up and started singing Trini Lopez's classic hit 'If I Had A Hammer', and we all joined in. Pretty soon we were all in time with Johnny's 'boot' hitting the floor above. We managed to sing all of two verses in three part harmony before there was silence. The next thing we knew, Johnny Harris appeared in the open doorway wrapped up in a bath towel, 'Hey Chris, turn your radio down a bit. I'm trying to concentrate upstairs.' Priceless!

15. MARY WILSON

We were packing away our instruments and suits backstage at the Flamingo after our final performance when Vince Silvestri turned up to say goodbye. The band had clubbed together and bought him a 'music themed' oil painting. It was a small token of our gratitude for all his kindness toward us. Vince was touched and thanked us. Then he asked us to accompany him to his office near the casino floor. Vince sequenced some numbers into the wall safe and when it swung open he produced four small cellophane bags. He tossed the bags, one to each of us in turn and said, 'Here take these silver dollars. The only hands to ever touch them was mine, there's five coins apiece for each of you. Pass them onto your grandchildren and let them know it's from Vince.'

The coins were uncirculated silver dollars dated 1922. It was a very special moment for us all. What a wonderful gift and what a wonderful man. The Vegas Mafia was very much alive and kicking in 1968, and we had heard stories from croupiers and waitresses about Vince's affiliations. Apparently he knew where all the bodies were buried in the big Nevada desert. But 'what are you gonna do?'. To us he was a diamond, a quietly spoken, unassuming gentleman, never to be forgotten.

On the day we were due to fly out of Vegas, Tom told us we were stopping off in New York on the way back to the UK, to make an appearance on *The Ed Sullivan Show*. The programme was a national event in the US each Sunday evening, and was the first exposure for foreign performers coast to coast. It enjoyed phenomenal popularity and was an American family ritual, with young and old gathering around the television. Sullivan was regarded as a kingmaker, and performers considered an appearance on his program a guarantee of stardom. The band was chuffed to bits as until now Tom had appeared solo on *The Sullivan Show*.

The American tour had lasted a little over eight weeks, and during that period Tom and the band had given forty-eight performances. We hopped on a Boeing from Vegas to New York and booked into the Goram Hotel again, a day ahead of our appearance on the show. We were scheduled to fly back to the UK directly after. The show went by in a blur and we left the gig in our stage gear, making a dash for the airport and our connection back to London. The security guys tried to get us to sign out of the studio, but we were already in the taxi speeding away. Arriving at Kennedy Airport we boarded a Trident airliner and, compared to the Boeing, it was a dream of a flight. The journey across the Atlantic was the most comfortable I had experienced. I have never understood why the magnificent Trident was pulled out of service in favour of the Boeing; it was the king of air travel.

Time changes everything, and number 4 Tonbridge Road was very much changed when I returned. Tony Cartwright, flush with the success of Freddie Lennon's hit record in Germany, had found himself a girlfriend, Pauline, and moved in with her. When I paid Mu my back rent she decided to take the family on a holiday to Southsea, 'the thing is Vern, I'm going to have to ask you for your keys while we're away.' I was shocked and asked her if she wanted me out. This was not the homecoming I had been expecting.

'Only for the fortnight Vernon. What with Noel Redding, Freddie Lennon and that lot treating the place like Piccadilly Circus, well I'm not here to keep an eye on things'. I was a bit crestfallen and wondering where I was going to find digs at such short notice. Mu was ahead of me on that score and had arranged accommodation at The Magpie Hotel in Lower Sunbury-on-Thames. All I could do was thank her and wish them all a happy holiday. 'I knew you'd understand Vernon. What do you bleedin fancy for dinner? What about a nice steak with all the trimmings? Mum get yourself down the butchers will ya, we're 'aving steak.'

The Magpie Hotel stood on the main road running through Lower Sunbury, which was an affluent and picturesque place. The Magpie was a popular pub and its white-pillared entrance led into a spacious bar and lounge. It backed onto the Thames and customers could take a seat on the patio and watch cabin cruisers, barges and row boats glide up and down the river. Once in a while you'd catch sight of a sea-going cruiser drifting by, its rich owners and guests sunbathing on the decks, drinking champagne.

The Magpie was run by Harry Pern and his Lithuanian wife, Elsa. They had teenage twin daughters, and were a lovely warm family. Harry was a heavy set fellow in his late fifties, and wore big horn-rimmed spectacles. He offered me the cheapest room in the pub, a second floor box-bedsit with a lovely view of the Thames. It would be my home for the rest of my time with The Squires, and for some time after.

After two weeks at The Magpie, I had been adopted by the customers and staff. It felt as though I'd lived there all my life, I became part of the furniture in no time at all. It was pretty special to just wander downstairs and prop up the bar at your local. Harry and Elsa very kindly said that they'd got used to having me around, so why not stay? I decided to make it my new home. I had been very lucky to stay with Mu. I'd really landed on my feet there and had some wonderful memories, but this felt like the right decision. Mu gave me her blessing and wished me all the best. We promised to keep in touch. I bought myself a small portable stove and lived off tinned food and fry-ups in Chez Vernon, my box-bedsit restaurant! I obviously missed Mu's cooking, but there was a decent curry house in the village and that was my blow-out venue, when I wasn't on the road with the band.

Ironically, both Tom and Gordon decided to move at the same time. The American tour had been an astounding success. They were now drowning in cash, and decided to sink some of the profit into new properties. Tom, Linda and Mark moved into Tor Point, a mansion in St George's Hill, Weybridge. Robin Eggar, the author of *Tom Jones: The Biography* described Tor Point as, 'a serious address, an indication of how far Tom had come from the basement rooms in Cliff Terrace. To a snobbish Englishman, living in St George's Hill was a sign not of breeding but of new money.' John Lennon and Cliff Richard lived nearby. Gordon and Jo Mills moved into a large Tudor mansion just down the road a little. Engelbert and Pat were also nearby, in Glenbank.

Tor Point was by far the largest property, a sprawling seventeen-room turn of the century pile. It could never make up its mind whether it wanted to be grand or comfortable. It was secure from rabid fans behind electronic gates and set in five acres of woods and carefully sculpted lawns overlooking St George's Hill Golf Club, one of the most exclusive courses in southern England. Despite Tom's proximity to the first tee and unlike many of his friends – Jimmy Tarbuck was a fanatical golfer and both Gordon and Engelbert became very keen – Tom never showed any interest in picking up a putter. Instead he invested thousands of pounds in building a state-of-the-art fitness centre, which included a tennis court, a squash court, fitness room, a sauna and an indoor L-shaped 25 metre swimming pool. The pool had a kiddie slide and a Welsh dragon in red mosaic tiles on the bottom.

No expense was spared in refurbishing the house. The interior decoration was closely supervised by Linda, who showed sophisticated taste for a Valleys girl. She eschewed modern furniture for classic, antiques and tropical hardwood panelling. There was an enormous drawing room with three chintz sofas and matching armchairs, a chandelier and a marble fireplace. The dining room contained a sixteen seater mahogany dining table, a crystal chandelier, silver candelabra and gilt mirrors. The kitchen was all mod cons, an electric hob in a melamine-covered central island and an old-fashioned Aga topped with a beaten copper hood.

Downstairs at Tor Point there was masses of stuff, each piece sitting dust-free and proud in its appointed place. Linda still did most of the cleaning herself. Copper ornaments, antique bellows, carriage clocks, bowls piled high with porcelain fruit, antique firearms on the wall, the mantelpieces crowded with ornaments, each tasteful in its time and place but indicative of mass purchase. Tom's wood-panelled study was packed with little knick-knacks, and had a phone with a gold leaf receiver. There were few books. Instead, the glass cabinets were full of framed gold and silver discs, Tom's Grammy Award and other assorted medals and presentation scrolls. The grate in the white marble fireplace was inhabited by an electric fire and surrounded by copper kettles and antique bed warmers. There were always vases full of flowers and fresh fruit on display.

The first floor contained four bedroom suites and a separate wing included two further bedrooms, a bathroom, Mark's playroom and a kitchenette for the live-in staff, who never came. The top floor was Tom's playground, with a full-sized billiard room, a bar with proper bitter in the barrel and a sixteen-seat cinema.

Tom had become eye-poppingly rich. It was hard to believe that just a few years previously we had all shared squalid digs together in the 'Calcutta', Ladbroke Grove. The rest of us didn't share in the enormous wealth. The band were pretty disgruntled as we were all working together touring and releasing new records, yet Gordon and Tom were pocketing the profits and we didn't even get a small increase in our forty pounds a week. It was a bitter pill to swallow.

Gordon and Jo's house was equally impressive. Gordon had christened his Tudor manse 'Little Rhondda', and it was set in three acres of landscaped gardens. It too had an indoor swimming pool, with an underground viewing gallery. There was a glass wall beneath the pool's waterline that allowed visitors to watch the antics of those in the pool. Almost immediately after settling in, Gordon installed a state-of-the-art high tech recording studio. Later he built a mini-zoo, with tigers, orangutans, chimpanzees and Ollie, a one-eyed silverback gorilla. Ollie absolutely hated men, but loved women; he had a particular soft spot for Jo.

Tom and Gordon would try to outdo each other in the luxury spending stakes. As soon as Tom caught sight of Gordon's zoo he bought a couple of racehorses and a yacht. Both of them were drowning in luxury cars with garages full of Rolls Royces, Bentleys and Mercedes Benz sports cars. During that summer, Engelbert also decided to join in the spending contest hysteria. This was very uncomfortable for the band to witness, but we just got on with it. Entreaties to Gordon about a more equitable split were met with a stony face and outright contempt. Tom refused to even discuss the matter, and fell back on his stock response of 'Take it up with Gordon, it's got nothing to do with me'. I pointed out that he was a board member of MAM, Gordon's company, and therefore it had everything to do with him. Tom always insisted he knew nothing about the business end of things, which was left to Gordon.

My new life at The Magpie sometimes introduced me to some unsavoury people: some of the pub's clientele were of the roguish variety. Don Henderson was a one-eyed old school villain. He always carried a gun and wasn't reticent about showing it off. Don practically oozed intimidation. He was around forty, thick set, dark and brooding. His lifeless glass eye gave him a particularly cold and menacing stare. I wouldn't see him for a few days, and then he would turn up laden with jewellery, stolen from some grand house or other. Don always told me Tom's house was on his hit list, but I think that was just bravado as this was accompanied by a little wink. I tried to keep out of his way as much as possible, he was bad news. He would sometimes be seated in a dark corner of the bar, in animated conversation with other rogues, maybe planning his next 'job'. A number of other regulars, usually there during the daytime, used to 'take orders' to knock off whatever you desired. Harry Pern wasn't fussy about who his customers were, or what they got up to in their lives, as long as they settled their bar bills on time.

At closing time, Harry would lock the pub's doors and all the regulars would take their drinks downstairs to a little basement bar. From outside The Magpie would look completely dead to the world, but below ground the party used to be in full swing. Being a pub fixture, I became a regular of the basement bar, when I wasn't on the road. Derek the barman, who wrote a couple of Hank Janson crime novels, would always see me okay for drinks until I got my wages from Chris Ellis on Fridays.

Chris was still lodging with Mu's sister in Thames Ditton. He eventually moved into The Magpie too. Our drummer, Chris Slade and his new bride, Lynne, were struggling with a mortgage. They'd found themselves a little semi-detached in Upper Sunbury-on-Thames. Lynne had secretarial work and their combined wages just about made the house purchase possible. Vic Cooper, our former keyboard player, was having a rare old time of it in Hollywood. Vic was on the set of the film *Toomorrow*, with Olivia Newton-John. When we spoke on the phone he would tell me all about his exploits in LA. Vic was living it up, good and proper. He told me that leaving the band was the best thing he ever did, and he couldn't understand how the rest of us could bear to put up with it a moment longer. Harry Saltzman, the film's producer had recently sent Vic and Olivia on an all-expenses paid holiday to Acapulco. He wanted them both fit and tanned for the movie. I remember mentioning this to Gordon at one of our rehearsals and he practically turned puce. He told me never to mention Vic's name in his presence again.

Bill Parkinson, our rhythm guitarist, and his wife Jenny were still renting a flat in Muswell Hill, just around the corner from

Mia's aunt and uncle. At that time, Bill and I began writing songs together. We would cut the demos at Regent Sound, Tin Pan Alley, where we'd cut the original demo for 'It's Not Unusual' back in 1964. One afternoon, a few weeks after returning from America, we went into the studio to lay down a new track. The song was called 'The Gardener' and was about a labourer falling in love with the grand lady of a country house. We had booked a keyboard player, but he didn't turn up. Denmark Street was awash with musicians, so we went out and found ourselves a pianist. He was a chubby young fellow who used to run errands for one of the sheet music publishers based in Soho. I remember him sitting at the piano and cleaning the lenses of his spectacles. I explained what we were after and we laid down the track. He gave 'The Gardener' a period, almost, classical feel, which much later became very much his signature. Job done satisfactorily, I paid him a fiver as agreed. I'll never forget him sauntering out of the studio with a grin from ear to ear, 'Just ask for Reg Dwight, next time you're stuck for a keyboard player,' he said. Of course Reg later became our national treasure, Elton John.

Not long after Bill left The Squires, he struck pay dirt with a song he had written about his mother, 'Mother of Mine'. It was recorded by the child star, Neil Reid, who had won *Opportunity Knocks*, and went racing up the charts, making Bill a very happy man in the process. 'Wee Neil Reid' was eleven years old at the time and the record sold over a quarter of a million copies in the UK.

At the beginning of May, Tom and The Squires were booked for another month at the London Palladium. The band joined up with our old friends the Ted Heath Orchestra to produce a full sound. We were delighted that Johnny Harris was also drafted in to conduct. He had lost none of his zip and went at it like a man possessed. Gordon thought he was a distraction and took Johnny to one side and told him to cool it. Johnny tried to calm down a little, but he loved his music and pretty soon he was like a wild man again, conducting with gusto and stamping his boot. Gordon lost patience and fired him. Johnny 'The Boot' Harris got the boot and never worked with Tom again; he took it in his stride and shrugged his shoulders. He went onto to create a fabulous album of music, *Movements*, one of the tracks from which, 'Footprints on the Moon', was used by news channels worldwide to introduce the Apollo space programme news alerts. Johnny also had a regular feature on Lulu's BBC show *A Happening For Lulu*. The show used to feature different Eurovision hopefuls each week along with one of Johnny's instrumental arrangements. Shirley Bassey became a great friend and loved his unique arrangement of 'Light My Fire' so much she recorded it on her next album.

Another familiar face started showing up on a regular basis at the Palladium, Mary Wilson of the Supremes. Since they met at the Bambi Awards in Munich Tom and Mary had kept in touch. She even visited him in Vegas before Linda arrived for the opening night. Tom was seriously smitten by the gorgeous Supreme, more so than any of his other conquests. I'd never witnessed him fall for anyone like he fell for Mary, he was besotted. Tom confided that he had never felt this way about a woman, other than Linda. He seemed totally at odds with himself, it was a real emotional ride and he was uncertain how it would work out.

Another problem was causing him sleepless nights. Tom was

very unhappy about how much tax he had to pay the Inland Revenue. Although he was a multi-millionaire he just couldn't get his head around the amount of money he was losing to the Exchequer; he told me his taxes were 'shocking'. Tom took it up with Gordon and demanded he do something about the current state of affairs. Gordon duly phoned Bill Smith, Tom's accountant, and gave him a rocket. He was told in no uncertain terms to 'sort it out or you're fired'.

It was typical Gordon to turn Tom's sleepless nights into restless nights for poor Bill Smith. Bill came up with the idea of putting all of Tom's affairs under the auspices of Gordon's company, MAM (Management, Agency and Music). Tom was able to claim expenses on running his fleet of gas guzzling Rolls and Bentleys, employing staff, and all the other costs involved in touring the world. The tax rate on company dividends was far lower and his tax bill was practically halved in one fell swoop. Gordon introduced Bill to Tom at the next MAM board meeting and Tom embraced him, grinning ear to ear. When Tom told me all about it later, I remember asking 'if you and Gordon can reclaim such huge amounts on allowances, why is the band stuck on such a meagre wage?' Tom was peeved that I'd punctured his euphoria and looked at me darkly. He was about to say something but I cut him off, 'I know, take it up with Gordon'. He wasn't happy with that and I guess looking back it was the beginning of the end for me. I've had a lot of time to dwell on it. They both certainly had no respect for us, it was a wonder to me that we were all still a band at all.

Our time at the Palladium came to an end and we were straight off to Bournemouth's Winter Gardens for another month of shows. It was the usual arrangement with two shows a night and three on a Saturday. Roy Castle was also on the bill, a very modest and extremely likeable character. Roy was a multi-instrumentalist, singer, tap-dancer, actor and man of boundless energy. This made it all the more poignant when he was struck down with lung cancer caused, he firmly believed, by the intake of tobacco smoke from performing in clubs and theatres in the UK. Roy's main instrument was the trumpet and being compelled to draw in huge gulps of air to play it, he was breathing in room's full of tobacco stale air at the same time. Roy left a legacy, and a charity bearing his name lobbied successive governments about the dangers of passive smoking, which helped lead to the ban in smoking in public places.

Bournemouth was truly exhausting, as there was no downtime. Gordon had also booked us into several television slots around our stage time. Being just an hour away from London, it was a case of straight off the stage and into a studio, then back to Bournemouth for the next scheduled show. By the end of the month we were all exhausted and Tom phoned Gordon to let him know just that, in no uncertain terms.

Tom was being a bit distant with me since our altercation about money, and this rancour started to enter our stage set, much to my distress. Tom used to introduce us individually on stage, 'This is Vernon, my bass player, this is Chris on drums' and we would all get a great round of applause and cheers from the audience. This now changed and Tom took to introducing us at every show with, 'An' 'ow about a round of applause for those bunch of 'ooligans at the back then? Don't clap too loud or they'll want a bloody rise in their wages!' The band was gobsmacked. It was a real low blow. We had been humiliated in so many callous ways over the years by both Tom and Gordon, but this was something new altogether. Our loyalty and respect for them was now all but spent.

Tom had rented a luxurious house in a secluded area of Bournemouth for the duration of the tour, and pretty soon Mary Wilson flew in from the States to join him. Chris Ellis was staying at the house, with his new Swedish girlfriend, Eva, an au pair. Linda, Tom's wife was still up at Tor Point, doing a pretty good impression of Howard Hughes. She was completely isolated in St. George's Hill, popping champagne corks, surrounded by acres of woodland and not a soul to talk too. She had refused to employ any staff and her only company was a flute of champagne. Blocked in, blocked out, it was bizarre, especially with Tom increasingly indiscreet about his fling with Mary.

Chris recounted a particularly hairy episode. Mary Wilson had offered to make dinner for Tom, Chris and Eva. Chris was sent out to buy a chicken and Mary cooked a delicious meal from a recipe of her grandmother's. They all ate well, congratulating Mary on a fine meal, and quite a lot of champagne was consumed. There was some food left over, so Mary popped it back in the oven for later. Everyone was feeling particularly enamoured after the meal and drifted off to their bedrooms. By all accounts it was quite an evening and everyone slept in the following morning.

That morning Linda was reading the morning newspapers. Splashed across the front pages was news of Tom and Mary meeting illicitly in Bournemouth. The phone rang in Tom's bedroom and the Supreme nudged him awake, passing over the receiver. Tom told us all about it, later:

'Hallo,' said Tom.

'Get that cow out of there now,' screamed Linda

Tom tried to bluff it out, 'What are you talking about, calm down.'

'I know that bloody Mary Wilson is in bed with you. Get her out now, or I'll kill the both of you. I'm driving down now and I'll be there in five minutes. Get her out!'

Tom was confused, it was over an hour from Tor Point by car, 'What do you mean, where are you?' 'I'm in the bloody phone box just down the road, you bastard!' and Linda slammed down the phone.

Tom sprang from the king-size bed like a cat with its tail on fire, screaming for Chris. Mary sat bolt upright wondering what the hell was going on. Tom leapt down the stairs in his dressing gown and practically dragged Chris out of bed. 'Wake up Chris, she's on to us, we're in big trouble. Come on, mun!' Chris was still half asleep so Tom ran back upstairs and ordered Mary to get dressed and pack her bags. She was obviously dumbfounded, but he explained that his wife was on her way to kill the both of them. That news got her packing, and Chris helped throw her suitcases into the Rolls Royce parked outside. Tom ran down the drive-way hysterically waving Chris and Mary away, and Chris drove like a bat out of hell back to her Mayfair hotel. Chris reported that Mary cried her eyes out the entire journey, listening to Tom singing 'The Green, Green Grass of Home' on a small portable tape recorder, over and over again.

After delivering Mary to the hotel, Chris made a U-turn and drove straight back to Bournemouth. He pulled into the drive-way of Tom and Mary's love-nest to be confronted by a lone figure staggering around in a daze. Tom had walked down the road to the nearest phone box to confront Linda, but there was no sign of her. He had checked every phone box within a mile radius, but with no result. Finally, giving up, he'd knocked on a neighbouring house and been welcomed inside for tea in a complete state of shock!

Linda eventually turned up later that afternoon, chauffeur-driven and accompanied by her black labrador, imaginatively named Blackie. She was in a rage, and stormed around the house looking for evidence of Mary. Her suspicions were confirmed by the long strands of dark hair she found in the en-suite bathroom. Confronting Tom, she pointed an accusing finger at the hairs in the bath. Tom pointed to Blackie and accused the dog of having jumped into the bath. Linda was fuming and headed for the kitchen, where she found the remains of the previous evening's chicken dinner.

'That looks nice Tom, did you cook it?' Tom stared awkwardly at the floor, avoiding her gaze.

'I don't know why I bother to ask. The only thing you ever cook up is a pack of lies.'

'Chris cooked it, honest,' said Tom, 'he's been reading up about cooking and everything. He's even gone and bought himself a bloody cookbook.'

'Don't talk bloody rubbish. Chris Ellis doesn't know how to boil an egg. That bitch cooked it.'

Chris was to witness many a row between Tom and Linda, enough to fill a book, he told me. He said that Linda had a fantastic aim, especially when it came to throwing crockery at her promiscuous husband. She could certainly get physical, lashing out at Tom until she had exhausted herself. Tom used to just stand there and take it, unflinching; he certainly knew he deserved it. You would have thought that after the beating from Linda, he would have cooled things down a bit with Mary. But he didn't, he was smitten, hook, line and sinker, and the liaison never let up. If anything it became even more passionate. I remember Tom telling me, 'Mary is so easy going, cool, calm and collected. The first time she undressed, it all seemed so natural and unaffected, like we were as one. You know Vern, its love, not lust.'

Meanwhile, Gordon was having kittens about their affair. He had bitten what was left of his fingernails to the quick. It was 1968 and things were not as enlightened as they are today. A relationship between a married white man and a stunningly beautiful black woman, let alone two superstars, was heavily frowned upon, especially in America, where attitudes to race and colour were a national issue. Gordon pleaded with both Tom and Mary to end their high-powered relationship, 'Can't you just be good friends? The public will settle for that.' Gordon's pleading fell on stony ground, neither one of them wanted to end it, and the affair continued.

16. FOUR SUITS

Tom and The Squires were glad to see the back of the Winter Gardens. Tom was still jittery after Linda confronted him over Mary and The Squires weren't happy with the acoustics of the large venue. The house PA was under considerable strain and the audience would sometimes complain that the Ted Heath Orchestra was overpowering Tom's voice. We were all glad of a few days break before embarking on another gruelling schedule of shows.

Mia was working the summer season in Jersey at the time. The island was a relatively short distance from Bournemouth so I took the boat and went to visit. Mia was on the same bill as the comedian Lenny Bennett, and the impressionist Paul Melba, both unknown at the time. Lenny went on to present the television show *Punchlines* during the 1980s and was a regular on the popular quiz shows *Blankety Blank* and *Celebrity Squares*. Paul would appear on the television series *Who Do You Do?*, *The Val Doonican Show*, and *The Comedians*. He was a regular performer at the Palladium and Talk of the Town. We all became great friends, and they persuaded me to take up snorkelling and water skiing, during my stay in Jersey.

Pretty soon it was time to head back to The Magpie, and we were back on the road again playing venues around the country. Due to our television appearances it became increasingly diffi-cult to leave the pub. The regulars would corner me as soon as I headed for the front door – 'Derek, pull Vernon a pint please'. Some of the customers thought I was loaded, and would tap me for money. I soon put them right on that score and took a leaf out of Tom's book: 'Take it up with Gordon!'

We were booked to appear at Caesar's Palace, a huge night-club in Luton, twenty miles up the M1 from London. We had appeared there a number of times. Cliff Richard, Shirley Bassey and the cream of UK and American talent regularly graced the stage. The manager, George Savva, was one of the most recognizable figures on the cabaret scene. He was nicknamed 'Mr. Show-business' and ran three of the most successful clubs in Britain: Caesar's, Blazers of Windsor and his own Savva's in Usk. George was responsible for bringing Johnny Mathis, Judy Garland, Jack Jones, Frankie Laine and a host of trans-Atlantic stars to his venues.

Whenever we appeared, George would be the perfect host. He made sure Tom was being looked after, of course, but also went out of his way to treat the band equally well. George was the kind of man who believed in equality. Whether the artiste had the star dressing room or the one next to the communal toilet, they were treated with equal respect. Shirley Bassey had appeared the week before us, and George was not best pleased with the diva's behaviour. Although he did say that once Bassey set foot on stage she transformed into a goddess, an absolute sensation, and any dislike he had for her melted away.

George told me that Shirley Bassey had summoned him to her dressing room, during a break in rehearsals. 'Are you the manager of this shithouse?' she asked him. George nodded and Bassey told him to sort out the dressing room. She wanted it re-decorated and a chaise longue found or she simply wouldn't perform. George rushed out and found a contractor to decorate the walls with gold embossed wallpaper. He bribed a local furniture store owner with some free show tickets and managed to borrow a chaise longue. When Bassey arrived that evening ahead of the performance she gave George a right ear bashing. The chauffeur-driven Rolls Royce sent to collect her was black and not white, as stipulated in her contract. There were no further complaints about the dressing room, but no thanks either.

The supporting act that evening was a ventriloquist and as part of the act he would chain smoke cigarettes whilst the dummy entertained the audience. George had ordered a stage hand to sweep up the dog-ends before Bassey made her spectacular entrance, but for some reason this had not been done that particular evening. Shirley sang her opening number and then paused; her eyes fell on the cigarette butts littering the stage. George was mortified; she had a face like thunder.

'Look at all this muck, ladies and gentlemen, can't the management afford a cleaner?'

There was laughter from the audience and one of the stage hands threw a broom onstage. George told me he died a thousand deaths. Shirley picked up the broom and swept up the dog-ends. The audience loved it and there were howls of laughter. But as soon as she came offstage there was absolute mayhem and she tore the place apart looking for George. He hid in the cleaner's closet near the reception cloakroom, and refused to come out until she had left!

George's favourite star was Iris Williams, 'the Welsh songbird', who had a number one hit with 'He Was So Beautiful', which was later used as the theme for the movie, *The Deer Hunter*. Iris was the complete opposite of Bassey, and George used to describe her as, 'pure class'. The Pontypridd-born jazz legend went on to have her own successful BBC television show,

The Iris Williams Songbook. Our paths would cross later in my career and I always found her to be a wonderful person.

The Caesar's Palace shows went really well, and on the last evening I was helping Chris Ellis load our equipment into the van. Suddenly Tom pulled over in his new silver Roller. The electric windows slid down and he poked his head out. He was puffing on an enormous cigar and casually flicked ash over one of the amps, 'Vernon, I've got three or four suits I'm chucking. You can 'ave 'em if you want.'

I exchanged glances with Chris, who looked startled; it was very unusual for Tom to give anything away. I nodded and said, 'Thanks Tom, I'd love to have them.' Tom smiled and said, 'Okay, come up to Tor Point on Monday, around two o'clock, and I'll have them ready for you.' Up slid the electric window and the Rolls sped off. Chris piped up, 'He can't be feeling well. I've never known Tom to give the skin of his shit away, let alone a suit.' I must admit I was a bit bemused also, but I appreciated the gesture. I possessed only one suit, the one I wore on stage. How wonderful it would be to wear a West End tailored suit. My luck was definitely on the up. When I arrived back at The Magpie in the early hours of the morning, Harry's wife Elsa had left a television set in my room as a surprise. They had installed a new set in the bar. I remember watching the first moon landing on that TV.

I also watched Elvis's comeback TV special on the set. It was his first public concert in ten years. It was amazing to think I'd been chatting with him in the Flamingo just two months previously. He looked cool and collected, dressed in a black leather outfit, and the magic was still there. Elvis was performing in an intimate setting. James Burton, the guitarist, and the rest of his musicians were all huddled together on stage. I really enjoyed watching them go through all the old rock 'n' roll classics. Suddenly I recognized a familiar face in the bottom left hand corner of the screen. It was our old friend from LA, Lance LeGault, the bit part actor who had pumped us for information on Tom. There he was at the side of the stage playing tambourine. I remembered meeting him beside our hotel pool when he told us he was on a 'covert operation'. In that moment all became clear. Elvis had sent him along to find out about Tom in advance of turning up at our show in Vegas. No wonder Elvis seemed to know a lot about Tom and the band before we met; Lance had reported everything back to him.

My appointment with Tom was at 2 p.m. Tor Point commanded St George's Hill, standing at its highest point, overlooking Weybridge. I drove there in my old green Triumph 2000, looking a bit out of place amongst all the luxury cars. The road rose steeply and there was no mistaking who lived behind the wrought iron gates to my right. The name 'Little Rhondda' emblazoned across the gates, I gave Gordon's Tudor mansion a toot on the horn as I passed by. It was a glorious summer's day and I pulled into the private estate full of the joys of life. I introduced myself over the intercom and the gates, complete with the Welsh dragon, swung open.

I knocked on the studded oak door, admiring the Greek pillars either side, and waited. After an eternity the door finally opened. Tom stood there, bleary eyed, wearing a white-towelling dressing gown. Letting out a large yawn he shrugged himself awake and said:

''Ow's it going Vern, alright?'

'Yeah, sorry to get you out of bed Tom.'

Tom didn't bother to invite me in.

'Come for the suits 'ave you?' and with that he left me standing on the doorstep. 'Wait there, I'll go and fetch them'. Tom shuffled off in his slippers and disappeared through a side door. I was quite stunned by the opulence on display in the vast hallway, it was crammed full of antiques and fine oil paintings. Eventually Tom returned, puffing away on a Monte Cristo, with four neatly folded suits clutched to his chest.

Tom handed me the suits. 'Right, there's four suits there. Dougie Millings the West End tailor made them for me. He's measured me for some new ones, and there's bugger all wrong with these.'

'Thanks Tom, I really appreciate it.' Arnold 'Dougie' Millings was known as 'the Beatles' tailor' and was famous for designing their collarless suits. He had even appeared in a cameo role in the Beatles movie *A Hard Day's Night*. I was chuffed to bits and couldn't wait to wear them. I could see that Tom wasn't going to bother inviting me in for a cup of tea so I smiled and said, 'Well thanks once again, I'll be on my way.'

''Old on a minute, where do you think you're going?'

Finally, I thought he's going to offer me a cup of tea. But it wasn't that. 'You 'aven't paid me yet,' he said. I was absolutely stunned and just stood there with my mouth gaping. 'Well you don't think I'm going to give them away for nothing, do you? I want six quid each for 'em.' I was incredibly humiliated and Tom seemed to be taking pleasure in my discomfort. I told him I only had the rent for my room at the Magpie, and passed him back the suits. He held up his hand, refusing to take them back, 'Don't worry about it. Chris Ellis can take six quid out of your wages every week, 'til you've paid them off.' Tom closed the door in my face, leaving me standing there. I was angry and upset; we had certainly come a long way from our days together in Ponty. I don't know why he treated me with such contempt. It might have been his way of getting me back for the Fender bass guitar, still gathering dust in Soho. Whatever the reason, it was petty and mean. Our friendship was all but now over. I paid off the suits in four weekly instalments, but I should have asked for a discount, the sleeves were too short and the pockets too deep to get money out of them.

At that time, Tom's parents Freda and Tom Senior came to Tor Point, not to visit but to stay. Tom also persuaded his sister Sheila and her husband Ken Davies to move in. Tom's parents had lived in Laura Street since the Second World War and had taken a great deal of coaxing to persuade them to leave their friends and neighbours. Tom's father was still a working miner and his camaraderie with his workmates was very strong. He was also used to the slower pace of Valleys life.

But Tom wouldn't take no for an answer and kept going until they finally relented. It was agreed that his parents would move into Tom's old home, nearby in Manygate Lane. Tom moved his sister, Sheila, and her husband Ken into the gatehouse at Tor Point. Tom employed Ken as gardener and odd job man. He was kept pretty busy, having five acres of landscape garden to look after.

Ken Davies was a great guy, affable and easy going. Sheila was a lovely girl too. Ken was a sensitive soul and he wasn't really cut out for Tom's high-powered, grand lifestyle. I used to bump into him regularly around Weybridge and we would catch up on the gossip from back home. He confided in me that Tom wasn't the same brother-in-law he remembered from back in

Ponty. Ken really missed the friendliness of the Valleys, and being able to meet his old pals down the local. Ken and Shelia liked a simpler life and didn't really take to the show business lifestyle of flash mansions and endless parties. Chris Ellis told me that Ken would cry, quite openly to him, about the emptiness he felt inside. He thought the whole of show business was a two-faced rat-race of money- motivated greed. He continued going through the motions but just wanted away from it, and this caused quite a bit of friction with Tom.

Sheila wasn't very happy at Tor Point either, because she hardly ever saw Linda. When they had lived in Ponty, just around the corner from each other, they were inseparable. Now, at Tor Point, they went weeks without seeing each other, despite living yards apart. When Tom was away on tour, Linda would wander around the seventeen room mansion, flower arranging, moving ornaments, a feather duster in one hand and glass of bubbly in the other, playing Tom's hit records over and over. Even when I bumped into Freda and Tom senior in Weybridge they complained that they never saw Linda, she was locked up behind electronic gates, hiding away.

Tom had wanted his father out of the mines, and quite rightly so. Any son would want the same. But it was a different proposition uprooting him from everything that was familiar to him back home in Wales. The only person who thought this was a good idea was Tom. Family members and friends were of a different opinion and tried to dissuade him, but he took no notice. Tom even tried to get his mother-in-law, Vi Trenchard to leave the Valleys and move to be near them. But Vi was having none of it. Her feet were firmly planted in home soil, and that was where she was staying.

Vi's younger daughter, Rosalind, had married Tony Thorne, the owner of the infamous Ford Corsair that Tom had taken without permission. Despite the trouble he had got into at the time, Tom bought the newlyweds a nice detached property in rural Church Village, on the outskirts of Ponty. Tom senior grumbled to Chris Ellis, that that would have done him and Freda quite comfortably, rather than uproot them. They hardly saw him and Linda anyway. Tom was always away gallivanting around the world, and Linda was a recluse. He reckoned they saw more of them both when they were back in Ponty and Tom and Linda would occasionally visit. Ken Davies didn't last at Tor Point very long. By 1974 he had had a gut full of it. Ken and Sheila were increasingly arguing about everything. Ken fell for another woman and he ran off with her. Tom was incensed, furious; he even threatened to pay someone to have poor old Ken 'worked over'.

Quite by accident, the house that Tom had bought for Rosalind and Tony Thorne, I had helped build. Back when we were starting out in Ponty and I was working at the local newspaper, I used to supplement my income with some labouring work. My fellow printer, Colin Donnallan, married the daughter of Fred H. Frey the owner of Ponty's only record shop. Tom and I spent hours in there every Saturday afternoon. With the help of his father-in-law, Colin bought the land in Church Village and decided to build a house there as an investment. Colin employed me to help him build it. During the late 90s, I happened to be passing Church Village and made a detour to see how the house was getting along; it was now part of an extended residential estate. Imagine my surprise when Tony Thorne emerged and called out to me, 'Hey Vern, how's it going?' I had no idea they were living there. Rosalind followed him out to see who he was talking to and they ushered me inside for a cup of tea. Tom could do no wrong in their eyes, having bought them such a lovely house. They pumped me for questions about Tom and The Squires and our rancorous parting. I was quite truthful about his behaviour, and Tony confided in me that he was forever getting into scrapes defending Jones' honour. Ponty was still a small place and it didn't go unnoticed that he was forever cheating on Linda.

I very soon became Harry Pern's favourite lodger at The Magpie. Chris Ellis had moved in and pretty soon Tom and Engelbert were regular visitors, along with the rest of the band. The pub was starting to become a bit of a celebrity hang out, and Harry was over the moon with the bar takings. He started to slip me the odd free pint with a nod and a wink, as a thank you. Then my old mates Mick Avory, the drummer with The Kinks, and Tony Cartwright started calling in regularly with all their mates. Harry took me aside and told me he thought he'd, 'died and gone to heaven'. Musicians are renowned for liking a drink or two and pretty soon his bar take had doubled. I must admit to feeling a bit sad at the time, standing there at the bar with Tom reminded me of the old days back at The White Hart in Ponty, when we were dreaming about stardom and trying to get a break. There had been a lot of water under the bridge since then, and things certainly hadn't flowed in my favour. But Tom was all smiles and mucking in with the rest of us, so I went with the flow.

I remember that when the bell used to ring for last orders, Tom would be in a bit of a panic. He was still tight-fisted and thrifty even then. He'd pipe up that it was so and so's round and to get them in quick as he'd bought an earlier round. He hated being out of pocket. It became a running joke amongst the band and we'd always programme the jukebox, around closing time, to play one of Tom's songs, 'Just Help Yourself', which was released in the autumn of 1968. The irony was completely wasted, as he would just sing along.

Gordon had decided to expand, with two successful acts on the books, Tom and Engelbert, he wanted to branch out. At the beginning of 1968 he latched onto an American singer, the larger-than- life Solomon King. Gordon brought him to the UK and he had a massive hit with, 'She Wears My Ring'. Unfortunately the partnership didn't last very long. Solomon had a quality tenor voice, but lacked a certain amount of sex appeal, and Gordon was disappointed with his next release, 'When We Were Young'. The song flopped and Gordon dropped him like a pancake. Pretty soon he was on the plane back to the States, cursing Gordon for all he was worth. Undeterred, Gordon latched onto Lee Graham, better known as the singer Leapy Lee. Lee had a worldwide hit with 'Little Arrows', which sold over three million copies and was awarded a gold disc.

Gordon, having seen Tom transplant his family from South Wales, decided he would do something similar. Gordon confided in me that he wanted someone from back home who was honest and reliable, but who would take orders without question. Charming, I remember thinking. It was all to end tragically. Gordon settled on his old school friend, Gordon Jones who had originally tipped him off about that new band called, Tommy Scott and The Senators. Gordon Jones was a laid back, unassuming guy with horn-rimmed glasses, who struck me as looking a lot like Roy Orbison. It was a considerable leap for him to uproot his wife and children and make the leap from the Valleys to Shepperton. Naturally he was very reluctant about taking the kids out of school and leaving their home in Tonypandy. But Gordon, as usual, won the day; he had a knack for wearing you down.

Gordon installed the Jones family in the property he had retained after moving to St George's Hill, a detached three bedroom bungalow. He let them live there, but there was a catch. He paid Jones a pittance, telling him he was taxing him at source for rent on the house. Things got so bad that Jones' wife had to take on a part time job, while the kids were in school, to make ends meet. Jones, having burned his bridges by making the move to London under pressure from Gordon, was now at the mercy of his ruthless fellow Welshman. Things did not go well for him, especially after he accidently dented the wing of one of Gordon's sports cars. Gordon went ballistic and demanded he pay for all the repair costs. The family could hardly afford to eat, let alone settle a garage bill for a luxury car.

In 1972 I married Mia, after a four year engagement. I happened to be in The Riverview, a little nightclub in Shepperton, celebrating with a few friends who had been unable to make the wedding due to tour commitments. It was almost three years since The Squires had disbanded. I had been playing in a trio with Leapy Lee and touring Australia whilst Mia continued her career in the UK. Gordon Jones suddenly appeared and came over to chat. He was in high spirits telling me that Mills had an unreleased album on his hands that he was raving about. The album was called, *Band On The Run*, by Wings, Paul McCartney's band. We caught up on old times and he toasted my recent wedding. Sadly it was to be the last time I ever saw him.

Gordon Mills sacked Jones rather unceremoniously a short time later. He was good at that, sacking people, and had a pretty long track record. Although his treatment of Jones and his family was an all time low. Jones had been at Gordon's beck and call travelling the world, watching him lose thousands of dollars gambling in Vegas, and wherever there was a roulette wheel or card game. Gordon had always been addicted to gambling. Jones had become accustomed to being treated with contempt by Gordon, but he had also become used to the thrill and glamour of a first division showbiz life. Suddenly that all came crashing down around his ears. It was a very abrupt and harsh end. Jones tried to struggle on to makes ends meet, but he had been left beggared by his former employer, especially after the family was turfed out of their home. He took up a position with Dyno-Rod, clearing blocked drains, but he was in debt and could barely make ends meet. Tragically, deeply depressed, he attached a hose to the exhaust on his vehicle and ended his life, leaving a distraught wife and children to cope on their own. Gordon Mills didn't even bother to send a wreath to the funeral. It was all a very long way away from the band I had formed in Ponty.

Tom was booked to appear for the second time on the Royal Variety Performance. The band had supported him on the previous occasion, but he felt confident enough to go it alone. But Gordon still booked us to augment the orchestra. It was quite a different scenario to our previous appearance. Now The Squires had to crawl through a tunnel beneath the stage, to change places with the rhythm section of the Jack Parnell Orchestra, before Tom's performance. The show went well and as Tom took his bow before the Queen, we scurried back through the tunnel to the dressing room. Gordon stopped off afterward to tell us we were all off to Germany.

Gordon had organized a tour of Germany with the Ted Heath Orchestra, under the musical direction of Ralph Dollimore, a brilliant pianist. Ralph had a real liking for his food and was rather rotund. He was a true gentleman. The Squires had worked with the Ted Heath Orchestra long enough to know what to expect. The only difference between Ireland and Germany was that they were now knocking back one litre steins of lager as opposed to Guinness. The tour covered the cities of Wiesbaden, Cologne, Hamburg, Berlin and Munich, and was dogged by gremlins. Tom's vocal chords were going haywire and several shows had to be cancelled and the money refunded. At one 12,000 seat venue there was a riot by disappointed fans.

Things didn't get any better. One night I was heading back to the hotel with Bill Parkinson. It was around 2 a.m. in the morning, when suddenly there was the most almighty crash between two speeding cars. It created a huge pile-up. We went over to help the survivors but by then a crowd had gathered and it was bedlam. When we got to Berlin we decided to take the opportunity to visit East Berlin. Arriving at Checkpoint Charlie, I was carrying a Little Richard album I'd bought in a small record shop. The American guards cheerily waved us through, but about halfway across the checkpoint we were collared by a bunch of Russian guards. We were ushered at gunpoint into a drab little room, forced to hand over our passports, and then searched from head to toe. Little Richard was immediately confiscated and tossed into a large bin, never to be seen again.

The Eastern side of the wall was laced with fierce-looking barbed-wire fencing. It seemed impossible for anyone to escape, but desperation works wonders and thousands managed to do just that, although many others suffered a terrible fate. We ventured about a mile from the Checkpoint into East Berlin. It was truly miserable. The city had suffered massive devastation by both Russian and Allied forces during the War. The West had invested and ensured that West Germany had recovered; West Berlin was a gleaming metropolis in comparison to its drab twin. The Russians seemed to have no intention of reconstructing East Berlin, it was quite bizarre. Office workers were in three or four storey buildings, where the top floor was missing, having been demolished under attack during the war. Walls were scarred by machine gun bullets and shrapnel. Wherever you looked, family homes were now down to using the upstairs bedrooms as the roof. It was a real eye opener. Just a couple of blocks away, the 'swinging Sixties' were happening. Everything lacked colour and looked very drab. All the food stores we passed looked practically empty. There was an eerie stillness. We would try to catch people's eyes, but they would hurry away. We couldn't wait to get back to the west, and made our way back to the Checkpoint.

Unfortunately the Russian Guards pulled Bill Parkinson out of the line and frogmarched him away. They tried to wave us on through but naturally we refused to leave our bandmate behind. We were all escorted to join him in another drab little room with paint peeling off the walls. Bill's passport photograph had been taken many years earlier, and showed him with neat, short cropped hair.

The guards sent for a barber who duly arrived and went to work on Bill, until he looked more like his passport photograph. We crossed back over to the west with Bill looking like Yul

Brynner. We knew we shouldn't have laughed, but we couldn't help ourselves, we were in hysterics. Bill was mortified.

On one of the last shows of that fateful tour we performed to an audience of 10,000 screaming fans. The noise was deafening. It's hard to believe today but back then we had no stage monitors feeding back. We couldn't hear Tom's voice or our vocals. We couldn't even hear the instruments, it was an absolute nightmare. We tried our best to belt out the set and at one stage I accidently trod on my guitar lead. The fact that the Fender bass had stopped playing fazed nobody, with all those kids screaming, no-one could hear a damn thing anyway. I remember shoving the jack plug back in and just got a loud crackling, the lead was broken.

I replaced the lead with a spare and carried on playing. Tom left the stage, sweating absolute buckets, the stage lights were blinding and no doubt the heat thrown off by 10,000 screaming fans had taken its toll. Back in The Squires dressing room, after the show, I fixed the broken lead and then changed out of my stage gear. Suddenly, Colin Berlin charged into the room looking for me. Colin was an agent from the Acuff-Rose Agency in London. He had represented Tom and the band from just before 'It's Not Unusual' and continued to do so. He was a bald headed, tubby little man, normally very friendly and easy-going. I saw a completely different side to him that evening. He pointed his chubby little finger at me and waved it under my nose, 'Tom wants to see you in his dressing room now,' he screamed, 'he's furious about that lead crackling!'

I thought he was pulling my leg, and looked to the rest of the band, everyone shook their heads, the noise had been so deafening on stage, no one had heard any crackling lead. I remember saying,

'You're kidding me, right?' But Colin turned puce and said, 'You're in big trouble young man.'

I decided to visit Tom to see what the fuss was about. I followed Colin to Tom's dressing room. Colin's nephew was there and opened the door to us, there were three other characters there I'd never met before. Tom was seated on a plush Regency style, gold-backed chair. He was in his customary white towelling dressing gown, a fat cigar in one hand and a flute of vintage champagne in the other. Something wasn't right, the whole atmosphere was incredibly cold and unnatural. Even though there was a very pretty young woman draped around Tom, he looked waxen faced. Tom, posing on his throne, looked right through me, he didn't even acknowledge my presence.

Suddenly the chorus of agents all piped up, hitting me verbally from all sides. They threw the book at me, going on and on about the crackling lead and how unprofessional it was, apparently I'd let down Tom and the band, it was a travesty and would harm the brand. The ridiculous rant continued *ad nauseum* and all the while I stared at Tom, just letting it wash over me. He had a look of utter disdain on his face, and kept staring through me as his latest conquest kept pawing at him.

Finally the chorus of agents exhausted themselves and fell mute. Throughout it all, I had said nothing, not a word. They waited for my response, there was a pregnant pause, and I smiled wryly at Tom, gave him a little wink, and turned on my heels and left the room. As I was leaving, Tom finally piped up, 'You want to get that fuckin' lead fixed before the next show, Vern.'

Back home in Wales I loved and admired Tom. I believe we had a high level of respect for each other. We were both proud young men, with shared views regarding the world around us.

Both bred in the Valleys, we were the closest of all the band members. We both came from tough backgrounds and strove to better ourselves. But what suddenly crystalized for me, in that dressing room in Germany, was that the Tom I had known, and struggled with on the road to stardom, no longer existed. He had now metamorphosed into someone I no longer knew, or even cared to know. Tom had become a mollycoddled, arrogant prick. He didn't even look like the Tom from back home, thanks to the facial reconstruction and mouthful of pearly-white crowns. Perched on his Regency chair like some king from past times, fawned on by acolytes, he had completely lost the plot. It was very sad.

17. MYRON AND BYRON

Christmas 1968 was upon us. Chris Ellis and I travelled back to Wales to spend time with our friends and families. Mia was also visiting her family in the Swansea Valley, and I spent some time with her. Mia, her seven siblings, parents and friends took me to the local pub, The Ancient Briton. I found myself sat at the old honky-tonk piano, belting out carols and sing-alongs, vamping out the chords and having a fine old time. Whenever I paused to take a break, the lid of the piano would be lined with free pints of Welsh bitter: 'Don't stop playing Vern!'

After the miserable German tour and my run in with Tom and the agents, it felt good to let my hair down and put the incident behind me. The icy manner of Tom and Gordon towards me and the band spoke volumes. None of us felt particularly confident that there would be a band to go back to in the New Year. Gordon would normally brief us about our tour schedule and commitments before leaving London, but he had been reluctant to meet and there were no dates marked in the calendar. I put it out of my mind and thoroughly enjoyed my stay in Wales. Spending time with family and friends helped restore my faith in human nature.

The reason for Tom and Gordon's demeanour quickly became apparent. A cold front from the past had settled in and was causing them sleepless nights. Myron and Byron, our former managers, had started legal action against them. They had been biding their time, observing with keen interest Tom's rise to superstardom, and more importantly his huge earnings. They had dusted down the old contract with Tom and the band and were intent on redress. They wanted their promised cut of profits from Gordon. Gordon had casually told both managers, 'your contract's not worth a light', but we all remembered his promise to them of five percent of Tom's future earnings when and if he ever became famous. Well, famous he now was, and they wanted to collect. Gordon never had any intention of honouring the contract, but Myron and Byron had called on Legal Aid and the case had reached the High Court.

Back in London in the New Year, I was seated in the bar of The Magpie, gazing into my pint, feeling sorry for myself. There had been no news from Gordon about any future tour dates. The bad weather had kept many regulars away from the pub, and that suited me just fine. I was in no mood for conversation. Upstairs, my room had zigzag patterns of ice forming on the inside of the window. I loaded the bed with old blankets and even my overcoat to try to keep warm. I'd found an old hot water bottle and was also putting that to good use. At precisely 10:30 p.m., Derek rang the final bell and placed tea-towels over the beer pumps, to call time. Almost simultaneously the phone started ringing off the hook. Derek answered and passed the receiver across the bar to me. A clearly agitated Chris Ellis on the other end: 'Vernon, I'm up at Tor Point. Tom needs you to do a favour for him. Tom and Gordon want you to testify for them at the Old Bailey tomorrow.' I was taken aback, 'What do you mean, Chris? They want me to take the stand? Testify to what exactly?'

'Well, you were at The Thorn Hotel when you all originally signed with Myron and Byron. I'm not sure what you're meant to say, I'm just the messenger. I'm sure Gordon and Tom will let you know in the morning. Tom's told me to pick you up first thing in the Rolls, is that okay?'

'I guess I'll see you in the morning,' I said and the phone went dead. I spent the night, shivering under the blankets, unable to sleep a wink. I was worried about what Gordon and Tom wanted me to say. This was the bloody Old Bailey and not some local magistrates court. Obviously I didn't want to be put in a position where I wasn't telling the truth: perjury is a serious crime and the penalties are pretty draconian. Chris picked me up in the Rolls around 7 a.m. and we collected Tom from Tor Point. I hoped he would fill me in on what was expected of me, but deprived of his usual morning slumber, Tom stretched out in the back of the Rolls and slept all the way to the front door of the Law Courts. I was having kittens. If I was called to the stand I had no idea what I was going to say.

The Old Bailey is an awesome and intimidating building named after the street on which it is located, which follows the line of the original fortified wall, or 'bailey', of the city of London. The initial location of the courthouse close to the infamous Newgate Prison allowed prisoners to be conveniently brought to the courtroom for trial. On the dome above the court stands a bronze statue of Lady Justice. She holds a sword in her right hand and the scales of justice in her left. Standing in the vast hall inside felt pretty surreal. I was wearing one of Tom's old suits for the occasion, which seemed somehow apt. There were so many familiar faces from Tom's past it was like an episode of *This Is Your Life*. I fully expected Eamonn Andrews to jump out clutching his famous red book.

Myron and Byron were standing in a huddle with their lawyer and were surrounded by a bunch of figures from the

Pontypridd area. Byron caught my eye and came on over, grinning from ear to ear. 'Vernon, how are you? Long time no see.' He put out his hand and I shook it. 'I hope you're keeping well. Sorry about all this, but it's all down to Gordon. No hard feelings.' I was reeling a bit and the back of my neck felt hot. Tom and Gordon were staring daggers at me from across the hall; Gordon looked like he might explode at any moment. I managed to find my tongue and said, 'Yeah no problems Byron, I hope you take them for all they're worth.' That drew an even bigger smile and he clapped me on the shoulder before re-joining his lawyer.

I spotted another familiar figure making his way toward me; it was Bryn 'The Fish' Phillips. Bryn told me he was there to speak on behalf of Tom, and talk about all the early shows with The Senators up and down the Valleys. Gordon wanted him to spell out that Tom and the band were getting nowhere fast until Gordon had shown up and led us to stardom. I was sorry to puncture the bubble, but I told Bryn in no uncertain terms that Tom might have achieved stardom under Gordon's tutelage, but it was a far different story for the rest of the band. He looked a bit confused and asked me if I was appearing on behalf of Myron and Byron. I had to be completely honest and told him I had no bloody idea who I was meant to be appearing on behalf of. Nobody had bothered to tell me anything.

Gordon was huddled in conversation with Tom and the agent, Colin Berlin. Then their bewigged lawyer and his legal team swept in and joined them in conversation. The atmosphere was electric; you could have cut it with a knife. It all turned a bit spaghetti western, with both camps facing off and staring daggers at each other. I was stuck in the middle, which increased the surreal feeling I had. With all the other cases waiting to be heard, the hall soon became an echo of manic conversation. White wigs and black gowns flitted every which way, carrying reams of documents. Gordon kept checking with Tom, the legal team and witnesses they had called to testify, he checked with everyone except me. I managed to intercept him and asked, 'Gordon, hold on a minute. Am I taking the stand today?' Gordon gave me one of his best put-down sneers and said, 'Probably, why is that a problem?' I had just about reached the end of my rope with Gordon Mills and said, 'Well what exactly am I expected to say, "Not guilty your honour"?' I swear I saw steam coming out of his ears. 'Piss off Vernon, I haven't got time for your jokes, just answer their fucking questions, and remember which side your bread's buttered.' Off Gordon scampered back to Tom and that was all the guidance I had. I was none the wiser on what to expect.

A few moments later Tom, Gordon, Myron and Byron filed into court number one, following their respective legal teams. It was like two international rugby teams walking onto the pitch at the Arms Park, ready to do battle. I stood with Bryn 'The Fish' outside the courtroom, with all the other witnesses, waiting to be called to testify. It was a nerve-wracking experience. Bryn, like Gordon, had a habit of biting his nails and I swear a pile of spent nails was gathering around his feet. After about two hours of waiting, Bryn launched into the latest material from his comedy act. Pretty soon he had drawn a crowd and everyone was in hysterics. Suddenly the court doors swung open and it was announced that both parties had agreed to settle the case. I breathed a great sigh of relief; I wouldn't be called to testify after all.

I found out later that Tom's lawyers were so concerned that the case was not going their way that they decided to fold and agree a settlement. Gordon had pressed the lawyers to ensure that there was a news blackout on the amount of the pay-out. He was adamant about their spurious contribution to Tom Jones rise to fame. Gordon insisted they had seen Tom and the band at the Green Fly and realised the potential for making a lot of money. Quite how that differed from him doing the same at the Top Hat I'm not sure. Gordon insisted to the court that Byron and Myron had been given over a year to prove themselves and had failed. On the other hand he had the experience, financial backing, power and influence to take Tom and the band into orbit, as was proved by the success to date. The judge listened and then awarded Myron and Byron £100,000. This was a massive amount in 1969 and they were both over the moon. Tom and Gordon were furious, but they just had to accept the verdict.

Byron stopped on the way out, with a tear in his eye, and shook my hand; he was too choked to say anything. I'd always had a lot of time for Byron. He was a real likeable guy and I was happy for him. Myron on the other hand strode out of court without saying a word to anyone. After the case, despite Gordon's proposed news blackout, it was widely reported that Mr. Michael Eastham, QC for Tom Jones, claimed the singer had agreed to the five percent payment, but only until he had paid off what might be due under the earlier agreement. But Myron and Byron had insisted that the original agreement stated that it was five percent in perpetuity. Mr. Justice Megarry was clearly taken aback, 'are you saying you want five percent of this man until the end of time?' Myron answered, 'Yes'. He could hardly be blamed for trying, but he got nowhere with that particular argument. Still, a £100,000 payout can't be sneezed at.

Byron and Myron even subpoenaed our old guitarist, Mickey Gee, to testify that they owned five percent of Tom for all time. Mickey said at the time, 'They wanted me to come and speak up for them because of a conversation I was supposed to have heard. I didn't want to go, but the court forced me too. But eventually it was all settled and I didn't have to appear. They got £50,000 each, which is a bit rich, as they did nothing for the band. They never got us a hit record. They just booked us into pubs and clubs in the Valleys. I wish every one of The Squires got £50,000. If anyone deserved it, we all did, but we got nothing apart from lots of heartache.'

Leaving the Old Bailey in the chill winter air I remember thinking, I haven't got a pot to piss in and I've been working my nuts off with Tom all these years, like the rest of the band. Myron and Byron had been a minor bump on the road to success and they had just coolly pocketed £50,000 each: it was madness. After the initial shock, Gordon and Tom realised they had got off quite lightly. £100,000 was nothing in respect of what was flowing through the MAM Empire, and it was a mere drop in the ocean in comparison to what they were making themselves. Gordon perked up and organized an impromptu party to celebrate the end of the case. Colin Berlin suggested the Wig and Pen in the Strand, which had a magnificent selection of quality champagne. I walked off towards the nearest tube station. Suddenly a familiar voice piped up, 'Vern, where do you think you're going? Come on, mun.' Tom motioned for me to join them.

The bar in the Wig and Pen certainly lived up to its name, it was crammed full of QCs and barristers enjoying lunch in a very liquid form. Tom stood in the corner with a customary cigar and flute of champagne, chatting with his lawyer. A waitress was doing the rounds topping up everyone's champagne glasses. I've never had a taste for champagne, so I bought myself a pint of bitter from the bar. Tom excused himself and came over to join me. ''Ow's it going, Vern. You alright?' I told him I was fine and pretty glad the case was over and I hadn't been called to testify.

'Yeah, too right the bastards. Myron and Byron? More like Pinky and fuckin' Perky. Look, Chris is going to drive me to the West End for a meal and a piss up. I won't be back 'ome till God knows when. Gordon is going to drive you back to The Magpie, he wants to have a word like. That okay?'

'Okay Tom, no problem. See you later,' I said. It would be much later before I saw him again, years in fact. 'Nice suit,' was his final comment as he re-joined his lawyer, obviously recognizing one of his cast offs.

Gordon fired up his sports car and we exited the underground car park in central London. It reminded of our journey to the south of France. Heading west out of the City, we were passing through Knightsbridge. Gordon lit a cigarette and said, 'Before I drop you off, do you mind stopping off at St George's Hill? I've got a song I want to play you.' I was taken aback as it had been quite a while since he'd asked my opinion on anything. 'Sure Gordon, I'd love to listen.' Gordon scowled and said, 'I want The Squires to record it and bring it out as a single. I'm sure it's going to be a massive hit.' I was confused. 'What do you mean, record it without Tom?' Gordon nodded, 'Yeah, the only thing Tom will be recording over the next few months is his new TV series. Lew Grade has finally given him a spot at Elstree

Studios. I can't have you boys twiddling your thumbs; we'll cut a disc in the meantime.'

It was all news to me, and I asked him if The Squires were to be involved in the new TV series? Gordon hummed and hawed a bit and I should have seen the writing on the wall right then. 'Well Vern, they've booked in a load of musicians who can sight read, it's that kind of show, I went to bat for you boys, but the decision's been made.' Gordon quickly changed the subject and talked up the new song, 'It's by Joe South, he's a great American singer. The song's called, "The Games People Play". It's already a hit in the US, if we cut it quick it'll be top of the charts in no time at all.' I smelt a rat but kept my counsel. We arrived at 'Little Rhondda', and Gordon played me the song in his state of the art recording studio. Joe South wasn't a particularly good singer, but the song seemed great. The opening bars positively zinged to the strains of a sitar. It was the first time I had heard one played on a pop record and the whole sound really blew me away. It was certainly a unique song and I could understand why Gordon would want to release it. But not without Tom on vocal.

Gordon passed me the demo and told me to get busy rehearsing it with the rest of the band.

He had booked us studio space, and told me the clock was ticking, so we needed to move quickly. I thanked him and turned to leave, but he wanted my opinion on another track. Gordon played me a song by a fellow called Ray O'Sullivan. I listened to the track and to be perfectly honest, the tune was okay but I thought the singer sounded like George Formby. Gordon scowled and said, 'He's from Ireland not the North, and the kid's got a future.' Of course, Gordon was right and I was wrong.

Gordon launched him as Gilbert O'Sullivan and went on to make millions of pounds with his compositions. Gordon dressed him up like the kid from the memorable Hovis advert, the one where the boy pushes a bike up a hill, and he went down a storm with the UK audience.

The band agreed that Bill Parkinson should sing the lead on 'The Games People Play'. We all felt that his voice had a certain edginess that complemented the metallic sound of the sitar. The rest of us piped up as backing vocal on the catchy-sounding chorus. Gordon had arranged for us to record the song in Barnes, South London. It was a pretty mediocre studio compared to what we were used to in Soho, and Gordon had booked us in after the midnight curfew to ensure it was cheap. We were all pretty pleased that Gordon had turned up to oversee the recording. However, he seemed completely disinterested in events, and didn't contribute at all. At one stage he pulled a pornographic magazine out of the sound engineer's briefcase, put his feet up on the consul and leafed through it for the duration of the recording. He seemed oblivious to what was going on in the studio. It was bizarre. Normally he was very hands-on for all our recordings. He just seemed to be going through the motions. As soon as the session was over, he picked up the tapes and made a hasty exit.

A few days later I nipped out of The Magpie to pick up the morning newspaper. I was leafing through it on my way back when suddenly my attention was caught by a glaring headline: TOM JONES AND THE SQUIRES IN AMICABLE SPLIT. My legs turned to jelly, I was in utter shock. It was the first I had heard of a split, amicable or not. The report contained a release from Tom's management that went onto explain, 'The Squires have been with Tom right from the start but there are reasons they now have to amicably split. Tom will be spending most of the year making his new television series, any future tours will be with the Ted Heath Orchestra. The Squires, have for some time, wanted to branch out on their own, and will soon be releasing a new single.'

Melody Maker and *New Musical Express* ran the same story. It was a huge shock. The band was stunned, especially as Gordon and Tom hadn't even had the courtesy to talk to us beforehand. Now everything made perfect sense. Gordon and Tom had obviously discussed getting rid of the band prior to the court case to limit any further liabilities. Gordon's proposed new recording had all been a sham, so he could point to it as being The Squires breaking out alone and splitting with Tom. It was very cunning and just what you'd expect from Gordon Mills. I don't know why I was surprised: the writing had been on the wall for quite some time. Still, it's a shock when you're hit with a juggernaut like that. We didn't know at the time, but a new employment law had just been introduced stopping an employer sacking staff summarily. Gordon had circumnavigated that by getting shot of us before the law was fully introduced, and he also had the Barnes recordings to point to as us deciding to leave Tom's employ. We should have taken a leaf out of Myron and Byron's book and started legal proceedings, but we were all just so tired and demoralized after the years of ill treatment at the hands of Gordon and Tom. In some ways it was a mercy to be shot of them both.

Lucy Ellis and Bryony Sutherland described the split in their biography, *Tom Jones, Close Up*, as 'Gordon creating the perfect scenario for dismissing The Squires. In offering them the opportunity of fame in their own right, he effectively separated them from Tom, while at the same time he determined to half-heartedly promote their record thus ensuring failure. Lack of sales could then be used as a legitimate excuse to let The Squires go. As Gordon had insisted that the group did not have written contracts he was able to sack them without so much as a week's wages, confident they had no legal grounds on which to sue for compensation. Chris Slade just about summed it all up when he said, "Gordon was a crafty sod, it was all oh, sorry fellas, you've failed, so you're out, bye bye. It was that sort of scenario".'

I never knew what happened to our version of 'The Games People Play'. I'm not sure it was even released. If it was there was zero promotion. To add to our disappointment Joe South later released the song in the UK and it shot straight to number 10 in the chart. The Squires insisted on trying to get hold of Tom for a meeting, but I told them to forget it because this was down to him as much as it was to Gordon. They persisted but got nowhere; he had gone to ground and refused to return phone calls. The final insult was when our band van was reclaimed by MAM. It was battered beyond belief after touring the UK incessantly for years and being regularly attacked by adoring Tom Jones fans. In all likelihood it probably wasn't worth its weight in scrap. But Gordon insisted it be reclaimed.

The band called an emergency meeting to discuss the future. We decided to go on but our hearts weren't really in it. We enlisted a new singer, Mike Stephens. The Cardiff-born soul singer had recently moved to London. It didn't really work out. Mike was never on time, we'd call for him at his flat and he'd be in the bath, or shaving, or eating, which made us late for gigs, and didn't go down well. We had a talk with him, but no change, it was like dealing with a tortoise. One night we caught a gig at

Ronnie Scott's Jazz Club, but by the time we had coaxed Mike into the van and raced across town, it was too late. Needless to say we weren't booked again. Disenchanted, we decided to call it a day and went our separate ways. I was really depressed; I didn't know what to do with myself.

The shabby treatment we received still hurts. It was premeditated, vindictive and downright unnecessary. How difficult would it have been for Tom and Gordon to sit down with us and just say, 'look guys we're moving in a different direction and your faces don't fit any more, no hard feelings, huh?' We could have lived with that and at least parted amicably. After all, we still felt that old Valleys bond. That's where we were all bred, and we lived by that code, or so I thought. Now Tom had renounced that history, and didn't even have the Welsh grit to face us man to man. He had delegated all the unpleasantness, and hidden from us. I feel an unbridled shame for Tom Jones. I feel even more shame for Tommy Woodward. This was a pathetic and sordid end to an enduring friendship, from the Valleys to the pinnacles of superstardom. Without The Senators there would be no Tom Jones, Tommy Woodward might still be plying his trade in the pubs and clubs of the Valleys for pocket money, wondering what might have been.

I was in a very dark corner. Luckily the pianist, Ralph Dollimore threw me a lifeline. Ralph was contracted to run the Ted Heath Orchestra, and approached me, Chris Slade and Bill Parkinson about becoming their rhythm section. We had fitted in well with them over the years, when they'd been hired to support Tom, so it was an easy decision to make. The Orchestra offered us £100 a week, which was a great deal more than we had earned with Gordon and Tom. Pretty soon we were boarding a plane for Germany. The Orchestra had been booked for a month-long tour. It was a great opportunity and we were very grateful to Ralph; it certainly kept the wolf from the door for a while.

Back in the UK after the tour, the Orchestra didn't have any further commitments. I stood in for a few local musicians, gigging in and around London. I also found employment driving a lorry, delivering parcels, furniture and bric-a-brac in the Home Counties. But it was spasmodic and insecure work. Then out of the blue, Colin Berlin got in contact. He was now working directly for the MAM Agency. Colin asked if The Squires were available for a special gig. I was about to inform him that the band had split, but he must have noted my hesitation because he quickly offered us £100 each for one night's work. The gig was for the investiture of Charles, Prince of Wales.

We were to play at a stately home near the ceremony in Caernarfon, where the royal family would entertain visiting dignitaries. It seemed too good an opportunity to miss, I told Colin I'd contact the rest of the band and get right back to him.

Unfortunately, Bill Parkinson and Chris Slade had prior commitments. Undeterred, I rustled up a really good local band I'd played with before. We quickly put a set together and the day of the investiture was upon us in no time at all. The historic ceremony was directed by the Constable of Caernarfon Castle, Lord Snowdon. The Queen invested the Prince with the insignia of his Principality and the Earldom of Chester: a sword, coronet, mantle, gold ring and gold rod. After the ceremony the Prince, along with the Queen and the rest of the Royal Family, travelled through the crowded streets to loud cheers from the people of Wales and the many international visitors. There was huge security around the town: soldiers, police and plain-clothed officers. Suddenly there was an explosion. Welsh Nationalist extremists had detonated a bomb. They were protesting at the crowning of an Englishman as Prince of Wales. It caused a stir, but the explosion was a good half a mile away, and no-one was injured.

After the ceremony we were given directions to the stately manor, and set off to unload the equipment and do a sound check. We were met by a butler who directed us to the back of the premises where a gigantic marquee had been erected for the occasion. It was so large it made Billy Smart's Circus big top look like a scout tent. I started to get butterflies when I noticed the huge stage inside. It needed to be big, the Ray McVay Orchestra were going through their sound check and they were a very big band. They had left a place for us on the right wing of the stage and we quickly set up. Looking out from the stage you couldn't help but be impressed. There was row upon row of tables resplendent with silver dinner services, bone-china crockery, cut glass crystal, champagne buckets and amazing floral decorations. A space had been left in front of the stage for dancing. We were all glad we had worn our suits; I had on one of Tom's for the occasion.

The dignitaries began to arrive and the Ray McVay Orchestra performed their set admirably. Our audience was a mass of penguin-suited gentry and elite, accompanied by ball-gowned companions, dripping with jewellery. There must have been fifteen courses of food, and nobody had the inclination or stamina to dance when the orchestra played. Toward the end they clocked on to the mood and laid off the foxtrots for something a bit slower, and one or two couples duly obliged with a circuit of the dance floor. I remember thinking at the time it was going to be a tough old audience, and I was proved right.

We kicked off with 'Resurrection Shuffle' but got nowhere fast, nobody took to the floor and we drew a lot of open mouthed stares. The band continued to up the tempo but seemed to be on a hiding to nothing. Changing tack we tried a few ballads, but everyone remained rooted to their plush seats. There was simply no response from the audience at all, which was very discouraging. We changed tack again and tried a soul number, 'Dancing in the Street'. Miraculously it seemed to work. Suddenly the entire audience was on their feet and clapping like hell. This was followed by loud cheering. At last, I thought, we've cracked it!

I was to be disappointed. The loud cheers weren't directed at us at all. A bunch of latecomers had sauntered into the marquee. It was the entire front bench of the Conservative Party, led by the Prime Minister, Edward Heath. I had to crack a smile because as Ted Heath led his cabinet and their wives across the deserted dance floor he broke into dance and started performing The Twist, showing the audience the appropriate response to 'Dancing in the Street'. Hats off to Ted, within a matter of seconds the marquee had erupted and the dance floor was packed with gyrating bodies. Pretty soon some other latecomers arrived and joined in the dancing: Princess Margaret and her husband Lord Snowdon, Princess Anne and her brother Prince Andrew. Perched up on the stage watching everyone let their hair down was pretty bizarre.

I remember phoning Colin Berlin afterwards to report on the gig. Colin told me that Tom had originally been booked to appear, but due to other work commitments he couldn't make it. Rather than lose the booking fee he had suggested The Squires play the spot. Gordon had been against it at first, but relented when he saw the size of the booking fee. Almost entirely to form, it took a few weeks to be paid for the event. Colin called and asked me to pop into MAM's accounts department in Bond Street to pick up the £400 in petty cash. I spotted in the accountants' ledger, as she was counting out the money, that MAM had pocketed a cool £4000 for the gig. As usual they paid us peanuts.

It had been a great final gig for The Squires, a real high. The venue put us up for the evening and when I woke the next morning I thought it was a fitting end. As I drove back to London, I decided to take the scenic route, travelling through the magnificent mountains of North Wales via Mount Snowdon, and down to the Black Mountains. That's when it all finally hit home, the rollercoaster of the previous years, the highs and the lows, the constant battles with Gordon and Tom. I found my peace, it was the closing of a chapter in my life, and I finally put The Squires to bed, and decided on a new direction.

18. SALAD DAYS

I sat on the edge of my bed in The Magpie, staring across the Thames and toward distant St George's Hill. With no band, no money and nothing on the horizon I pondered my next move. Tom had embarked on a six-month world tour. I had been surprised to receive a phone call from Chris Slade. Gordon had approached him to join the tour. Naturally, after the unpleasantness of The Squires' demise, he had reservations. Chris had phoned ex-band members to ask our opinion. We all gave our blessing and wished him the best, though with the natural proviso of 'watch your back!'. Chris took up the offer and joined Tom's new band for the tour.

Big Jim Sullivan had replaced Bill Parkinson as guitarist and the ex-Shadows bassist, John Rostill took my spot. Big Jim was one of the most sought-after guitarists throughout the 1960s and 1970s, and together with Richie Blackmore and Pete Townshend, persuaded Jim Marshall to make his now famous amplifiers. He toured with Tom for five years and eventually left to set up his own label, Retreat Records. Both Chris and John Rostill left Tom and Gordon's employ a good deal sooner than expected and in very different circumstances, one tragically. John Rostill was found dead in 1973, electrocuted by a guitar that was believed to be improperly grounded. It was a tragic loss, John was way ahead of his time and used to include double-stopping in his technique. He also played bass finger-style, rather than use a plectrum which was very unusual at the time.

Chris Slade soon found that Gordon hadn't changed. He was

shocked when Derek Watkins, Tom's leading trumpeter, inadvertently let slip that Gordon was paying him £1000 a week for the tour. Chris was getting paid a fraction of that, but what really made his blood boil was the fact that this was more than four times the combined weekly wages The Squires had received. Chris confronted Tom about this unfairness. He pointed out that the new musicians had been with him less than eight weeks, whilst he had been with Tom for eight years, through thick and thin. Tom rolled out his stock, 'Go and see Gordon, it's got nothing to do with me.' Chris did just that and was told to take it or leave it. Chris left it, after telling Gordon, in no uncertain terms, exactly what he thought of him. He wasn't out of work for very long, he joined Manfred Mann's Earthband, which became a platform for even greater things.

With the summer now drawing to a close, the other Chris, Chris Ellis, returned to The Magpie after working on the world tour. Chris had been kept on, after we were unceremoniously dumped, to work as Tom's road manager and fixer. We caught up and Chris told me he was moving out. He and his Swedish girlfriend, Eva, had decided to move in together. They rented a top-floor flat nearby in Ashford. Around the same time Mia moved out of her uncle's house in North London and we decided to live together too. Harry Pern, owned a listed Georgian mansion nearby, 'Orchard House', in addition to The Magpie, which he had converted into five flats.

We rented the top floor flat of the impressive three-storey building. It was a handsome property with a massive walled garden. About the only furniture we owned when we moved in was a bed, a table and two chairs. But we were deliriously happy. When we had visitors, they had to make do and sit on empty beer crates, courtesy of The Magpie.

Mia had been disgusted by our treatment by Gordon's MAM Empire, and now that the Acuff-Rose Agency had been bought out and subsumed by MAM, she wanted out. She instructed Colin Berlin to terminate her contract and inform MAM she would find representation elsewhere. Our situation gradually improved with me picking up local gigs playing bass, and Mia securing regular gigs in workingmen's clubs in the area. We took each day as it came, and weren't responsible for anyone other than ourselves. We were young and carefree, and just got on with life.

The first winter in the flat wasn't so carefree. Tony Cartwright called and couldn't get over just how cold the flat was. Tony had come a long way since Tonbridge Road and his days of managing Freddie Lennon. He was now a recognized and reasonably successful manager of some fine up-and-coming talent. When he called we were huddled around the ancient gas fire to keep warm. Having once been a grand house the lounge and two bedrooms were very spacious but difficult to heat. In honour of our guest we lit the three gas rings on the stove and kept the oven door open to create a little more heat. Tony thought it was hysterical and with typical Liverpool humour put the word around that poor Vernon and Mia were sitting around a 'polo mint' to keep warm.

Tony was a great friend and contacted me a few weeks later. The singer Leapy Lee was enjoying huge popularity on the back of the success of 'Little Arrows', and was looking for a new bass player for his band. Tony told me he was offering £50 a week, which was £10 more than I'd ever got with The Squires. Even better, all the scheduled gigs were around London and the Home

Counties, which meant being able to get back to Mia after each gig. I leapt at the offer. The job was a godsend and Leapy was a very generous person. It was a pleasure to work with him. My new band mates were a cracking bunch of lads and I really took to them. Pete Kircher, on drums, had formerly been with the band Honeybus, who had enjoyed a hit single with 'I Can't Let Maggie Go'. They were the comedian Kenny Everett's favourite band and he was devastated when they split. Mick McNeil was our guitarist and had previously played with the Irish balladeer Val Doonican. This was just the tonic I needed after the debacle with Mills and Jones.

It was at that time, in 1972, that Mia and I decided to 'tie the knot'. Leapy and his wife Mary were our witnesses at Ashford Registry Office. The guests came back to the flat for a lavish buffet and pretty soon we all staggered across the road to The Magpie for a knees-up. Not long after the wedding Mia became part of an established cabaret act working in and around London. They were very popular and were offered a season playing in the Bahamas. Things were looking up for Leapy and the band as well. We were offered a summer tour of Australia and jumped at it. Returning to London after a successful tour I hopped onto the next available plane and joined Mia in the Bahamas.

While I was away Leapy was involved in a serious incident that resulted in a three year prison sentence. The afternoon Leapy arrived home from the Australian tour, jet-lagged after the forty-eight hour flight, he went back to his spectacular house in Sunningdale to get some rest. The manor was a grand residence in two acres of landscaped gardens. It was painted bright pink, typical of Leapy's colourful character. The actress

Diana Dors lived nearby and Leapy had become very friendly with her family. Dors was the English equivalent of the 'blonde bombshells' of Hollywood, and was regularly described as a home-grown Marilyn Monroe. Her film career was on the wane at the time, but she was still hugely successful through cabaret work and regular 'celebrity exposé' tabloid headlines, mostly in Rupert Murdoch's *News of the World*. Dors was renowned for throwing adult group parties and the Archbishop of Canterbury once famously denounced her as a 'wayward hussy'. Her parties were notorious, being heavily publicized in the press, and she ensured that a number of celebrities and young starlets were brought into close contact, with ample supplies of alcohol and drugs, against a background of soft and hard core porn films. As her former lover and party attendee, Bob Monkhouse, famously commented, 'the awkward part about an orgy is that afterwards you're not sure who to thank.'

Diana Dors' husband, Alan Lake, was there to meet Leapy at Sunningdale that afternoon. Alan persuaded Leapy to join him for a drink at the local pub, and refused to take no for an answer. Lake had his baby son with him, so Leapy assumed it would be a quick drink and relented. They went to Sunningdale's the Red Lion, and Leapy told him all about the Australian tour. They arranged to meet in the pub the following evening. They were ordering their first drinks when the landlord demanded payment for a Babycham that had been ordered for Lake's baby son the previous day. Both Alan and Leapy denied any knowledge of ordering the Babycham and said it must have been one of the customers, having a laugh.

Events quickly became heated and tempers boiled. The landlord got physical and it degenerated into a punch up with some of the customers joining the fray. Leapy was fairly short and quite slightly built, and in no time found himself on the floor. The landlord had armed himself with a golf club and now stood above Leapy, raining blows on him. Alan Lake thrust a pen-knife into Leapy's hand and the Landlord received a two-inch cut to his forearm. There was bedlam and the police were called.

When I returned from the Bahamas the case had just gone to court. Leapy was sentenced to three years for stabbing and Alan Lake was sentenced to eighteen months. On his release, Diana Dors presented Alan with a mare named Sapphire. He was a keen horseman, but he was unseated when the horse ran into a bough, which resulted in him breaking his back. Alan eventually recovered, but he had begun drinking heavily. Leapy's career was in tatters. The Judge had wanted to set an example and he had certainly accomplished that. Leapy's marriage broke down when he was in prison and his reputation was shot. There were no further bookings for the band.

Leapy worked in the prison hospital wing and with good behaviour was eventually transferred to La Verne Open Prison, on the South Coast. With further exemplary behaviour he served half his sentence and was released. He found it impossible to get work and emigrated to Majorca, where he eventually remarried and began a family.

Tragically, Alan Lake eventually committed suicide after the death of Diana Dors, who had succumbed to cancer. Grief stricken, he burned Dors's clothes, took their son to the railway station and put him on a train to stay with relatives, then returned to their Sunningdale home and killed himself.

I talked over our options with Mia and we decided to form

our own duo act, Two's Company. We played a few local gigs and got a warm reception. Pretty soon we were approached by the Wally Dent Agency, and agreed to representation. It was a good fit and before very long we were appearing on the television programmes, *Rising Stars* and *New Faces*. It certainly helped with our bookings and everything was going well. We then started to pick up slots supporting household names like Jim Davidson, Frankie Vaughan, Tom O'Connor, Freddie Starr and a host of other familiar faces. Then Mia became pregnant and we took a break until our lovely daughter Tara was born.

Tony Cartwright phoned to congratulate us on the news of Tara's impending birth. Tony asked what I was up to and I truthfully told him I was considering my options. He said he might have just the thing to keep me occupied. Tony was managing the handsome and fair-haired singer, Malcolm Roberts. Malcolm had arrived in the music industry through a previous career as an actor; he had appeared briefly in the ITV soap, *Coronation Street*. It was while appearing in *West Side Story* in London that he got his first big break. Lionel Bart spotted him and cast him in a number of West End productions, the most notable of which was *Maggie May* at the Adelphi. Malcolm had gone onto enjoy a number of hit singles: 'Time Alone Will Tell', 'May I Have the Next Dream With You' and the Les Reed and Barry Mason penned 'Love is All'. At that time Malcolm had broken big in South America where he was idolized. Tony was quick to capitalize and was putting together a band to tour South America; we quickly agreed terms and I was on board.

The very next thing I knew I had been summoned to Malcolm's magnificent house near Guildford for rehearsals with the rest of the band, prior to embarking on the South American tour. I was working with the legendary guitarist, Mick Green, a founding member of Johnny Kidd and the Pirates. They had enjoyed numerous hit songs, the best-known being 'Shakin All Over' and 'Please Don't Touch', but their influence on future musicians was profound. Their stage act was very theatrical, and anticipated and influenced rockers of the 1970s like Alice Cooper and Marc Bolan, and helped usher in the whole glam rock phenomenon. Led Zeppelin, in their early days, covered all of their songs. It was great to meet Mick, it felt like we were old mates, and we had a mutual friend in keyboard player Vic Cooper. The drummer, Pete Wolfe, had just completed work on the famous West End musical, *Jesus Christ, Superstar*.

We set off for Buenos Aires in the spring of 1974 for the first leg of the tour. Tony Cartwright accompanied us and we arrived just as winter was approaching. We were whisked into the city centre by two black limousines. It was Malcolm's fifth tour and he turned to me quite puzzled: there were no billboards or posters announcing the tour. Apparently this was very unusual. The whole city seemed to be wall-papered with posters of Juan Domingo Peron, President of the Republic.

Peron had recently returned from an eighteen-year exile in Spain. On the day of his homecoming, a crowd of left-wing supporters had gathered at the airport in welcome. Camouflaged snipers opened fire on the crowd killing at least thirteen people and injuring over three hundred and sixty. The Ezeiza massacre, as it became known, precipitated an armed conflict between left and right wing factions, and soon death squads were targeting opposition parties. The 'dirty war' was in full swing and we had landed right in the middle of it.

We booked in at the American-owned Hilton Hotel and I was

unpacking my suitcase when an enormous explosion rattled the windows. I quickly went out onto the balcony and the stench of acrid smoke stung my nostrils. Below, near the entrance to the hotel, were the charred and twisted remains of a flat-bed truck. A bomb had been detonated, injuring a number of pedestrians. The hotel staff informed us anti-Peron terrorists were to blame. They also said that the bomb was probably to mark the anniversary of the blowing up of the Hilton's thirteenth floor a year earlier, which was still empty. We didn't sleep easy: the tour party was all booked into the fourteenth floor, just above. Apparently Peron had the full backing of the United States, so American interests were prime targets, and the Hilton was a favourite. We all just wanted to get this leg of the tour over as quickly as we could.

Tony Cartwright arranged for two armed bodyguards to follow us everywhere. They became part of the family for the whole six weeks we were in Argentina, accompanying us to every gig, TV show, radio show and press interview. On one memorable occasion we passed Peron in our car, being driven the other way in his armoured limousine flanked by a cavalcade of police motorcycle riders. We were advised not to venture too far from the hotel, and absolutely never to get into a taxi with a red and black ribbon tied to its aerial. We might be mistaken for Americans and never be seen again. We made sure we only ever flagged down a taxi with a blue and yellow ribbon from then on.

One afternoon, taking a rare break from the hectic tour schedule, we were in a bar close to the Hilton. Suddenly there was the unmistakable sound of heavy gun fire outside. We tentatively looked out of the bar and witnessed five masked terrorists dragging drivers from their vehicles and shooting up their cars.

It happened at the height of rush hour traffic, and was replicated throughout the city, causing traffic grid lock. By the time we headed for the airport we were a bunch of quivering wrecks. I arrived back in London with perfect timing for the birth of my daughter, and was so glad to be still in one piece!

In 1975 Mia and I began performing as a duo again, Vernon and Maya. We made our act a mixture of mainstream, country, soul and rock 'n' roll, and were soon booked solid for the year. The Wally Dent Agency was over the moon as they were turning down bookings because we were so busy. It was incredibly liberating not to rely on another artiste for our income; it was a very happy time. Since being sacked by Gordon and Tom my finances had blossomed, and I was a world away from living hand to mouth. I was very thankful and my faith in human nature was all but restored.

Pretty soon a local venue asked us if we would become the resident band around our touring commitments. It was regular money and close to home, so we couldn't refuse. The John O Gaunt in Walton-on-Thames sits between Sunbury and Weybridge. Our residency became very much a family affair and we built up a fanatical following. Our friends from show business regularly dropped by, and joined in the odd spot. I don't think I've ever been happier, it was a great period in our lives. One particular Thursday during mid-summer we had returned from another tour and were due to play our regular gig at The John O Gaunt. I pulled into the pub to park in our reserved spot and was pretty shocked to see a white Rolls Royce hogging our parking space. I remember commenting to Mia, 'Maybe it's a record producer?' The Wally Dent Agency had recently sent out our latest demo with a view to releasing it. We were both pleasantly surprised and intent on performing a great gig.

We set up on stage and went through a quick sound check. To my surprise Tom Jones waved at me from the back of the room. Tom was accompanied by two stunning blondes, one draped on each arm. His PR, Chris Hutchins, hovered a little behind. My jaw practically hit the floor. Mia noticed and asked what was wrong. I pointed to Tom cheerily waving and smiling from the back of the room; she told me to ignore him. The last time I had seen him was in The Wig and Pen. He had left Gordon to deal with the axing of The Squires, yet here he was as bold as brass. I should have listened to Mia but naturally curiosity got the better of me and I walked through the packed room toward him.

''Ow's it going, Vern? Wanna a pint?'

I was speechless, so he turned to the barman and ordered a pint of bitter. I regained my composure and asked him what brought him to this neck of the woods, 'I'm taking these birds up the West End to make a night of it. I'd ask you to join us like, but you've obviously got a gig on.' It was turning a little weird; I was flummoxed by the whole situation.

''Ow are things? Are you doing alright?'

I managed to find my tongue, 'I'm doing okay Tom, and you?' Tom looked at his two blonde companions and smiled. I was disturbed by his presence and told him how let down I felt by the whole manner of the end of the band. Tom lit a cigar and looked me in the eye, 'Well Vern, you know that was all down to Gordon'. What a brazen cheek, I thought. 'Well Tom, after all we've been through together don't you think it would have been a bit more dignified if you and Gordon had sat down with the band to let us know it was over?' Tom looked uncomfortable and asked Chris Hutchins what time their reservations were arranged up West. I couldn't just leave it there, 'For God's sake Tom, we all had to read about it in the papers.' He was about to say something, but I cut in, 'I know, take it up with Gordon.' I turned on my heel and made my way back to the stage.

Picking up my guitar, I announced the opening number of our set. Normally it would have been a blaster to set the pace for the evening. Instead I chose a song that Tom had originally introduced me to, way back when we spent our Saturday afternoons together in his mother-in-law's front room. I could almost picture Tom dropping the stylus on his Dansette record player. The song was called 'Wolverton Mountain'. It was the hit that launched Claude King's career and was based on a real character, Clifton Clowers, who lived in Arkansas.

'This song should strike a chord with someone tonight,' I announced over the microphone. 'I remember a very long night a long time ago, and an even longer walk home the next morning, covered in pigeon shit. This song kept our spirits up.' Halfway through the song, Tom and his companions passed within feet of the stage without so much as an upward glance, and slipped out of the pub. Shortly afterwards he emigrated to the United States, for tax reasons. It would be another twelve years before our paths would cross again.

Most people remember where they were when someone famous dies in tragic circumstances: President Kennedy, Princess Diana, John Lennon, Elvis. On August 16th 1977 I had nipped out of the flat for a pint in The Phoenix, in Lower Sunbury. At approximately 10 p.m. the radio behind the bar announced the death of Elvis, at Graceland. It came as a complete shock to everyone. The pub's jukebox had been playing away non-stop most of the evening and as a tribute to The King a customer chose an Elvis song. The jukebox packed in, and we couldn't get it started again. The next morning, Mia and I travelled up to the West End for a publicity photo-shoot, organized by the agency. Elvis was on everyone's lips and all the radio stations were playing his records non-stop. Everyone was in shock at his sudden death.

The following year things were going really well and we moved to a semi-detached house in nearby Shepperton. In 1982 we moved upmarket again and bought a lovely property nearby on Old Charlton Road. The day we moved in we had no running water, but thanks to our kindly neighbour we were supplied with bowl upon bowl of fresh water until the problem was fixed. Our kindly neighbour became a great friend; his name was J.G. Ballard.

Jim Ballard was an unassuming gentleman in his early fifties. He told me he had been born in Shanghai in the 1930s and was interned by the Japanese during the war. After his release he came to England and studied medicine at Kings College, Cambridge. He was also a qualified pilot in the Canadian Air Force. It wasn't until sometime later that he told me he was a novelist. Typical modest Jim. I got some of his books and found out he was a *great* novelist. His best-known books are *Crash*, made into a film by David Cronenberg, and the semi-autobiographical *Empire of the Sun*, also made into a film, by Steven Spielberg. I'll never forget the premiere of the movie in 1986, in Leicester Square, attended by the Queen and Prince Phillip. Jim gave us a wave as he was chauffeured away from Shepperton in a black limousine, and we watched him on television, lining up with the stars to shake hands with the Queen. He told me later he was over the moon, but it didn't stop him from publicly refusing the CBE he was offered sometime later. Jim described the honours system as 'a Ruritanian charade that helps prop up our top-heavy monarchy'. He was a real character.

Over the twenty-three years we were neighbours we spent a lot of time in each other's company. Jim is to blame for my writing this memoir. First, he told me to write a novel. He was kind enough to point out I had more than one sitting in my head, waiting to be released. I'll never forget Jim telling me, 'take ideas from all your adventures in show-business, the lows as well as the highs, and create a novel. You can distil the characters from all the many entertainers you have bumped up against.' After I moved home to Wales, we kept in regular contact by letter and phone. I was shocked to receive his letter, in 2007, revealing he had been diagnosed with prostate cancer and given two years to live. Jim was typically philosophical about it all and reckoned that aged seventy-seven, these things were to be expected. He insisted that I go for a PSA blood test as a precaution, something that hadn't occurred to him and which was now too late. The letter upset me and I phoned him immediately. We had a long conversation and it was evident that Jim was calm and philosophical about being struck down, but there was also a raging fire about the situation, an incredible frustration. Sadly, Jim passed away from prostate cancer in 2009. It was a tragic loss, but his influence on popular culture is undiminished and enduring.

A few months after Jim's death I was driving to a gig and happened to catch *The Archive Hour* on BBC Radio 4: the author Will Self was narrating the life and times of J.G. Ballard. I was struck by how well the programme had been put together; it was a fitting tribute to the great man and his novels. The accuracy and poignancy of Will Self's personal narrative was incredibly moving. The following day I was inspired to put pen to paper and wrote a letter to Self explaining just how affected I had been by the programme. I shared some of my wonderful memories of Jim Ballard, his generosity, kindness, wisdom and advice. It was a heartfelt letter and quite unexpectedly Will replied, thanking me and requesting permission to read the letter at a memorial service being held for Jim at Tate Modern in London. I was deeply honoured and humbled to have my tribute read aloud to Jim's family and friends.

We took a break from touring in 1986. Mia wanted to spend more time with our wonderful daughter, Tara. I decided to take up the offer of a six-month summer residency at the Potters Holiday Complex in Great Yarmouth. I shared the bill with an up and coming young comedian, Shane Richie. At the end of July, a fellow entertainer stopped me and asked if I had heard the news? Gordon Mills had died, aged fifty-one. Naturally I was taken aback. I had wished Gordon his comeuppance for many years, but I never wished him dead. Johnny Laff, the comedian, reported that the article said he had been ill for some time. I guessed that it was stomach cancer. Johnny asked me how I knew and I explained that Gordon had always lived on his nerves, and that in turn exacerbated his stomach ulcers. I had seen him throw up on more than one occasion when he was suffering a severe bout of stress. Stress and stomach ulcers are a clear pathway to stomach cancer. I needed some time alone to gather my thoughts and made my excuses to Johnny and left.

Gordon had also thrived on stress, especially when the rewards from enduring it were so high. Since he had begun

310

managing Tom, Engelbert, and later Gilbert O'Sullivan, he had
gambled everything; it was inherent to his make-up as a human
being. It hadn't entirely escaped my notice that over the preced-
ing few years things had begun to unravel for Gordon. He was
not the kind of person to take a setback lying down and, no
doubt would have been raising the stakes to ever greater heights.
Perhaps events had finally taken their toll.

Just prior to his death, Gilbert O'Sullivan had taken Gordon
to the high court. Gordon must have experienced a sense of déjà
vu after his last visit to the Old Bailey with Myron and Byron.
Gilbert was demanding millions of pounds in back pay. The
crux of the case was that Gordon had fraudulently 'fleeced'
Gilbert of all his earnings. Gilbert's lawyers argued that the
singer had been living on just £10 a week pocket money, the
whole time he was topping the charts. I remember thinking, no
change there then. The lawyers claimed that even when Gilbert
had become an international performer Gordon had only paid
him £150 a month. When the shy and diminutive singer eventually took the stand, he reported that whenever he queried his
royalty statements, Gordon would scold him. The revelations
dumbfounded the judge, who summed up that Gilbert was, 'an
honest and sincere young man, the same can't be said of his
manager.'

The court ordered all of Gordon's accounts to be seized and
when they were examined thoroughly it was found that millions
of pounds had disappeared. It was widely reported in the press
that from 1970 to 1978, Gilbert's singer/songwriter royalties had
grossed £14.5 million, but that he had received just £500,000.
The judge awarded him £7 million and ordered Gordon to pay
O'Sullivan's costs. Chris Ellis was in court and reported that

Gordon had been tied in knots by Gilbert's lawyers, something he had done to others for many years. Gordon left the courtroom tail between his legs. He hated losing. His gambling addiction had taken hold and losing the court case had effectively bankrupted him. The judgment blew the finances of MAM apart and it never recovered. Within weeks the offices in Bond Street were closed and MAM was finished.

Gordon was back at square one with only Tom on the books. Engelbert had jumped ship and retained Tony Cartwright as his new manager. Colin Berlin and the rest of the old Acuff-Rose Agency had seen which way the wind was blowing and deserted MAM some time previously. It was a very unceremonious end, much like the way of The Squires' abrupt demise.

Chris Ellis wasn't to last much longer either. He had kept in touch over the years, and we continued to meet up when he was back in London. Chris was Tom's road manager, fixer and did just about everything required to keep Tom happy when touring. Chris was very bitter after being dumped shortly after the O'Sullivan case. He confided in me exactly how it came about. Chris, Tom and his son Mark were staying in a rented farmhouse on the outskirts of Paris. Tom wasn't able to enter the UK, for tax reasons. They had recently arrived from LA for rehearsals in Paris prior to a European tour. Tom had asked Chris to carry on to London to pick up a white Mercedes for his use on the tour. The evening before Chris was due to leave they went on a bit of a pub crawl. Chris said that by the early hours of the morning, Tom was thoroughly depressed; he'd had quite a bit to drink and was very maudlin. Tom wasn't happy about the direction of his career and the fact that he wasn't selling many records. Chris reassured him that things were cyclical and that his time would come around again. Chris left a weepy Tom and flew on to London.

Back in London, Chris was kept pretty busy. He had been tasked by Gordon with getting all the necessary permits and documentation for all musicians who were taking part in the European tour. In his downtime he drove Linda to various shopping engagements. Then the day before the tour began he received a phone call from one of Tom's agents, telling him he wouldn't be needed on the tour after all. Tom's son, Mark, would be filling in for him, due to 'cutbacks'. Chris was gobsmacked and immediately phoned Gordon. They had a massive row, screaming down the phone at each other. Chris asked Gordon why Tom hadn't just told him at the farmhouse in France that his services were no longer required. Gordon told him to get over it and hung up. Chris immediately phoned Linda at Tor Point, who told him it was all news to her. She said that Tom had been talking for some time about taking Mark on, but she never imagined it would be at Chris's expense. Linda asked if there was anything she could do, then she offered to phone Tom in France and demand an explanation. Chris asked Linda, 'Talk to him and tell him to call me, I want to know what's going on. If I'm out I want to hear it from him, not one of his bloody agents. I've been with him too damn long for it to end this way.' Linda promised to call, and Chris waited patiently, but he would have some wait, Tom never ever contacted him again.

19. TOM JONES

Mark Woodward now cared for all his father's needs; he had learnt all about the trade from Gordon Mills. Tom widely reported that after Gordon's death he 'felt lost, completely lost'. Mark settled into Gordon's shoes and took over his father's management. He had a tough job on his hands; Tom's career was at rock bottom. Mark has done an admirable job, and Tom has become an icon. But I would run into Tom again, long before he had regained his place in the firmament, before his son's expert management returned him to superstar status.

One February Friday evening, I was getting myself spruced up, ahead of a solo gig in Kingston-upon-Thames. The phone rang and I was pleasantly surprised to hear a wise-cracking Liverpool accent, it was my old friend Tony Cartwright, 'Bespopo, it's Tony.' For some reason Tony had christened me 'Bespopo' since sharing digs together. 'I've got a message from Tom. He wants to see you. He's pining for you.' Tony was always a joker.

'Yeah, pull the other one, it's got bells on,' I laughed.

'Seriously, I'm going for a curry with Tom tonight in Weybridge. He wants you to come along.' Naturally I was shocked, but also a little curious. But I'd committed to a gig and told Tony that. Tony tried his best to get me to cancel, but I stuck to my guns. 'I just can't, I'm already getting into my coat to head over there. Maybe next time.' Tony could see I wasn't for changing my mind, so we said our goodbyes and arranged to catch up soon. I was baffled by this turn of events. Twelve years had passed since Tom had unexpectedly turned up at my gig in The John O Gaunt. What on earth was he up to, wanting to meet up after all this time? I put it out of my mind and headed for the gig.

The following Monday, Tony called again. 'Hey Bespopo, Tom was really disappointed you couldn't make it. Look, he's playing over at Lakeside tomorrow night and wants you to come along.' I was taken aback. Tony went on, 'Look it's only twenty minutes from Shepperton. Tom's expecting you. He's left instructions at the box office, what have you got to lose? I can't make it, but I'll tell Tom you'll be there, okay.' The line went dead and I had some thinking to do. Part of me didn't want to bother; the ditching of The Squires was still painful even after all these years. But I was curious as to what he had to say. I also thought it might provide the perfect opportunity to find out whatever happened to my song, 'With a Little Luck'.

In 1984 the miners had gone on strike, resulting in soup kitchens up and down the country and families living hand to mouth. The conditions inspired me to write a song, 'With a Little Luck', about riding out the storm. It was a country song focused on a family getting by during bad times. My publisher, Teedes Music, recorded the demo with Mia and I performing the vocals, and sent it out to potential artistes. Gordon Mills had received a copy in LA, and Chris Ellis was with him when he listened to the demo. Chris told me at the time that Gordon was interested in Tom recording it. But I had never heard anything further. Some time after Chris had been sacked he'd popped around for a catch up over a beer or two, and the song came up in conversation. Chris asked if I'd ever made any money out of it and I was a bit confused and asked him what he meant. Chris told me, 'Well, Gordon played the track to Tom and asked him if he knew who was singing it. Tom shrugged his shoulders and Gordon told him it was you. They thought it might be a hit so they recorded it in LA.' This was the first I'd heard about any recording and I contacted my publisher, but they confirmed they'd never heard back from Gordon Mills. It was all very mysterious. I pumped Chris for information on the recording, who told me Gordon had hired some top LA session musicians and Tom had laid down the track. It was missing the strings section and female backing vocals, which he assumed Gordon would have added later. I was interested to find out what had become of the recording, and with Gordon now dead the only person to ask was Tom.

It was raining heavily when I arrived at the plush nightclub in Lakeside. My name was on the door and they had been expecting me, so I was past the waiting queue. I settled myself near the bar, a fair distance away from the stage. I don't mind admitting I was pretty nervous about seeing Tom after all this time. The place wasn't as packed as I had expected. Tom was in a trough at the time, but would soon bounce back as Mark found his touch as a manager. The houselights went down and Tom's band appeared. I didn't recognise a soul; Big Jim Sullivan and Derek Watkins had long departed. The band kicked off and Tom made his entrance. It was the first time I had seen him in the flesh for almost twelve years. Tom's voice was superb as always, and showing no signs of wear and tear, but his once lithe stage movements were a little restricted. Time stands still for no-one and Tom was feeling his age.

I felt a pang of sadness. As I watched the hour-long set my mind wandered back to our time together in Ponty, starting out, and then roughing it in London. The tough times at the 'Calcutta', and all the experiences we had shared right up until success came flooding back. Nothing can take that away from me. It had been an emotional rollercoaster, certainly, but there were plenty of good times to remember. It was too sad for words that it had ended as it did. Tom took his final bow on stage. I was undecided whether to join him in his dressing room. I wasn't sure I could handle it, as I was feeling pretty emotional. Then I caught sight of Jimmy Tarbuck and a whole entourage of people filing backstage to meet Tom. That made my mind up, and I slipped out to the foyer and then home. As I collected my coat the club's PA system crackled into life, 'Can Vernon Hopkins please make his way backstage. Tom Jones is waiting for him.'

A few seconds more and I would have been walked quietly away. Now I found myself heading backstage and knocking on Tom's dressing room door, which was opened by a bodyguard who invited me inside. Tom was standing at the mirror, in his dressing gown and towelling his hair, fresh from a shower. There were about a dozen people milling around, though the only person I recognized was Jimmy Tarbuck. Tom tossed the towel aside and we shook hands. Then completely unexpectedly he embraced me. 'How's it going, alright?' Tom's face gave nothing away and I noticed his diction had become far more refined, perhaps the result of all the interviews he had given over the years. After getting over my initial shock I told him, 'I'm good. I caught the show, you were really good. It felt a little strange watching you perform though, I'm so used to standing behind you on stage.'

Tom smiled, 'Yeah I was thinking that too as it happens.' Tom took me by the shoulder, 'Let's go over to a quiet corner for a chat. Do you want a drink?'

'I'll have vodka if you have it?'

'Vern this isn't a pub, its champagne or nothing. I suppose you heard about Gordon?' I nodded. 'I went to see him at the hospital in LA. He was on his death bed. He looked awful. There were tubes running from his nose and mouth, and his eyes were rolling around. He asked me what his chances were and I told him the doctors had given him a 50/50 chance. You know how Gordon liked to gamble; even though he was full of pain killers he told me the odds weren't good enough. I told him not to worry, if it came to the worst I'd be there for his family. The next day he was gone.'

Tom looked visibly shaken; he was obviously taking Gordon's death very hard. He was clearly still in mourning and wanted to talk about Gordon, and we reminisced for quite some time. The rest of the people in the room were looking a bit restless, so Jimmy Tarbuck wandered over to get Tom to meet and greet everyone. Tom seemed lost in thought; he clearly just wanted to carry on talking and remembering Gordon. Jimmy made a crack about Tom and I having a love affair, which backfired. Tom gave him a rotten look and I really thought he was going to knock him out. Jimmy picked up on the vibe and quickly scampered away. The entourage left a little later, barely acknowledged by Tom.

We had both lost our fathers and the conversation soon turned to commiserating with each other about that. Tom Woodward senior had passed away in October 1981, aged seventy-one. With a lifetime working underground behind him, his lungs had succumbed to all the coal dust he had inhaled over the years. My father, Evan, passed away in 1983, aged eighty-one, after suffering a massive heart attack. Having been so close in Ponty, we knew each other's fathers very well and we keenly felt the loss. We both got a little misty. As he was changing into his suit I told him it had been good to catch up and I'd better head on home. Then I asked him about my song, 'With A Little Luck'. He remembered recording it in LA; 'Gordon wanted me to do something with it, but it got shelved after he became ill.' I nodded and told him I'd like to hear the track, 'Okay I'll try and dig it up when I get back to LA.' I turned to leave and he stopped me, 'I'm playing the Albert Hall tomorrow, why don't you come along?'

The following evening I parked my car near the Albert Hall and made my way to the foyer. I looked around, hoping to see a familiar face, maybe one of Tom's agents or PR guys, and then ran into Barry Clayman, his agent and Mark Woodward. We had not seen each other since 1968 and quickly caught up on all the latest news. Barry told me Tom was in his dressing room getting ready for the show, he told me to grab a seat in the public bar and he'd let him know I'd arrived. I hung around in the bar for ages; Tom had asked me to come along before the show started. About five minutes before curtain, Steve Montgomery, Tom's bodyguard, materialized and led me up to Tom's dressing room. It was an entirely different scenario to the previous evening. I got the distinct impression that Tom wished I wasn't there. In my uneasiness, so did I. Tom was a bit stilted and uncomfortable. I think it was a relief to both of us when he said, 'Oh well, time to go on. See you around, Vern.' The dressing room door opened on cue and the bodyguard led me to my seat in the auditorium. I only watched half the show having seen it the night before, and slipped out wondering what on earth it had been about.

Driving back to Shepperton I had time to think, and the only reason I could imagine for the sudden offering the olive branch was that Tom wanted someone to reminisce with, someone who knew Gordon as well as he did. I had listened patiently to Tom as he rambled about Gordon, and had been happy to share my memories. But I had told Tom that, in my view, Gordon was a vindictive and callous man. Of course I was sorry for his death, but there was no escaping the way he had treated the band. I'm not sure Tom saw things in the same light; Gordon could do no wrong in his eyes. I had expected some sense of atonement from Tom regarding the way we had been treated, but none was forthcoming. He couldn't even bring himself to enquire about the rest of the band, and when I had tried to let him know what everyone else was up to he had seemed disinterested and quickly changed the subject.

About a month later a parcel was delivered with 'Tom Jones Enterprises' in embossed gold lettering above my address. Inside was a cassette tape with a song 'Matador' printed on the A-side and 'With A Little Luck' on the B-side. I believe the A-side was a song from a prospective Broadway musical which had never got off the ground. I don't think the song was ever released, but it was a real kick to hear Tom singing 'With A Little Luck'.

Sometime later, I was getting on with life when I received another unexpected visitor. I was playing a gig in Wimbledon when I recognized a familiar face in the audience – my old band mate Vic Cooper. He had been booked to appear at the same venue the following week. It had been over twenty years since I'd last seen him, heading to Hollywood. It was a pleasure to catch up, and he filled me in on the last two decades. Vic had

VERNON & MAYA

ALL ENQUIRIES
Wally Dent Entertainments.
121a Woodlands Avenue.
West Byfleet. Surrey
Tel BYFLEET 47885 & 51444

Publicity photo for Vernon and Maya, for the Wally Dent Entertainment Agency.

Top. On tour in Australia with Leapy Lee, visiting Captain Cook's house in Botany Bay, 1972.

Bottom. And in Majorca, my daughter Tara, her husband Richard, and the grandchildren: Liberty, Bradley and Brittany.

Publicity photo, mid 1980s, for the Wally Dent Entertainment Agency.

Freddie Lennon, Tony's first client spruced up for the release of his record.

With my old friend Tony Cartwright, manager to the stars.

Top. Rockin' it up in Puerto Banus in Spain with Vic Cooper, for a summer season in Joy's Bar.

Bottom. With my father, a talented musician who bought me my first guitar. He died, aged 81, a few months after this was taken in 1983.

Bryn 'The Fish' Phillips.

Singer Johnny Bennett, who persuaded Gordon Mills to check out Tommy Scott and The Senators.

Top. With Iris Williams at the launch of her album, *Catch My Dreams*, which includes my 'Travelling Through The Valleys', sung beautifully by this legend.

Bottom. With Alex Parry, my doppelganger in *Tom: The Musical*.

Future album cover.

lived the LA high life. Unfortunately his movie had bombed at the box office. It had been released in 1970 and the plot centred on a group of musicians who encountered aliens from outer space. A sound track had been released to accompany the movie, but that didn't do a lot better. Vic had naturally been disappointed but he had still accrued a tidy little nest egg. He even showed me a parting gift from the legendary movie producer, Harry Saltzman; it was a three thousand pound gold watch with the inscription, 'Fine Cockney Role', engraved on the back.

Vic and his girlfriend had moved back to the UK, but were increasingly spending most of their time in Spain. He had steady bookings along the Costa del Sol and the upmarket resort, Puerto Banus, which was frequented by all the stars. He mentioned that there was lucrative work in the Swiss Alps and asked if I would I be interested in performing with him as a duo. In 1990 we found ourselves practicing yodelling and skiing the slopes of a village called Chateau D'oex. We were booked into a sumptuous hotel as the resident band, with free à la carte, free drinks and a black London taxi, with dodgy brakes, ferrying us to our free skiing lessons.

'Vic and Vernon', as we were billed, belted out a steady stream of rock 'n' roll to the affluent skiing fraternity throughout the winter season. Vic was a Jerry Lee fanatic, so that formed the bedrock of the set along with Elvis, Little Richard, Chuck Berry and the Everly Brothers. Vic had been correct about it being a lucrative gig, we each got £600 a week and didn't have to spend a penny as everything was complimentary. After the season was over I returned with Vic to Spain and we were soon booked solid in Puerto Banus, along the 'Golden Mile'. It was a regular celebrity hang out at that time and we kept running into a lot of old and new celebrity acquaintances: Rod Stewart, Engelbert Humperdinck, Peter Stringfellow, Frank Bruno, Des O'Connor, the list was endless. You never knew who you were going to bump into in Joy's Bar.

Things were going so well that Vic and I discussed reviving The Squires; there seemed to be a lot of interest. We contacted Chris Slade to enquire if he would be up for re-forming the band. Chris's career had soared since his parting with Tom. His cv was amazing, it looked like a Who's Who of top rock bands: Manfred Mann, Uriah Heep, Led Zeppelin, Pink Floyd, AC/DC. Sadly all the years of touring with those bands had had a strain on his marriage. Chris and Lynne had divorced, though they remained the best of friends. Chris still lives in LA. His two children, Callum and Cerys are both based in there, and Callum has followed his father's 'foot pedal', becoming a great drummer. Cerys works for a record company. At the end of the 90s Vic and I teamed up with Chris, and The Squires were re-born, with Ricky Purcell, ex-Fortunes lead guitarist. It gave us an opportunity to get together for old times' sake and wallow in nostalgia. It was fun while it lasted but pretty soon Chris had been summoned back to LA to begin another tour with Asia.

In the dawn of the New Millennium, 12th August 2000 brought a very special occasion as I proudly walked my darling daughter Tara down the aisle of St Nicholas Church in Shepperton. I had a tear in my eye as I watched her husband-to-be, Richard Smith, nervously slip the wedding band onto her trembling finger. It was a magical day and two years later Mia and I were overjoyed to become grandparents to Bradley Lewis Smith. In 2004 came our second grandchild, Liberty Beatrice Smith. But before then, after a great deal of consideration, the family decided to re-locate back home to Wales. We settled on the charming village of Pontardulais, on the edge of Gower, near Swansea.

The name Liberty, for our second grandchild, was no accident. Although my daughter had always adored the name, I had also recently composed a battle hymn, 'The Liberation Hymn (Let Truth Be My Guide)'. It was inspired by the First Gulf War, which was mercifully over in two weeks, but I hadn't written it until Saddam Hussein was defeated in 2003. The Treorchy Male Voice Choir recorded it at the Pop Factory in Rhondda, and all proceeds from performance went to charity, in support of the Armed Forces, the wounded and their families. The Hymn was picked up by the BBC and aired regularly on radio. It became very popular with listeners who asked where they could buy it.

Unfortunately we had been unable to persuade a major record company to release it. Then the comedian Jim Davidson rang me one morning. I had worked with Jim for many years supporting him on shows throughout the UK. He had heard 'The Liberation Hymn' and wanted Katherine Jenkins to record it in aid of the Falklands Veterans Foundation. I gave my blessing, and a release was planned for the 25th Anniversary. As the date came closer it was announced the Mark Knopfler of Dire Straits was releasing 'Brothers In Arms' in support of the Foundation. It seemed crazy to release both at the same time so 'Liberation Hymn' was put on hold.

In 2008 I took some time out and flew to Chicago with fellow musician and friend, Roger Simmonds. The plan was to take in America without all the rigours of a touring schedule. We had a great trip which included time in LA and then Vegas. Tom was playing at the M.G.M. at the time. I wrote him a personal note. It was by no means a berating letter, just a note clarifying some of the unresolved issues now raised in this book. I never expected to hear back, and I wasn't disappointed. Tom had never been a letter writer. It had been almost forty years to the day since I had first seen Elvis and his entourage sweep into the Flamingo to watch Tom and The Squires. It was now a very different hotel but I stood in the foyer in exactly the same spot, and Roger took a photograph of me re-enacting the moment. We goofed around and had a fantastic time in Vegas re-visiting old haunts.

I returned to the UK re-invigorated and determined to get 'Liberation Hymn' released in aid of the Armed Forces. I contacted Kevin King, the owner of Optimum Records, who set about helping me, and on 22nd June 2009 'Liberation Hymn' was finally released as a CD, in support of Help For Heroes. It included two other tracks, 'The Brave Bar None' and 'The Bridge to Wales', which Jim Davidson had persuaded me to compose for Katherine Jenkins. Thanks to Kevin King's resolve and hard work the CD flew up the charts. I received many letters of support for the project, the most notable from Prince Charles, and the Prime Minister, Gordon Brown. The Hymn was adopted by our Armed Forces and is regularly played at military events in the UK and abroad. I was surprised and incredibly proud when Cardiff City Football Club adopted it for the opening of their new stadium, and it's now played before every home match. Treorchy Male Voice Choir and I were invited to perform the song at their home match against Newcastle FC in 2013, on the pitch during half time. There were 30,000 fans in the stadium and the match was televised to over 200 countries worldwide, watched by up to a billion viewers. It was a sublime moment: I sang my heart out!

Kevin King was a workaholic, with interests in music publishing, his record company and artiste representation, there didn't seem to be enough hours in the day to cram in all the business he got through. Kevin contacted me in 2010 about a new album he was putting together in support of the three Welsh regiments. It was to be an entirely Welsh affair. The album, *The Brave Bar None*, is a compilation of songs by Welsh artists, including Iris Williams, Rob Allen and many others. Iris performed one of my compositions, 'Travelling Through the Valleys' which made me a very happy man. It was a real honour to see her perform the song supported by the Treorchy Male Voice Choir on her successful 2011 tour. Iris is a legend; she has a successful singing career and has appeared a record fourteen times in the Royal Variety Performance Show.

Things had been going so well that it was a shock to receive some tragic news around that time. On a bitterly cold day in January, I attended the funeral of my dear old friend and band mate, Mickey Gee. Mickey had passed away aged just 64. After acrimoniously leaving The Squires, Mickey had gone on to record with a host of music business luminaries. We had kept in touch and The Squires' demise would inevitably crop up in our conversations. Mickey had taken the way he had been treated by Tom and Gordon very badly. We were all bitter about our treatment, but Mickey more than any of us; he had a very sensitive nature and never really got over it. Micky would curse Tom and Gordon, and really work himself into a rant. He would always end with, 'Why Vern, can you explain it?'. None of us could.

Micky suffered more than his fair share of tragedy. His

brother had committed suicide and his long-term girlfriend had died in a car crash. The poor man was carrying a lot of emotional scars.

When his father passed away he cared for his sick mother, until his own death from emphysema. It was heartbreaking to see him toward the end; he was choking for breath and could barely hold his beloved 1965 Fender Telecaster. He knew he was on the way out and his last words to me were, 'I'll never get to ask Tom why he did it, Vern.' It was very sad.

The funeral service was held at the crematorium in Cardiff. It was very well attended by over three hundred mourners, Mickey had touched a lot of people, and nobody had a bad word to say about him. A lot of fellow musicians came to pay their respects to a great guitar picker. After the service I walked away lost in my own thoughts and saw Mickey's aged wheelchair-bound mother about to be lifted into the limousine and went over to help. I offered my condolences and she turned to me and said weakly, 'Thank you Vernon. He's an evil man.' I was taken aback; for a moment I thought she was referring to her son. Then she looked at me and said, 'Mickey never got over the way Tom treated him. He thought he was a friend.' I watched the limousine pull away.

Over the years there have been many biographies published about Tom Jones. I've willingly agreed to contribute to a great many of them. Biographers have so much information to squeeze into the pages that there has to be a certain conciseness regarding the interviews with people connected with Tom Jones. The biographer has to limit the material used, otherwise the book would run to a mammoth length. A biography is a report, in many respects it is a clinical, logical, unemotional observation.

Unlike a conventional biography these pages hold deep, emotional and heartfelt accounts of exactly what went on and I hope they help set the record straight. Writing this has been an emotional rollercoaster. Much of it I wish I didn't have to write, but it had to be said. Shakespeare was right when he wrote in *The Merchant of Venice*, 'but at the length truth will out.'

The rest of the band had spoken to me for some time to put our side of the story across. After Mickey's death it hit home that none of us are getting any younger. Curiously, my intention to put the record straight was speeded up by the BBC. Twenty-five years after the release of 'The Green, Green Grass of Home' I was contacted by a producer at BBC Wales asking me to be involved in a documentary about the anniversary of the number one hit. The show's director, Suzanne Phillips asked to interview me in Ponty's YMCA, where it had all began. I agreed on the condition I could speak my mind about what had gone on behind the scenes. I'll never forget the shocked look on Suzanne's face when I advised her on what to expect. She assured me she would do her best to see it included in the final programme. I put my faith in her, but understandably I was a little sceptical that the hierarchy at the BBC would allow this.

The day of filming came and the camera rolled. I duly answered all the questions right up to the story about smuggling light ales on stage for Tom's first appearance with The Senators. Then came the question I had been waiting to hear for such a long time: 'Vernon, when Tom parted company with The Squires, the newspapers reported that it was an amicable conclusion, is that correct?' I explained just how far from amicable it had all been. I was heartfelt and emotional, and afterwards Suzanne told me she was interviewing Tom next. When the programme aired a few weeks later, my segment had been cut back considerably but my closing statement was included: 'Tom didn't care for the rest of the boys after the success of "It's Not Unusual". He betrayed us through and through, and when it all fell apart he left us stranded. It was a pathetic end, and it didn't have to end that way.' Immediately after, Tom's segment appeared, in which Suzanne challenged him about the band. Tom coughed into his hand, something he always did when he was nervous or in a tight spot. 'Well no, it was like this, I had to get rid of the band because they couldn't read music. But they understood.'

Understood? Well hardly. The Squires had performed on almost every major stage around the world, thousands of TV appearances, Royal Command performances, the London Palladium. We were good enough to perform in front of Elvis, who had even tried to entice our drummer away. Then quite suddenly, four years after 'It's Not Unusual', we were unceremoniously dumped in a newspaper article.

'They understood,' Tom shrugged into the camera lens.

True, we couldn't read music, but that had never held us back. If our faces didn't fit why not sit down with us and agree to split in a proper manner? Nothing lasts forever, but it was a brutal way for the band to end. The documentary was later released in Sweden and Chris Ellis was glued to the screen. He phoned me after the programme in a huge temper and told me he had thrown his shoe at the screen. We had a laugh about that.

A few months after the documentary, Robin Eggar phoned me. He had seen the documentary and was intrigued by my comments. Robin wanted to interview me for a biography he was writing about Tom. Robin is a prolific author, and I was familiar with his work, so I readily agreed. Over a three hour interview I gave him my insights into the band's years on the road and our dismissal. A short time later he contacted me again and asked if I would accompany him to Sweden to interview Chris Ellis. Chris wanted me to be there for support. It was great to see my old friend and his lovely wife, Eva. Robin interviewed Chris for three days, as he had such a wealth of information having continued to work for Tom long after the band was dismissed. Robin Eggar's biography, *Tom Jones*, was published in 2000 and was the definitive version of his life. It became the subject of an ITV documentary in which I was included, and given the opportunity to clarify things.

Ten years later I received another call from the BBC asking if I would appear in another documentary, *Tom Jones at 70*. It was planned as a celebration of his birthday on 7th June. After the previous programme I thought this was a wind up, and insisted on phoning them back to ensure it really was the BBC. It was and I took part. The producer was aware of the acrimonious split, but nevertheless thought it would be disappointing if I didn't make a contribution. I've always regarded Tom as head and shoulders above any entertainer in popular music, and I've always expressed that opinion so was happy to go along with it. I nearly burst a blood vessel when at the end of the interview I was asked to turn to camera and wish Tom a happy 70th birthday. My phone was ringing hot after that: I didn't half cop some flak from the band. Sadly, the broadcast of the programme was delayed because Stuart Cable, the drummer of the Stereophonics, was tragically found dead on the morning it was due to go out. Transmission was delayed a week, out of respect.

The documentaries and the Robin Eggar interviews had

certainly helped me remember all the early days with Tom, and were really useful in writing this book. The final push that I needed came from BBC Drama. They contacted me about a proposed drama about the formation of The Senators – Tom joining the band and all the events leading up to the success of 'It's Not Unusual'.

They asked for permission for one of their researchers to pay me a visit and record my voice and mannerisms, apparently this would be helpful for the actors they were lining up to play Tom and the band. Naturally I was flattered: who wouldn't like to see themselves immortalized in a film? I remember asking, tongue firmly in cheek, if they could get Clint Eastwood to play me; I'd met him once, long ago and thought he would be perfect. The Drama Department tried to get in touch with the rest of the band and I helped as much as I could. But Dai Cooper had long ago disappeared to South Africa, Mickey had passed away, and Chris Slade had permanently moved back to LA and was always touring. The project fizzled out. So I thought why not write this book, and here it is, the story warts and all. It has been a pleasure and a privilege to work the stage with Tom Jones, from the moment he first joined The Senators at the Ponty YMCA to the Flamingo in Las Vegas and meeting Elvis. Tom drove the band and the band drove Tom, and the audiences responded. It all worked beautifully, it was a beautiful time, and a beautiful bunch of boys from the Valleys in South Wales followed their dreams and against all the odds got noticed. Now who could argue with that?

20. POSTSCRIPT

In December, 2016, my lifelong friend Chris Ellis, loyal, dedicated road manager to Tom Jones and The Squires, sadly passed away in Sweden. Chris was 73 and had suffered a long and painful illness with cancer. Over the many years after the demise of The Squires in 1969, we never lost touch even when he moved to Sweden in the late Seventies, after his own cruel dispatch by Tom Jones. Chris was a great, loveable character, loyal and a defender of the band. He had retired from being a theatre lighting technician in Sweden, and as is sometimes the case when someone retires, particularly after having the challenging working life as Chris had had, being at a loose end may have affected Chris's health and happiness to a degree. In the years of his retirement, he would often ask if I would send him a typical British dish, a Fray Bentos steak and kidney pie, unavailable in Sweden. I think he had started to feel homesick, which his favourite pie may have alleviated, at least for as long as it took to enjoy demolishing the overseas delivery to his Swedish front door.

Aware that my old friend only had weeks left, I emailed Mark Woodward, Tom's son and manager, that Chris hadn't long to live and to let his father know the sad news, in the hope that Tom would at least give Chris a phone call or send a message saying that he was thinking of him. Considering how long he had known his personal road manager, and the prominent role Chris had played, I thought he would want to know. Confidante and close friend would describe their relationship, though Chris was on a wage the average plumber would have sniffed at.

Tom had even been best man at Chris's wedding to his softly-spoken Swedish wife Eva on September 16, 1973. The simple service was held in a tiny chapel in Las Vegas. Tom and Linda also acted as witnesses at the ceremony which had been held at 3 a.m., after Tom had finished his second show at Caesars Palace. Many years later, Chris would repeat an anecdote about the wedding gift Tom presented to the newly-married couple. A case of Dom Perignon champagne, the singer's favourite tipple, which Chris said he then got stuck into at the reception that lasted long after dawn had risen on the Strip. Tom polished off the lot before retiring to his penthouse suite at Caesars.

I could well believe Chris's story. Considering how the gift went AWOL at the reception, that part of the anecdote and the way Chris told it, was quite amusing. However, when the parting of the ways came between the roadie and the singer, there wasn't even a farewell handshake from Tom, though Chris had been with him for fourteen years. Instead, Chris had received a short telephone call from the Jones camp.

I had hoped for a response from Mark to my email, but shouldn't have held my breath. When Mark was born, his father, in his own words, leaving the hospital: 'No one can touch me now'. Why would he think that? A deep sense of insecurity? Listen carefully and you can hear it echoing through these pages. The desperation of backing into a shell at the slightest sign of being fair and square, and not evasive on issues that need addressing can be resolved by the repetitive mantra. "No-one can touch me now."

I sent several more emails to the Jones camp, each including Chris's telephone number and address in Sweden. Apparently another member of The Squires also notified Mark at his home in Maidenhead, but these efforts fell on deaf ears. Chris passed away, and I emailed Mark again, asking them to at least send a message of condolence to his devastated wife Eva. When that failed, I contemplated paying him a visit to give him a piece of my mind. Having fussed little Mark and made him laugh back in Ponty while Tom got himself ready for the evening's gig, it doesn't take much imagination to realise how he now perceives me, and perhaps how he perceives himself.

There is a telling comparison to be made between this apparent callousness and the response of Sir Paul McCartney in similar circumstances. When the brilliant guitarist Mick Green, one of the original members of Johnny Kidd and The Pirates, and who I have played alongside, passed away eight years ago, Paul was on tour in America. Mick Green had backed him on previous tours and Paul made his apologies for not being at the funeral. He sent his widow Karen a bouquet of flowers and a hand-drawn sympathy card, and love. Little things can mean a lot.

During the past few years, showbusiness seems to have had more than its share of singers, musicians and actors taking the stairway to only God knows where. It seemed like every other day, a major entertainer left the planet. My old friend, singer Leapy Lee expressed the mood, typically light-heartedly: 'From now on, Hoppy, I'll be looking over my shoulder.'

While trying not to sound too morose, I feel that when a close friend, neighbour, anyone who has made a positive impact on your life dies, out of love and respect for that person the right thing to do is to personally send your condolences to those grieving over their loss. I'm afraid I've been doing that too often of late, and I was shocked to hear that Tom's wife Linda had passed away in America. I had known Linda, way back, straight after Tom joined The Senators. Attractive, soft-spoken, a warm smile and gentle personality, while having those qualities she was fiercely protective of her husband, should anyone say negative comments about him or his singing. As much as Tom led her a tidy dance throughout their marriage, Linda loved him deeply, putting up with his wayward Woodward ways. She would never have walked away from their marriage. Being a Welsh village lass, she was brought up to believe, "Now that you've made your bed, you will have to sleep on it". Any suggestion of divorce was out of the question, which perhaps gave Tom the confidence 'to be his own man'. However, Linda was no pushover whenever she found out about his infidelities, usually through the newspapers. By Tom's own admission, when the sparks flew, he would scarper out the door a fraction ahead of well-aimed crockery, and more to follow if she could lay her hands on him. Linda had plenty of spirit.

The last time I met her, we didn't actually meet each at all. It was just after we had been unceremoniously sacked by Tom and Gordon. Linda and Mark, thirteen at the time, were walking in my direction along Walton-on-Thames High Street. I was about to say hello, when she suddenly bowed her head and hurried past. I know it wasn't in her nature to do that, it must have simply been that she felt hugely embarrassed by her husband's action. Having had a great friendship with Linda for such a long time, this lovely woman was too painfully embarrassed to say hello. It made me want to cry inside, and for her.

I sent Mark my condolences for the loss of his mother. He must have been devastated, like his father. But like every other email sent to him, it wasn't acknowledged. Perhaps Tom was upset by the first version of this memoir, published in 2012. It would have made uneasy reading for him, that's for sure, the way he treated his fellow Pontypridd musicians, with such flagrant disrespect, disloyalty and dishonour. I am unsurprised by the way he's always avoided mentioning The Squires during interviews. Tom plays his cards close to his chest, it being such a delicate subject. The band dealt him four loyal aces on the road to stardom but it meant nothing to him back then, nor today, it seems. I trusted Tom absolutely implicitly, even when other members of The Squires began to doubt his integrity, and warned me that my gullibility could bite me back. How true and painful those words would become. When Gordon Mills saw us at the Top Hat Club in the Valleys, the band had been together for over three years and was on top form. Gordon, unknown to the rest of the band, had slyly made up his mind to concentrate only on Tom's career, and to exploit the rest of us. Tom had been primed for it. We were duped by sanctimonious pretence. Gordon realised Tom would never go it alone in London, not without the rest of us. He knew which side his bread was buttered, so we became a means to their end, promising us the world, eventually revealing their true colours.

Robin Eggar had this to say in his award-winning biography on Tom Jones: 'Stardom changes everything. People, relationships, previous certainties dissolve in its glare. Every star says the same thing, "It won't change me." And they believe it. But while a star may not change, his circumstances do. In the presence of power, people defer, an off-hand suggestion becomes a royal command. Protection becomes sequestration. Access equals power. A star is, by definition, the centre of his own solar system. At best, preternaturally self-centred. At worst, self-obsessed.'

Being born with the gift of an amazing voice and becoming a star, is no guarantee against immunity to criticism. In fairness to Tom, Gordon Mills is the definitive panto villain in this story. Tom succumbed to his manager's evil influence from day one, swallowing the bait, hook, line and sinker, hanging on to every word of Mills's dictatorial direction, not only navigating Tom's career, but embodying his own nature into his protégés' psyche. Gordon has been dead for over thirty years, The panto villain has been booed off the stage, but the show goes on and the curtain yet to fall.

*

Earlier I mentioned my song, 'With a Little Luck' and how Tom Jones came to record it during the Eighties. Gordon Mills had insisted that Tom recorded the country song, believing it to be a hit. But when Gordon passed away in 1986 it had not been released. However, a few years ago, the track was brought to my attention, by chance, through a friend in America. 'With A Little Luck' had been included on a US album, *Tom Jones from the Vaults*, on the Mercury label in 1998. Although not released in the UK, I managed to obtain a copy and was astounded to see that the track was listed as 'Composer Unknown'. This meant that my royalties for the song were paid to Tom Jones's publishing company, Valley Music. You could have bowled me over with a feather! Go back to page 315 and you will understand why.

I Immediately contacted Tom's management office and spoke to Mark's secretary, who confirmed that my song had been released and that she would chase up the royalties that were due to me. I then contacted the Performing Rights Society which confirmed that 'With A Little Luck' was registered to me in 1984 by my then publishing company, Teedes Music, proving beyond doubt that I owned the copyright to the song.

I wasn't going to hold my breath waiting for a response from Mark, the innocent kid I used to bounce on my knee. There was no response from him. I did some detective work by contacting the royalties department at Universal Records. Mercury Records, a satellite company of theirs, reported that the album was still available on the internet, and had sold in excess of 12,000 copies since its release. During these investigations I emailed Mark's office with the situation. I didn't expect to receive a life-changing amount in royalties, far from it! Instead, I asked if he and his father would consider releasing 'With A Little Luck' as a charity record to mark the thirtieth anniversary of the 1984 Miners' Strike. There are convalescent homes for ex-miners operating throughout the UK and run through public donation. I explained that I had already contacted a miners' charity, which was thrilled at the possibility that Tom might release the song. Tom was aware that the lyric, written in 1984, was about a mining family living on the breadline, inspired by the ongoing strike.

I made a point of saying to Mark that his grandfather, Tom's father, was a miner affected by the strike, and that alone would be a good reason to release the record. Tom wouldn't have to go into the studio to record it, the track was already up and running. After receiving no response to the email, I tried again. This time, I found that my emails had been blocked. Of course, the miners' charity was disappointed by the outcome. It was an opportunity for the ongoing saga of 'With a Little Luck' to bear fruit for a very good cause.

*

I described in the previous chapter how 'The Liberation Hymn' came into being, inspired by the Gulf War. After the first version of this book was published in 2012, my dear old friend Tony Cartwright came back into my life, having not been in contact for thirty years or more. Living in Ascot, he had somehow got hold of my book and was keen to meet up again. To say that I only mentioned Tony once or twice in the book would be an understatement! We arranged to meet half way between Ascot and Swansea, in the impressive hotel and golfing resort, The Celtic Manor, close to Newport.

Obviously we had both changed in appearance somewhat after such a long time, and with glint of a tear in our eyes we greeted each other warmly. We sat in the sumptuous lounge of the hotel, ordered tea and fine sandwiches, and started reminiscing about our time at Mu's house, laughing so loud at what we got up to that we annoyed a number of people nearby. The hotel lounge was library-like refined, the only thing missing on its walls, a QUIET PLEASE notice.

Having exhausted our reminiscing, we began filling in the past thirty years. Tony had retired, having been personal manager to many stars since the Seventies. Aged 71, he filled his days playing golf at the exclusive Wentworth Golf Club, which he deserved it after managing the outrageous and unpredictable, but loveable comedian Freddie Starr.

Later, saying our farewells for now, we went our different

ways. The day had been memorable and my mood was high. But when I reached Swansea, I was shocked by the news that my brother Norman, the ex-policeman who had been instrumental in getting The Senators their TV appearance on *Discs-A-Go-Go*, had been rushed to hospital with pneumonia. Three weeks later he passed away, aged 77.

I had taken to the Celtic Manor a screenplay I had written entitled The Bells of Santiago. After reading the story about a terrible fire in Santiago, Chile, where 3,000 lives were lost in a cathedral in 1863, and in light of the Chilean strong connection with Swansea at that time, Tony joined the project, using his business acumen and contacts in the movie industry to acknowledge the potential of The Bells of Santiago as a blockbuster movie.

With Tony on board, it became a serious venture. The hugely talented Swansea artist Jeff Phillips became involved and immediately set about creating a storyboard. Each finely detailed drawing, pencil, water colour or oil painting, was painstakingly created, nothing less than miniature masterpieces. Three years later, the epic project was ready to convince a major film producer to believe in its potential.

Meanwhile, I was aware that Tony was looking delicate and had lost weight. He had developed bowel cancer and was operated on in October of that year, followed with six months of chemotherapy. The operation was successful, as was the subsequent therapy. Tony had been a driving force with the film project and his prowess for cutting deals as manager to the stars, his finely-tuned persuasive talents were vital for the next stage. The dreadful disease had knocked him for six and convalescing was an important part of full recovery, so we took a breather from the project's final stage. Tony was nearing his 75th birthday and his recovery was a priority. But then something even more dreadful happened to my old friend. Having heard the great news that his six month course of chemotherapy had been successful, Tony's wife Pauline, who I had known for as long as I had known Tony, was diagnosed with cancer and tragically passed away within a week. It was devastating.

Tony, the larger-than-life showbiz character who I had known for so long, didn't show his heartbreak to those around him. He was strong in that respect. His two children, Paul and Sarah, and his grandchildren are always there for him and these days, he passes his time, usually with Paul, visiting Wentworth Golf Club.

In 2018 *Elegy to the War Horse*, a beautiful EP, was released to coincide with the unveiling of a magnificent bronze statue of a war horse on a plinth. The reason for inclusion of 'The Liberation Hymn' on the EP is the result of a remarkable chain of events.

Tony Cartwright's son Paul had contacted John Kaufman, an established London music publisher, literary agent and owner of Right Recordings Ltd, and an influential businessman who could perhaps pass the screenplay of *The Bells of Santiago* to a potential producer or director. John, a warm, knowledgeable man, after discussing the possibilities of moving forward with the film project, was also interested in publishing any songs I had. My previous publisher had recently passed away and my catalogue had reverted to me, ready to be established with another publisher. Initially, I sent John 'The Liberation Hymn', with two other war anthems that I had written and sung on. He loved the tracks, particularly the Treorchy choir's rendition of

'The Liberation Hymn', and said he was very impressed with the poignant lyrics, musical arrangement. Full marks go to friend and brilliant musician Carl Simmonds who arranged, performed and recorded the dramatic backing of 'The Liberation Hymn' at his Pinewood Studio, Pontypool. I had known Carl for some twenty years or more and it was well worth the journey from Swansea to record there. I've lost count of how many sessions we've worked on together from scratch. Over the years, I have composed music in almost every genre and Carl never fails to fulfil what I hear in my head as the basic arrangement, and then surpasses my expectations with his superb musicianship and mastership of the mixing desk. After adding my vocals, I can drive back to Swansea with a contented smile.

Unknown to me – a secret kept between John and my daughter Tara – John and his associates were involved in a project to commemorate the millions of war horses, mules and donkeys that were killed during the 1914-18 First World War. In 2018, the centenary of the end of the war, a magnificent statue of a war horse was unveiled in Ascot, near the racecourse. The £250,000 cost of the monument was met by generous donations; that generosity and the statue itself are a fitting tribute to those animals killed on the battlefields.

John had been involved with the War Horse Memorial project for the previous four years, and was asked to create and release a four track EP of classical music for the memorial, royalties from sales going to charities associated with the welfare of horses, donkeys, dogs and other animals that serve mankind, The Household Cavalry among them. He put forward 'The Liberation Hymn', along with many other pieces of music from which the organisers of the memorial would select for the CD.

He had asked Tara not to tell me about this in case it wasn't selected. But 'The Liberation Hymn' finally made the cut and their closely guarded secret was out. John asked Tara to give me this fantastic news which they had kept to themselves for over a year. A number of military artefacts were placed in a brass shell case, along with the EP, inside the statue's plinth.

*

I was listening to Radio Wales in my car when I first became aware that a theatre company had developed a musical based on the early days of Tommy Scott and The Senators, about the most challenging time an undiscovered band from Wales could live through. Some of the cast of Welsh theatre company, Theatr na nOg (Theatre of Eternal Youth), were being inter- viewed, to publicise the show's premiere on St. David's Day, 2014, in Pontypridd.

I pulled into a layby and turned up the radio. This is what I had been waiting for, recognition of how The Senators were far more than just a footnote in the success of Tom Jones's rise to stardom; the incredible odds against it becoming a reality. The band were not simply 'instrumental' in beating those daunting odds, The Senators were the pivotal force behind it. Tom hasn't done much to acknowledge his past with The Senators, mostly giving a standard answer in interviews, 'I had this band, see'.

I listened intently as Geinor Styles, the production's director, explained how the script was given to her by writer Mike James in 2012, the same year that the first version of this book was published. I was keen to help in any way possible to promote the production, which was performed by a great cast of actor-singer-musicians. How close could a stage performance be to what happened? I later discovered just how close when I was asked to attend the opening night in Pontypridd: an amazingly talented cast lifted the curtain on my band's past on an unforgettable night!

Three seats had been reserved for myself, Tara and her husband Richard. Travelling from Swansea, we entered the grade 2 listed building, The Municipal, affectionately called The Muni. The last time I had been there was on a New Year's Eve, welcoming in 1964. Tommy Scott and The Senators provided the music. Within six months, the band would be slumming it in Ladbroke Grove.

I was pleasantly surprised to find The Muni had long ago been refurbished, and catered for major bands and solo artistes who loved the venue. Settling in our seats, with the hall packed to capacity, the show began. Tom Orton epitomized Tommy Scott, and I say that unreservedly. It felt strange, me-watching-me on The Muni's stage during the musical, played by an actor-musician capturing the essence of my character with such ease. There was a sublime moment during the show when The Senators were belting out a selection of familiar songs we used to play. That was when I suddenly realised that fifty years earlier, almost to the month, the real Tommy Scott and The Senators had played to an audience from that very same stage. Here I was, an old rocker, going 'back to the future' as real as could possibly be imagined! Mesmerised by it all, these old eyes welled up.

The climax of the show had the audience dancing in the aisles and singing along to the hits, from the time 'It's Not Unusual' secured Tom's future. I was so pleased to see my lovely niece Nadine and her partner Tony, dancing near the stage. Afterwards, Geinor Styles introduced us to the cast, who said they felt boosted by me being there on the crucial opening night of the production. They had felt nervous about what I would think of their performances, and how authentically they had acted those days gone by. Believe me, it had all the qualities of playing the London Palladium for a season.

Geinor told me that Tom's management had been approached, hoping that he might lend his support for the opening night, even if he couldn't be there in person, him being a Ponty boy done good. Perhaps a good luck message that Geinor could announce. It would have been a wonderful gesture for him to make, even an honour, considering how hard the production team had worked to honour him. Sadly, it never happened.

Amanda Lloyd is a Tom Jones superfan, who clearly believes Tom can do no wrong. Fair enough. Her home is a mass of Tom Jones memorabilia, walls papered with photos of the star, and every space dedicated to her idol. Her obsession has even created enough interest for a TV item on her collection. And why not? We all have dreams we'd like to fulfil, and for this person one of her dreams came true.

Tom Jones was made a Knight of the Realm in 2006, being a man of honour required by the Queen, for services to music. Through her tireless, endless campaigning for it to happen, Amanda Lloyd's dream came true. She is now set on another conquest for Tom, a bronze sculpture in Pontypridd to mark for all time what 'the boy from nowhere' did to help keep the town from its gradual decline. The once vibrant mining town is now almost down on its knees. The town centre had a thriving indoor and outdoor market, attracting visitors from miles around, and especially shoppers from the Rhondda Valleys, but the arrival of superstores and on-line retail have crippled high streets in towns and villages everywhere, and Ponty is no exception. Would a statue of Tom Jones erected in the centre of a potential deserted High Street help revive the town?

It doesn't take much to figure out why Tom shied away from wishing the show good luck. As usual, it's not unusual for Tom to barely acknowledge any connection with the town, let alone the band's struggle on the road to stardom.

As for the success of the musical, after the opening night in Ponty, it toured the length and breadth of the UK, selling out in every theatre. In 2016 Geinor Styles gave me the very good news that it was to be performed in Cardiff, at the prestigious Wales Millennium Centre in its breathtakingly stunning theatre. I sometimes wonder about Tom's thoughts on such a triumph. Try brushing that under the carpet!

*

I am the proud father of one child, yet blessed with the love of a dozen daughters. These days, Tara, husband Richard and my beautiful grandchildren spoil me far too much. Perhaps falling downstairs and breaking my hip in three places almost two years ago is the cause for their concern. Dammit, I was sober as a judge when it happened. I was left with *no* excuse, other than admitting to a senior moment... my leg suddenly giving way. Sadly, it was also a watershed moment. From that day on, performing on stage around the country, belting out rock 'n' roll numbers, was over. Having spent a month in hospital and months on crutches, I reluctantly hung up my guitar. After first getting up on a pub stage as a naive teenager, even before forming The Senators, my very last gig was to be a local country pub-restaurant on New Year's Eve, 2016. Little did I know that would be the end of my career as a performer. It began on a pub stage, and ended in a cosy pub-restaurant venue, The Lewis Arms, Llanelli booked by my agent Terri Dean.

As luck would have it, the venue being close to home, all my family were there to enjoy the New Year celebration. What a perfect book-end finish to my career as a singer-guitarist, seeing all my family there, having a great time on the dance floor. It was the most memorable New Year's eve ever. For the record, the following New Year's eve was the first time I wasn't singing on some stage or other since 1965, the year 'It's Not Unusual' was released. It really hit home: I now had that special night off, not having to go out gigging somewhere...for the first time in fifty-three years!

Ending my career as a stage performer does not mean that I am now retired, pottering about in the garden, doing the school run for my grandchildren, particularly in winter when inclement weather means they arrive home warm and dry. No, the time when I retire will come when my time is up. Until then, I believe I will still be involved in various projects; composing music, writing screenplays and novels.

21. WHERE ARE THEY NOW?

Of the five members of The Senators, before Tommy Woodward joined the band, two have sadly passed away in recent years: drummer Brian Price and singer Tommy Pitman. That leaves myself, Keith Davies and Jeff Maher from the original line-up.

The passing of Micky Gee, aged 64, is described on page 328. I have tried to locate rhythm guitarist Dave Cooper without success. It was rumoured that he eventually settled in Bristol. Dave was a great musician and great company, and I hope he's still around and doing well. Our brilliant drummer Chris Slade is based in LA, undoubtedly with a famous rock band. Chris joined The Senators when he was just sixteen, and no-one could be prouder than me of what he has achieved since, becoming one of the greatest drummers of the time.

I certainly know the whereabouts of my lifelong friend Vic Cooper, who joined the band after the cruel disposal of Dave by Gordon Mills. Vic and I had a great time as a duo years after The Squires disbanded. Afterwards, he performed on super cruise liners, sailing to exotic destinations and tickling the ivories of a grand piano in one of the cocktail bars on board. His programme began with Sinatra and Bublé and other cool singers before breaking into classic rock 'n' roll including the Jerry Lee Lewis hit, 'Lovin' Up a Storm' – perhaps an odd choice for a ship in the Caribbean. Eventually Vic dropped anchor for the last time and while playing in a piano bar in Altea in Spain he was introduced to Patricia, a lovely lady and widow of the owner of the men's outfitters, Fosters. They moved in together and when I visited them – hobbling on a crutch having broken my hip – we had a wonderful time, out on the town every night in perfect company.

Bryn 'The Fish' Phillips, the larger than life comedian and lovable character who provided the laughs in The Senators concert party, sadly died in 2013 at the age of 79. Jo Mills, beautiful model and the wife of Gordon, died a year later. Her warm nature was as beautiful as her face but it didn't stop Gordon from preferring the company of other women, which led to their divorce. She gave him vital support in the financial hard times before Tom and The Senators got our break, and provided the majority of the lyrics for 'It's Not Unusual', though without a credit. She lived as the wife of a multimillionaire before their divorce, but afterwards her life was less and less comfortable, and Gordon died penniless in 1986. She almost became destitute and relied on her children until her death. Had she had the credit for those well-known lyrics she would surely have had financial security.

Welsh singer Johnny Bennett, who introduced Gordon Mills to Tommy Scott and The Senators in 1964, died early in 2017. I had been able to attend the funeral of Bryn Phillips, but two days after Johnny's death I broke my hip and was hospitalized. Johnny was a gentleman, quiet-spoken and always immaculately dressed. Handsome, he had Hollywood charisma. He played an important part in Tom Jones' eventual rise to stardom but as with so many others, his death remained unacknowledged by the man he helped.

INDEX

INDEX